The People's Guide to RV Camping in Mexico

Carl Franz
with Steve Rogers

Edited by Lorena Havens

John Muir Publications
Santa Fe, New Mexico

For my brother Rob, and the adventures we've shared.

John Muir Publications, P.O. Box 613, Santa Fe, NM 87504

First edition. First printing

Library of Congress Cataloging-in-Publication Data

Franz, Carl.
    The people's guide to RV camping in Mexico/Carl Franz with Steve
Rogers; Lorena Havens. — 1st ed.
      p. cm.
    Includes index.
    ISBN 0-912528-56-7
    1. Camping—Mexico.   2. Recreational vehicles—Mexico.   3. Camp
sites, facilities, etc.—Mexico—Directories.   4. Mexico—Description
and travel—1981- —Guide-books. I. Rogers, Steve, 1938- . II. Havens,
Lorena. III. Title.
GV198.67.M6F73   1989
647.9472—dc20   88-43537
                                                    CIP

Distributed to the book trade by:
W.W. Norton & Company, Inc.
New York, New York

Typeface: Melliza
Typographer:Copygraphics, Inc.
Designer: Susan Surprise
Printer: McNaughton & Gunn

Contents

Acknowledgments

Special thanks to Steve Rogers, Tina Rosa, and Churpa Rosa-Rogers for their research and good-natured support, to Linda Ellis for editing and tedious etceteras, to Richard Harris for inspiration, and to Mary Hartsfield for heroic calm among the computers.

Introduction

Lorena and I will soon be celebrating twenty years of traveling together with another camping trip in Mexico. As usual, we've compromised on our itinerary and selected a route that runs vaguely north to south, with an occasional jog to the east or west. We plan to kayak to our favorite desert islands in Baja and stretch our hammocks on a Pacific mainland beach. The preliminary wish list for this celebratory adventure includes searching for a certain lost crystal mine in north central Mexico, birding and fishing in several isolated lagoons south of Acapulco, more birding and wildlife watching in the rain forests of Chiapas, and a long-postponed float trip to a remote jungle ruin. From this point, planning is still in flux. Continue east to Yucatán and Quintana Roo for more ruins and skin diving? Or turn north to beachcomb the Gulf Coast and hike the forested mountains of eastern Puebla? Or what about continuing south to the Belizean cays and the cool, volcanic highlands of Guatemala?

To our usual motto, ''Wherever you go, there you are,'' we've added a camper's postscript: ''Never a dull moment.'' Although we seldom know exactly where our travels will take us or what adventures we'll have, one thing is certain: in addition to meeting new and old friends, we'll be crossing paths with the usual cast of amazing characters who migrate to Mexico every year just as surely as the butterflies and whales.

What is it about Mexico that draws us back, year after year, one adventure after another?

The answer is easy. Virtually everyone who travels in Mexico for any length of time considers the country's greatest attraction to be its people, the Mexicans themselves, rather than its mountains, deserts, or colonial cathedrals.

Though poor in terms of material goods, Mexico is rich in natural beauty. Its people have a sense of pride, self-reliance, personal warmth, and old-fashioned hospitality that seldom fails to impress and influence the visitor. Like many others, Lorena and I have been changed and strengthened by our friendships with Mexicans, and our lives have been enriched. Once you've opened yourself to Mexico, it's difficult not to go back.

One of our favorite pastimes in Mexico is exchanging information and hot tips with other travelers. Frustrated by a notable shortage of reliable guidebooks and maps, more than one camper has had to rely on the gringo grapevine for advice about conditions south of the border. Information on Mexican campgrounds is particularly limited. Other than sketchy references in general tourism-style guidebooks and bare-bones listings in handouts from travel clubs and insurance companies, travelers usually depend on luck and word of mouth to find good campgrounds and RV parks.

Although I personally enjoy traveling in Mexico with a very loose itinerary, many campers prefer to know what lies around the next corner. This is particularly true if you're a newcomer to Mexico or find yourself traveling with limited time or money. Nothing is more frustrating than passing by some noteworthy camping place or natural attraction simply because you didn't know it existed. Even if you speak Spanish and are willing to ask for directions, reliable information is difficult to come by. Ironically, most Mexicans are woefully unaware of what their country has to offer.

The expression "Ignorance is bliss" does not always apply to traveling and camping in a foreign country. If you're headed to Mazatlán, it can be very reassuring to have the name and location of a comfortable, cheap place to camp for the night rather than winging it. By the same token, tips on highway conditions, bird-watching, or where to launch a boat can take a great deal of uncertainty out of a trip and allow more efficient use of your time.

Who Are We?

The publication of the first edition of *The People's Guide to Mexico* in 1972 marked the beginning of my career as a travel writer. In that book, I related many of the adventures and insights I'd enjoyed while traveling through Mexico with Lorena, Steve Rogers, and two very noisy parrots. Since that time, the *People's Guide* has undergone several revisions and expansions. There have been other changes as well: after years of crisscrossing Mexico in a series of camper vans, Steve and his partner, Tina Rosa, have turned their considerable knowledge of the country into two great books, *22 Days in Mexico* and *The Shopper's Guide to Mexico*.

Once he had officially become a travel writer, I didn't have to twist Steve's arm very hard to interest him in a long-discussed project: a personal review and directory of our favorite camping places in Mexico. Steve, Tina, and daughter Churpa would be our "field team," while Lorena and I handled the writing and editing. To avoid burnout, we'd take frequent research trips ourselves, primarily to Yucatán, Oaxaca, and Baja.

"This means I'll have to refresh my memory on a few Pacific beaches this winter," Steve said, looking rather misty-eyed at a fresh road map of Mexico. Before it was over, in fact,

Steve and family completed a 10,000-mile camping odyssey that stretched from Ensenada to Isla de Mujeres, with a lot of interesting side trips along the way.

This book, then, represents our "team" effort, not to mention the considerable contributions and support of many other campers we met along the way. We hope that you share our good experiences in Mexico and find the information (reasonably) up to date. Mexico is both charmingly traditional and changing very fast. Expect surprises and learn to enjoy them; that's what traveling is all about.

PART I

Preparing for Your Trip

CHAPTER 1

Camping in Mexico

Every good camping trip to Mexico begins with a daydream, whether it is a vague desire to feel warm sand between your toes and drink coconut milk or a lifelong urge to search for a Lost City. Whether you're traveling in a luxurious motor home, in a rented VW bus, or on public transportation, you'll undoubtedly experience a sense of camaraderie and shared adventure with other campers you meet along the way. Foreign travel is a great equalizer, and it's common to find people from all walks of life and economic levels in the same campground.

In a casual census of one small RV park in the Yucatán, we met campers from a broad range of American states and Canadian provinces. They included an ex-crop duster pilot, a retired Army noncom, college students, a carpenter, commercial salmon fishermen, housewives, an antique dealer, a CPA, and a realtor. There were several Mexicans and Europeans, including a French longshoreman, a Danish bus driver, and a commercial artist from Mexico City. Mix these diverse personalities, languages, and backgrounds together in an exotic location and it's no wonder that every day spent camping in Mexico is a memorable experience. Camping styles in Mexico are limited only by your imagination and budget.

Motor Homes and Trailers

Interest in retirement in Mexico has surged in recent years. Mexico's low prices, warm climate, and hospitality are tempting more retired American and Canadian RVers to cross the border. These RV retirees tend to be much more adventurous than their contemporaries back home. One couple in a trailer park near San Miguel de Allende complained that traveling in the United States was "too crowded, too expensive, and too predictable." They came to Mexico to find a little excitement. They were knocking around the country in a small motor home, learning Spanish on the street and having the time of their lives.

Quite a number of parks and campgrounds in Mexico cater to the "residential camper" and "snowbird." These parks are most common in Baja and along the Pacific beaches. RV retirees also congregate in Guadalajara, Cuernavaca, and other popular cities. Some campgrounds have become residential, with time-share and leasehold spaces.

A typical resident camper will drive to Mexico in October or November, park the RV in a comfortable space, and then stay put until spring. When summer beach temperatures get too warm, these people migrate north again, or move into the cooler Mexican highlands. RV residents often develop close friendships with Mexicans and can be gold mines of local information. Though this style of "camping" may not seem very exciting to some, others find it both satisfying and quite economical.

RVers who prefer more active travel follow an unofficial circuit of trailer parks and campgrounds. Although Mexico has many opportunities for safe and easy free camping, RVers often feel more comfortable in an established park with hookups. Mexico's campground circuit is extensive, but it doesn't begin to match the facilities available north of the border, at least in quantity. Mazatlán, one of the country's most popular destinations, has less than a dozen RV parks, including some semiprivate residential parks.

"I guess you could call us hopelessly middle class," one woman said to me. We stood on a grassy campsite near the edge of a rather rundown trailer park. She and her husband had been coming there for years; their van was parked to take advantage of a fine view of the Pacific Ocean. A cool breeze ruffled the tarp they had erected over a set of folding chairs and a card table. They had hammocks, a barbecue pit, and even a badminton net. This was it, their home for six months of the year. I looked around their camp again, thinking of people at home, fighting winter weather, frustrated at rising prices and decreasing incomes, struggling to enjoy their free time or retirement.

"Hopelessly middle class?" I took another bite of her delicious fresh mango pie. "I don't think I heard you quite right."

A retired gringo described his life-style to me like this: "I've got my little boat (a 12-foot aluminum runabout), my outboard, and my fishing poles. I drive around Mexico, looking for good water. When I see some, I stop. I hardly ever fish the same place for more than a week. I've been doing this for years now and still haven't seen it all. Probably never will."

He had an encyclopedic knowledge of Mexican fishing spots, but getting it out of him would have taken bamboo splinters and truth serum. "Down Michoacán way," was about as close as he'd come to divulging information.

Caravans

RV caravans have been popular in Mexico for many years. Several companies offer full-service caravanning, including insurance, wagonmasters, mechanics, organized sightseeing and shopping tours, and campfire songfests. Caravans are sometimes accompanied by Green Angels, special tourist assistance patrol trucks provided by the Mexican government.

Many RVers use caravan travel as an introduction to Mexico. Several caravan veterans have told us that the experience they gained on a caravan gave them the confidence to return to Mexico on their own. Others enjoy not having to worry about logistics, repairs, and security.

One of the primary disadvantages of caravanning is the inevitable clannishness that such regimented travel can produce. Meeting Mexicans is especially difficult in a tightly organized caravan with schedules that don't allow spontaneous side trips and explorations. Caravans also have a tendency to consume everything in their path, especially ice cubes, gasoline, cold drinks, and fresh bread. ''They're like army ants!'' one angry independent camper complained after a caravan of over one hundred RV rigs made a shopping blitz through a nearby town.

Other campers, myself included, try to look on the positive side. Caravanners often stock up at home on food, hardware, and other unavailable goodies. I know gringos who ''work the rigs,'' trading everything from books and seashells to Mexican trinkets for treats from home. Caravans inevitably include vacationing handyman types who jump at the opportunity to help a fellow traveler with a problem. On the Caribbean coast, Steve and I were both given considerable assistance by the members of an RV caravan when our vans were struck with hard-to-solve breakdowns. (For a list of RV caravan companies, see the Appendix.)

Van, Pickup, and Car Campers

Vans, pickup campers, delivery trucks, cars, and converted school buses make up the next largest group of recreational vehicles found in Mexico, though most of their owners seem to shy away from the term "RV." Some van campers look down their noses at RVs and motor homes, just as the owners of classic, wooden sailboats tend to sneer at the fiberglass boats of the "Tupperware Fleet." As history recycles itself, however, more and more ex-VW van drivers are beginning to kick the tires on used motor homes, daydreaming about that perfect camping spot at the end of a long Mexican beach.

In my opinion, the biggest advantage of a van or pickup camper in Mexico is maneuverability. In spite of great feats of highway building in recent years, the better part of Mexico—in terms of both area and adventure—is still off the beaten path. If you stick close to the pavement, whether it's on Baja's 850-mile-long Transpeninsular Highway or Mexico's endless two-lane highways, there's no real limit to the size of rig you can drive. Lorena and I just happen to be addicted to narrow streets, cul-de-sacs, dead ends, side trips, back roads, and vague, dotted lines on badly creased maps.

Is It Safe?

In the many years it has taken to research and write this book, I've asked a number of people, "Do you think camping is safe in Mexico for gringos?" The answer I've gotten from archaeologists with years of field experience in remote areas of the country, from cops, *federales*, soldiers, ranchers, guides, tourist officials and other campers was an almost unanimous "Yes!"

The popular gringo image of a mustachioed *bandido* thundering over a cactus-studded hill brandishing a rifle in one hand and a smoking pistol in the other went out with silent movies and the decline of the narrow gauge steam locomotive. Today, Mexican bandits are as rare as war-painted Indians firing arrows into a circle of motor homes in Yellowstone. The people of rural Mexico, compesinos and Indians, are basically very honest, hardworking, proud, and willing to give visitors more than a fair chance to prove themselves worthy of trust and friendship.

And among this nation of Scoutlike folks there are the inevitable drunks, petty thieves, and vandals who can so easily give an entire area a bad name. Dealing with this latter group tends to overshadow the good qualities of people you'll meet while camping in Mexico. Paul Theroux wrote, "Travel writing is a funny thing. . . .the worst trips make the best reading." What better way to get someone's attention, either in a book or sitting around the living room swapping tales, than with some horror story? It doesn't matter if you have to exaggerate the drunk into an armed bandido, the point is to hold your audience's attention at any cost, even if the cost is truth and accuracy.

Take reasonable precautions while you are camped, and chances are you'll never have a problem with thievery. Be especially careful, however, while in the larger cities. Ironically, we've heard of more campers being robbed on their way to Mexico than south of the border. Professional rip-off artists in the United States know that a loaded motor home or van makes a fat target.

Most rip-offs take place on the beach (or in large cities) and are often the direct result of a camper's own laziness and lack of even normal vigilance. It is very common to see excited campers fling their valuables to the sand and run into the surf, only to return ten mintues later to find they've been robbed. Let's face it, the temptation is incredible when a thief or poor person is presented with a golden opportunity to snag a camera or a wallet. If you must leave things, ask someone (in a store, restaurant, or another camper) to keep an eye on your stuff.

Backpackers should keep their gear neatly stowed at all times. We like to keep our things out of sight as much as possible, without being obviously paranoid. "Don't touch that!" is no way to deal with a curious visitor. Rural people are very open about handling your things, though they'll often make polite hints before looking at something. Sleeping bags, stoves, lanterns, tools, and kitchen gear interest them a great deal. Oblige their curiosity, but don't leave things lying around carelessly lest you tempt someone beyond reason to take it with them.

Camping in Mexico is very safe, but it can, and probably will, make you slightly nervous until you've become acquainted with the country and its new night sounds and activities. You don't expect a burro train of firewood to pass by at 3:00 a.m., so when it does, it'll probably startle you. It's not easy to be completely relaxed when you don't fully understand what everyone else is doing and why.

A friend had the wits scared out of him on his first night in Mexico. He parked his van on the edge of a recently harvested cornfield, well away from the nearest highway. He woke in the middle of the night to the sound of gunshots and shouts, some quite close. Before he could gather his wits and flee, a very excited campesino farmer appeared, yelling something about rabbits. Once our friend had regained his composure, he realized the farmer only wanted to know if he'd be interested in buying a freshly killed *conejo* (rabbit). He'd camped in a popular hunting area.

Accept the unknown gracefully. Don't be scared off by your own imagination; once your fears have been explained, you'll be glad you didn't overreact.

Alone? With Children? With Friends?

Camping alone in Mexico is a lot easier for men than for women. I wish it weren't true, but machismo can ruin camping for single women and even for groups of women. The relentless attention of Mexican men can be unnerving, irritating, and potentially dangerous.

Children find camping in Mexico a true delight. I wouldn't hesitate to take a child camping or even backpacking. Mexicans are literally crazy about kids. Friends who camp with children, from toddlers to teenagers, are almost unanimous in urging others to take their kids south rather than leave them at home. Some kids make better campers than their parents, happily ignoring minor discomforts and taking pleasure in simple camp chores.

Camping with friends, especially on a trip to Mexico, requires cooperation and mutual respect. Sharing expenses is the most commonly used rationale for traveling in groups. In my opinion, it should be the last consideration, especially if you have any doubts that your group can get along under the normal pressures of traveling and camping in a foreign country. The few dollars you'll save by sharing expenses won't seem very important when your friends refuse to wash the dishes or complain endlessly about mosquito bites.

Pick your group carefully. Discuss plans in some detail, and if conflict arises, don't be afraid to resolve it by saying, "Maybe I'll meet you in Mérida." I've seen a number of groups (including some I was in) explode under pressure. Don't let a break-up become irreconcilable even if it means gritting your teeth and saying, "See ya later," before it's too late.

Some people think group camping requires drinking out of the same cup and pitching tents side by side. I prefer cooperative camping, where each member of the group maintains a certain independence and respects the needs of others for moments of privacy, solo side trips, and so on.

What Will It Cost?

In celebration of finishing the first edition of our book on camping, boating, and backpacking in Mexico in 1981, Lorena and I rewarded ourselves with a "bus driver's holiday": six months of camping and low-budget bliss on one of

Mexico's most beautiful beaches. Our total costs for this half-year idyll were $1,200. Our major expense, $600 for lodging, went for labor and materials to build a very comfortable palm frond house. The balance was spent on food, ice, and miscellaneous supplies, plus gasoline for an outboard motor and frequent short side trips in the van. On just $200 a month we were more than comfortable—it was heaven!

Since then, Mexico's economy has suffered tremendous shocks, including repeated devaluations of the peso and sometimes rampant inflation. These seesawing economic forces have created a great deal of instability and confusion about prices. Using our $1,200 beach trip as a benchmark, however, today a similar trip would cost about the same.

In general, campers will find that prices in Mexico for staple foods, dry goods, and basic services are lower than in the United States and Canada. Some things will be very cheap. To promote "social stability," the Mexican government heavily subsidizes many staples, including tortillas, bread, bus tickets, propane, and sugar. Consumer goods, imported foods, and luxury items, however, can cost as much as they do at home or even more. Of these, gasoline is the best example. As of this writing, gasoline costs slightly more per gallon in Mexico than it does in California. Meat and chicken often cost more in Mexico than in the United States, even though the average person earns just a few dollars a day.

The key to saving money is to imitate Mexicans: avoid pricey tourist resorts, and buy only what you need for the next few days. Buy fresh, locally grown meat and produce rather than packaged, imported, or out-of-season foods. Go easy on liquor, nightlife, souvenirs, and toys. In other words, live simply and modestly.

Such measures, combined with careful bookkeeping and a moderately paced travel itinerary, allow Steve, Tina, and their daughter Churpa (our collaborators in the Campground Directory) to travel throughout Mexico in their van on $600 a month (not including insurance). This includes some free or very cheap campgrounds, RV park fees, occasional restaurant meals, and lots of gasoline.

Steve and Tina's average daily costs break down like this:

Campgrounds	$ 5-$6
Gas	$15
Food	$10
Total	$30 *(for an average travel day of about 250 mi.)*

Tina advised that days of rest cost less and days spent sightseeing and moving around cost more. In estimating your own costs, start with unavoidable expenses such as gas, oil, and insurance. Insurance runs a minimum of about $2.50 a day, depending on the value of your vehicle and the extent of the coverage.

If you live more than a day or two from the border and hope to travel for a month or more, it's easy to put 5,000 miles on the odometer. At roughly one dollar per gallon for gas, I can see that just getting to and from Mexico in our guzzler, plus a thousand-mile loop of the Yucatán peninsula, is going to cost $600 in gasoline alone. That's a lot of bus tickets and cabs.

Most campers save money by doing their own cooking and mixing their own drinks. Partying, even for one person, can take an amazing bite out of your pocketbook. Liquor is relatively cheap in Mexico, but its cost often adds up fast, especially if you "drink out" regularly.

Campers who are willing to "free camp," either on their own, with a Mexican family, or in one of the country's many "unofficial" campgrounds, will see a considerable savings. Catch a fish now and then, barter a pair of pliers for a lifetime supply of papayas, and cancel that subscription to the *Wall Street Journal*. In short order, your living expenses will plunge to near-Mexican levels. I frequently talk to backpack vagabonds and shoestring budget van campers who consider $200 to $300 a month reasonable or even generous. Some of my best trips to Mexico have been spur of the moment, with only a token thought for planning and preparation. For example, I once spent a week in Chihuahua's Copper Canyon with nothing but a couple of changes of clothes, a sleeping bag, a camera, and a few comb-and-toothbrush personal items hurriedly stuffed into my backpack. Though I might have wished for more gear, I certainly had enough to cover my basic needs and to support a very enjoyable camping/cheap hotel trip.

My favorite example of casual trip planning was related to me by a fellow I nicknamed Robinson Crusoe. He was strolling idly down a street in San Francisco when a chalkboard notice in the window of a travel agency caught his eye. It advertised a super-cheap round-trip fare to the Pacific coast of Mexico, an offer he literally couldn't refuse. As he was self-employed and accustomed to poverty, he wasn't afraid to blow most of his remaining money on the ticket. There was just one catch: the last flight available left in eight hours.

"I bought my ticket and ran like a maniac for the nearest discount store," he said. "It took about an hour to buy bug dope, a frying pan, water jugs, and a cheap sleeping bag. I didn't have any spare clothes with me, either, so I took a cab to the Goodwill and got a suitcase and a whole wardrobe. I climbed on the plane wearing an Al Capone-style suit. It felt kind of ridiculous, but when I got to Mexico I traded the suit to a cab driver for a ride to the beach."

That's where I met him one morning, while I was beach-combing and surf casting for a breakfast fish. He'd been on the beach for ten days, hiking back and forth to a nearby village for food and water, conserving his money as carefully as possible. "One catch on that discount fare," he explained, "was that I had to stay three weeks."

When he left, he traded his hobo camping outfit for a ride to the airport. For what most tourists spend on a long weekend he had enjoyed a round-trip three-week vacation on a beautiful Mexican beach.

Such a casual approach to planning might seem reck-lessly carefree if you're headed to Mexico in an RV or van, but the point is to avoid overplanning, especially if this is your first or second trip. Once you've got a general idea of what you'd like to do and see in Mexico—or a specific fantasy to be fulfilled—you're ready to get down to brass tacks.

Travelers who say, "After we get our marlin in Baja, we'll try hiking near Puerto Vallarta and then bird-watching in Campeche and exploring ruins around Chetumal and then . . ." are biting off much more than they can chew in less than several months of determined travel.

Unless you've got unlimited time, you can't possibly see all of Mexico in one trip. I must have met hundreds of travelers in northern and central Mexico who left home bound for the tip of South America. In most cases, once these people reach Mexico and begin to relax, their ambitious travel plans quickly dissolve into thin air. As many of us have learned, the often-ridiculed "mañana syndrome" is actually a healthy sign, especially when it infects perennially hyper-active gringos.

Once you've got an idea or a daydream to plan around, what's the next step? For once, the answer is simple: Don't overplan.

I firmly believe that exercising your imagination is at least as important as making detailed lists or selecting the best possible equipment. Unless you've traveled extensively in Mexico before, you can't anticipate what you'll actually find there. Mexico is often bewilderingly foreign. Such apparently straightforward questions as, "Will we find gaso-line?" or "How do I arrange a hiking trip?" seldom have easy or even reliable answers. Complex plans have a way of turn-ing into hair-tearing chaos, even for the most experienced travelers. This is particularly true if your time is limited. In Mexico, "planning ahead" is often a waste of time and energy. The more flexible your approach to traveling, the more enjoyable and relaxed your trip is likely to be.

Preparing Your Camper

Unless you're driving a factory-made RV, you'll probably test your carpentry skills by building your own camper. A nifty kitchen cabinet, perhaps, with a fold-down table for the stove and a cutting board that slides out of sight. When the building urge strikes, consider having it done by a Mexican carpenter. The materials may not be cheap (wood is generally expensive in Mexico), but the labor will be a bargain. Look for a shop that is turning out good furniture; many Mexican craftsmen do fine hand joinery work and decorative carving. Just make sure they use plenty of *tomillos* (screws) and *resistol* (wood glue) to withstand hard road use.

Do-it-yourself cabinets and furnishings should be securely attached to the vehicle while traveling. A rubber-burning emergency stop or unexpected speed bump at 50 mph can turn the best organized camper into a mess.

Water Storage

Built-in water tanks aren't worth the expense or trouble. When a hose for filling them is not available (often the case in Mexico), you'll have to do the bucket brigade trip, so you might as well start with portable jugs. Two five-gallon cans should be a sufficient supply of fresh water for two or three people for a considerable length of time.

If your camper already has a built-in water tank, check its plumbing carefully. As a backup, and to extend your supply, I'd also carry one or two collapsible water jugs.

Refrigerators or Ice Chests?

If you're unsure whether to use an ice chest or a portable refrigerator on your trip, Steve says emphatically, ''If you can afford it, get the fridge! In fact,'' he adds, ''I'll never travel without one again. It completely eliminates the hassle of finding ice in Mexico and has saved a lot of our food from spoiling."

Steve uses a small propane refrigerator and through it meets his not-inconsiderable needs for cooking while traveling. He warns, "This is not an alcoholic's model. It will only make one small tray of ice cubes and chill a reasonable number of sodas or beers."

I've met a few campers in Mexico using portable electric refrigerators that resemble ice chests. The general consensus was that these "cold boxes" were very small and expensive but nonetheless convenient.

A sturdy ice chest that can be easily removed for use outside is much more convenient than a permanent built-in one. An ice chest with a lift-up top is also better than an upright model when large slippery chunks of ice are used— usually the case in Mexico.

Propane System

Propane is widely used in Mexico, but the selection of parts and fittings is limited and the quality low. Inspect your propane systems very carefully and check closely for leaks and loose fittings. RV systems designed for American freeways may not hold up well to the sustained bump-and-grind of Mexican highways and back roads. Assemble a kit of spares and tools to take care of obvious repairs.

Rugs and Carpets

Carpeted floors in vans and motor homes can drive you to distraction when camped near sand or mud. After I reached the point of asking guests to go through a series of foot cleansings as complicated as those given to diseased cattle, Lorena suggested we remove our van carpet. I immediately relaxed again, though I quickly tired of the bare metal floor.

The solution was simple: we bought cheap *petates* (woven reed mats) of various sizes and one bright handwoven Mexican blanket to spread over them. The mats make a good rug pad for the blanket. They can also be used on the ground as doormats. The combination is much more attractive than carpeting and insulates against road noise. As a bonus when we get cold, we pull up the rug and sleep under it.

Interior Lights

The interior lights in a car or camper rarely shine when or where they're needed. Because light is important for cooking and reading, take the trouble to install lights that are really useful. When you wake up in the middle of a long night with the burning desire to reread *War and Peace*, you'll be glad you did.

Lights are available in auto junkyards, discount stores, auto supply stores, and, if you can afford the high markups, trailer and RV supply outlets. I prefer portable, rather than permanently attached, lights; they are more versatile and easier to install. Buy the type that plugs into the car's cigarette lighter. Spotlight models use a lot more juice than bulb types but also give considerably more light. Replacing your regular battery with a deep-cycle RV battery can solve starting problems and extend your reading hours. (For more on batteries, see chap. 3, On the Road.)

If your vehicle is a nonsmoker model, clip the plug off the portable light cord, strip the insulation from the two ends, and crimp (soldering is better) alligator clips to the bare wire ends. This light won't have a switch to turn it on; just attach the alligator clips to two connections on the vehicle's main fuse panel. Clip one to any fuse holder, and then touch the other alligator to other fuse holders until the light comes on. You can also bare part of a hot wire for one clip and put the other on any good ground. (There is a risk, however, of an accidental short circuit should something later touch the bared spot, but you can't have everything.)

Our light has a magnet built into the case. It almost sticks to the van's body. Magnets can also be glued to cabinets or strategic points that aren't metal.

A friend who burned down his "fireproof" van, complete with all his worldly goods, suggests that candles be used with extreme caution. The votive type, sold in reusable glasses, can be held in plastic or metal devices sold as drink caddies.

Curtains

Unless you're an exhibitionist, put curtains on all windows or you'll be playing to standing-room-only audiences when camped in most areas of Mexico. This is especially true if you spend the night in a town, schoolyard, soccer field or other public place. When sleeping by a highway, the lights of passing trucks can keep you awake with their near-lighthouse intensity. Dark curtains are especially good for blocking out unwanted headlights (and daylight , too, if you enjoy an occasional siesta). Curtains also protect your possessions from greedy appraisal by would-be thieves when you are not inside.

Bug Proofing

Some type of bug screening is essential. Rig drapes or curtains of mosquito netting over side and back doors. The netting should be long enough to prevent mosquitoes from crawling underneath and loose enough so that you won't punch a hole in it with a foot or elbow.

I prefer a rectangular canopy of mosquito netting rigged over the bed. This allows all doors and windows to be opened without having to screen them. The canopy arrangement, however, forces you to stay in bed when the mosquitoes are out. This isn't necessarily an inconvenience if you're into reading, sleeping, and other bedtime activities.

Mosquito nets can be suspended from the ceiling of a van or RV with wooden or plastic clothespins. If the surface is smooth, install small screws at strategic points or glue strong cloth or plastic tabs to the interior. With a little practice, you'll be able to put a mosquito netting in place in just a couple of minutes.

In many places where we've camped, bugs weren't a problem *most of the time*, but when they did attack it was merciless and all-out. This may happen during the day as well as at night. A screened refuge can mean the difference between evacuating a nice campsite or holing up for a short time.

Awning

Living outside is more comfortable with some sort of protection from the sun and rain. We use a light tarp and telescoping aluminum tent poles. The tarp is attached to the rain gutter of the van (drill small holes and make wire hooks or loops for tie points) and extends out from the side. Adjustable poles are convenient for irregular ground, but anything will do. Two eight-foot lengths of light bamboo are ideal. Secure the tarp with lengths of twine and pegs. I tie strips of white rag to the twine so that when I trip over it, I know what's happened. Other tarps can be rigged as side walls for more privacy.

If your tarp, poles, lines, and pegs are kept stowed neatly, you'll be able to find them and erect a shelter within five minutes of parking. This can make even a brief highway lunchbreak much more relaxing and comfortable. The advantage of protection from the rain is obvious, especially if your vehicle isn't very roomy.

Skylights and Windows

Skylights and extra-large windows, even heavily tinted, act as heat collectors during the day. The Mexican sun may be more than you bargained for when you installed that skylight in Minnesota. Our VW van had two skylights, each capable of heating us to the baking point on a hot day. To avoid this, we blocked them from the inside with newspaper, aluminum foil, a foil-backed blanket, or whatever else could be taped or jammed into place.

Carry a good supply of silicone seal for emergency repairs. Skylights and plastic windows are notorious for leaking. When repeatedly softened by the heat of the sun and then subjected to vibration, they may develop annoying cracks and splits. A brief tropical shower can hammer through the tiniest of cracks. Lorena actually put her head through one of our skylights. It took a full tube of silicone seal and several feet of heavy-duty duct tape to make it almost watertight again.

When bugs or rain force you inside, you'll want as much fresh air as you can get. If your vehicle is short on windows, install a few more with strong, tight bug screens. Windows that open will provide extra air, light, and a better view. Crank-open overhead ventilators are also good.

Plumbing

Unfortunately, there are few places in Mexico's backcountry where dumping a holding tank will be appreciated. RV owners we've talked to suggest that you find a remote spot, dig a deep hole, and flush. Don't do this near water, please.

Self-contained campers must also deal with dishwater and, perhaps, shower runoff. Make every effort to dispose of these wastes away from the campsite; there's nothing worse than discovering you've pitched your tent on an unpleasant wet spot. Think of others before pulling the plug. I know of one case where an uncooperative motor home owner was ''invited'' by gringo vigilantes to leave his campsite after he refused to do anything about various obnoxious drains.

When nearby campers tired of the smell and health hazard, they spontaneously organized an Unwelcome Wagon.

Luggage Rack

A sturdy *parilla* (luggage rack) ranks high on my "must have" list of van and car camping equipment. There's no point in denying it: no matter how often I vow to "go light," we always take more gear to Mexico than our van can neatly hold. To avoid overcrowding and chaos, I use the luggage rack as a traveling attic for spare tires, lawn chairs, camping equipment, interesting driftwood, stalks of bananas, and other vital flotsam and jetsam. I cover the load with a strong tarp and plenty of rope. Valuable items are locked to the rack with chains or cables, but in many years of travel, I've never (knock on wood) lost anything to thieves.

A thin plywood floor can turn a large roof rack into an interesting tent site. John Muir, author of *How to Keep Your Volkswagen Alive*, used to pitch a bright orange pup tent on top of his VW van. Steve's daughter Churpa uses their van's roof rack as a combination playhouse and bedroom.

In the Yucatán, where rough, rocky ground and plentiful ants can make sleeping out in the jungle difficult, having an "upstairs" room is very convenient.

Dashboard Compass

Although I have a good natural sense of direction, I always carry a keychain compass in Mexico and use it frequently. After driving four hours in the wrong direction in West Texas, I also have a compass mounted on the dash of my vehicle.

Mexican road signs have improved considerably in the past ten years, but they're still less than obvious to the casual visitor. Learning to navigate with a compass and a road map is an easy way to reduce the chances of getting lost. I say "reduce," because getting lost on occasion is almost inevita-

ble. The Yucatán peninsula, for example, has an odd shape
that often throws travelers off by 90 degrees. *Glorietas* (traffic circles) can also scramble your sense of direction. Whenever possible, we have given compass directions to RV parks
and campgrounds listed in the Campground Directory portion of this book.

Locks and Alarms

According to statistics, the greatest chance of being ripped off
in Mexico occurs while parked in large cities. As in the
United States, most thefts in Mexico are done by urban
teenagers. The usual entry method is to jimmy a vent window with a screwdriver or flat bar and then release the door
lock. Because virtually any lock can be broken or bypassed
by a determined thief, your best protection is to be extra cautious when leaving your vehicle unattended in the city. It is
best to take the following precautions:

- Never leave valuables in view inside a locked vehicle.
- Close the curtains, if you have them.
- Park in supervised lots or within sight of a security
  guard.
- Use additional locks on vent windows and sliding
  windows.

Electronic alarms tend to be ignored in Mexico, where
such sounds merely add an interesting new flavor to the
background city noise. Because tourist vehicles often attract
attention and admiration, it isn't unusual to have young people and even adults sitting on your bumper or fenders or
peering curiously into your car. Sensitive electronic alarms
will only "cry wolf" in such situations.

The most practical security device I've used to protect
cameras, tools, and other small valuables was a heavy-gauge
steel strongbox bolted to the floor of a van. The footlocker-
sized box was closed with a serious padlock. The top of the

box was padded and made a nice seat. This simple concept can be adapted to virtually any vehicle or boat.

Fans and Small Appliances

If you'll be staying in RV campgrounds and don't have air conditioning, a small 110-volt fan can be very useful. Besides beating the heat, fans are a wonderful way to keep mosquitoes at bay while you're sleeping.

In RV parks, van and car campers often don't take advantage of electrical hookups that are included in the space fee. Van campers can benefit by carrying a few small electrical conveniences. Electric skillets, blenders, crock pots, popcorn makers, rice cookers, and even ice cream machines work almost as well in Mexico as they do at home. I say "almost" because voltage fluctuations do occur, especially in campgrounds that aren't wired for power-hungry foreign RVs. Expect "brown-outs" and "hot flashes" from time to time. If your electrical appliances are sensitive to these fluctuations, use a surge protector. Most kitchen gadgets can handle Mexican current just fine. Unlike European plug-ins and connectors, Mexico's electrical outlets will accept U.S.-made appliances, however, so carry one or more adapters (3-prong to 2-prong).

Red Tape

Tourist Card

American and Canadian citizens visiting Mexico need just one simple document to cross the border: a tourist card. This card, actually a slip of paper, can be obtained free of charge at the border, at Mexican consulate and tourism offices in large American and Canadian cities, at travel agencies, or from an airline. Tourist cards will be issued on presentation of proof of citizenship: passport, birth certificate, military discharge papers, or notarized proof of citizenship. Naturalized citizens must have a passport or naturalization papers. A driver's license is not proof of citizenship and will not be accepted.

Tourists under 18 years of age must have their parents' notarized consent if traveling alone or with just one parent. For example, a father and son must have the mother's notarized consent in order for the boy to enter Mexico. This rule is not always enforced, but it may be. Children under 15 may be included on their parents' tourist card, but the child cannot leave Mexico without the parent or the parent without the child. It's easier to have a separate tourist card for everyone.

Your tourist card must be validated by Mexican immigration authorities at the border or at the airport when you land in Mexico. The length of your stay is determined at this time. Some tourist cards, especially those issued by airlines and tourist agencies, may have 30, 60, or 90 days in the space preceded by the words *Authorized to Remain in Mexico Days from Date of Entry*. If you want to spend more time in Mexico (up to a legal limit of 180 days), ask the immigration official to change the number. If the space is blank, the officer will ask how long you intend to be in Mexico. Give yourself a wide margin; once the number of days is written down, you're stuck with it.

The best way to convince a skeptical official that you should be given the amount of time you want in Mexico is to be very polite and respectable-looking as possible. Also, have enough money on hand to prove that you aren't a bum. When nothing else works (see Bribes, below), you'll have to take what you get or try crossing into Mexico at another border point.

Tourist cards can be extended (though not beyond the 180 days). Visit an office of *Migración* (Immigration) or *Turismo* (Tourism) inside Mexico before your tourist papers expire. They'll tell you what to do next, but if you don't have proof of solvency (money) you may be out of luck. It all depends on the mood of the official you talk to and your gift of gab.

Vehicle Permits

If you are driving into Mexico (beyond the border zone where casual visits do not require tourist cards), you will be issued, free of charge, a combination tourist card and temporary vehicle importation permit. This permit is issued on presentation of proof of citizenship, valid driver's license, car title or registration (or, if the car is not in your name, a notarized affidavit authorizing you to take the car into Mexico), and current license plates. If your plates are about to expire, don't worry about it; the Mexican police are supposed to overlook this.

Your combination tourist card/car permit will also have noted on it any large accessories such as air-conditioners, radios, tape decks, and small trailers. All these accessories must leave Mexico with you and the car or you are liable for a very stiff duty. This isn't always checked when you leave Mexico but you never know. Along with the car papers, you'll be given two tourist stickers. This decal is pasted onto your windshield and rear or side window and identifies the vehicle as belonging to a tourist. "Tipping" can often speed up the paperwork, and I suggest you view these few dollars as valuable grease to lubricate the bureaucratic machinery.

Note: Car permits are not required for the Baja states, but if you intend to cross to the mainland from Baja, you'll need to visit the customs office in La Paz. (See Baja Ferries, chap. 10.)

You must leave Mexico, with the vehicle and all of its accessories, within the period of time noted as your authorized stay.

Boats, Trailers, Motorcycles, and Towed Cars

A monthly fee and a registration fee based on weight are charged for sport boats taken into Mexico. Depending on the official who issues your papers, this fee may be applied to cartop boats or it may not. Boats over 22 feet in length must be bonded.

Boats, trailers, and towed vehicles are usually treated separately, though they may be included on your car permit if the official at the border decides that would be easier. In other words, your motorbike might need its own papers or your boat, bike, trailer, and hang glider might all be lumped together as accessories. The more things you take into Mexico, the more patient you must be while the *papaleo* (red tape) is being unraveled. Be helpful, patient, calm, and understanding. You have nothing to gain by losing your temper. Tourists who fly off the handle may find themselves refused entry into Mexico. As a visitor, it is your responsibility to be cooperative.

CB radios were once banned in Mexico, but the government has now authorized their use by tourists and private citizens. CB groups are becoming popular in Mexico. However, public use is restricted to channels 11 (emergencies), 13 (caravans), and 14 (general chatter).

Yachts and Private Aircraft

Clearance papers may be obtained at Mexican consulate offices or from marine customs brokers. They must be shown at ports of entry and departure. Boats under five tons are exempt from entry charges (theoretically, anyway). If you or your crew intend to go ashore, you should obtain tourist cards in advance.

The regulations for aircraft are basically the same as for cars. You must also send a written report of your flight plan to authorities of the international airport closest to the point where you intend to cross the border. There are other requirements and I suggest that you visit the nearest Mexican consulate or write to Departmento de Transporte Aereo Internacional, Dirección General de Aeronautica Civil, Secretaria de Comunicaciones y Transportes, Avenida Universidad y Xola, 2 Piso, Mexico 12, D.F. (phone 5-19-81-83 or 5-19-76-25). Or, easier yet, write to Aircraft Owners and Pilots Association, 421 Aviation Way, Frederick, MD 21701, (301) 695-2000. They have a packet of comprehensive information for anyone considering flying into Mexico, including aircraft entry information, customs guide, weather service companies, sample flight reports, a checklist for flight information, and survival equipment sources.

Car and Boat Insurance

Very few insurance policies issued in the United States or Canada are valid in Mexico. There are a bewildering variety of insurance offices on both sides of the border who will quickly write up a policy to cover you and your vehicle (and boat). Basic insurance rates are government controlled, but most companies tack on additional clauses—and charges— that send the price much higher than the legal minimum. Read the policy carefully; the most basic cover only liability (no payment to you, for example, for body work, medical expenses, or theft). Rates decrease significantly for long-term policies.

It is important to understand that in Mexico, insurance isn't just a way to pay off damages, it's also *stay out of jail* protection. In the event of an accident, especially one that involves injuries, all parties may be locked up until claims have been settled. Innocent or guilty, you could find yourself behind bars. Your insurance agent will deal with the police for you. This puts a whole new light on insurance, and for this reason, I heartily recommend that you buy at least minimum liability coverage.

Larger companies (Sanborn's, AAA, and others) give away free guidebooks, road maps, and other information with their policies. Boats and trailers in addition to cars and other vehicles are insured. Most car policies are not valid if the car is used to tow an uninsured boat or trailer. Does your policy cover anyone who drives your car? Check it carefully to be certain. You also won't be covered (in most policies) if you have an accident while driving another vehicle.

Immunizations

There are no immunizations required for tourists visiting Mexico, but campers should have a recent tetanus shot. Some doctors also recommend paratyphoid immunizations; others say it isn't worth it. Consult your family doctor.

Pets

To take a dog or cat into Mexico, you must present a veterinarian's certificate stating that the animal is in good health and has been inoculated against rabies within the past six months. This certificate must be visaed (stamped) by a Mexican consul for a fee. Go to the nearest consul before you leave for Mexico; each consul may certify pets only within the immediate area.

Pets are often a problem while traveling in Mexico, primarily because few hotels or motels (or even trailer parks) will allow them on the premises. Tourists are frequently shocked to find how rigid these rules are. Don't take your pet unless you're willing to put up with this. Keep a close eye on your animal, especially if it bites.

Mexican Customs Inspections, Bribes

Tourists are given a customs check when entering Mexico. This is done at the point where your car papers are issued or tourist card is validated and occasionally at "flying checkpoints" on major highways in northern Mexico.

The customs check is usually quick and casual, but if you're traveling with a vehicle and a great deal of camping gear, you might find yourself subjected to a more detailed inspection. Firearms are the main point of these searches, but, in reality, some customs inspectors use the opportunity to coax a bribe out of tourists who are eager to be on their way. Stay calm and pay the bribe. It probably won't be very much, but if you argue and complain, the price will go up fast. The official policy is that bribes are absolutely prohibited; the reality is that they are often sought out and accepted. Any minor discrepancies in your paperwork or any imagined violations (too many cameras, too much whiskey in the cupboard, etc.) can usually be straightened out with a few dollar bills.

Keep your tourist card, car papers, and other official documents close at hand and in neat, clean condition. Fast checks go even faster when you're prepared for them.

Fishing and Spearfishing Licenses

The rules covering sportfishing and spearfishing seem to change about every two months in Mexico. Local officials often don't know what the rules are and play it by ear. Your best bet is to buy a fishing license (which also covers spearfishing and seafood foraging) and not worry too much about details unless someone questions what you're doing. Some popular bass fishing lakes, for example, fall under local management, and such things as closed seasons and license fees may be changed at any moment.

Fishing licenses, fortunately, are inexpensive. I suggest that you get one before you enter Mexico, especially if you have a boat. Licenses are sold within the country, but it is often difficult to find out exactly where and when they are available. If you fish for bass, take special care to have a license; game wardens seem to concentrate their efforts around popular bass lakes.

Although enforcement of game laws, especially those concerning fishing and diving, is both lax and erratic, tourists shouldn't take advantage by neglecting to buy a licence. This will only bring stricter enforcement in the future (and a higher fee for licenses to pay the costs). Tourists comprise the greatest number of sportfishing enthusiasts in Mexico; set a good example by complying with the law.

For details on Mexican fishing regulations, and to buy a

fishing license by mail, write to Mexican Department of Fisheries, 1138 India Street, Suite 125, San Diego, CA 92101.

Hunting and Guns

The Mexican government has a very definite attitude toward firearms—they don't want tourists to have them in Mexico. The rules, regulations, and fees required for legal hunting are so stiff that I won't bother to detail them here. If you are a very serious hunter write to Wildlife Advisory Services, P.O. Box 76132, Los Angeles, CA 90076, or call (213) 385-9311. They'll explain everything and help you through the mass of paperwork involved.

Illegally importing a gun or ammunition into Mexico is extremely stupid. If you are caught with a gun while traveling in Mexico, the *least* that will happen will be a stiff fine, the loss of the weapon, and a long hassle with the cops or army. Mexicans often ask tourists to bring them guns, but nothing will ruin your vacation faster than getting caught.

Mexico: It's the Law

Tourists enjoy almost all of the rights of full Mexican citizens. When tourists do run afoul of the law, it is usually the result of drugs, auto accidents, or immoral behavior. For full details, I suggest you read *The People's Guide to Mexico,* Tourists and the Law. Briefly, it is illegal to possess and use drugs (the usual types, from marijuana to pills and heroin) and dangerous to be around anyone who does. The Mexican police operate on the principle that it's easier to arrest everyone at the scene of a suspected crime and then sort out the guilty from the innocent later (sometimes a lot later). Uninsured motorists involved in an accident are almost assured of a visit to the local jail, especially if there is an injury. An insurance agent is much cheaper than a lawyer and works a good deal faster to get you out on the street again.

Immoral behavior almost always means public nudity, which is absolutely illegal and very offensive to most Mexicans. This is a constant problem for the Mexican authorities, especially with sun-loving European tourists who think nudity is natural rather than offensive. I don't like to involve myself in other people's affairs, but when campers start stripping, I consider it self-protection to ask them to go elsewhere. If they won't, we consider moving.

Crossing the U.S. Border

"Are you United States citizens? How far into Mexico did you folks travel? How long were you down there? Do you have any agricultural products with you, any eggs, meat, or fruit? Do you have anything else to declare?"

Questions such as these will be your greeting on returning to the United States. Though tales of long intensive vehicle inspections and "strip-down" drug searches by zealous customs agents are true, millions of people cross the border every year without a second glance. A few simple preparations should make your border crossing as brief as a few minutes.

1. Answer all questions simply and forthrightly. There's no reason to be nervous, but if you are, don't overcompensate by joking around or telling fish stories. Customs agents are serious law officers, not Welcome Wagon volunteers.

2. If you've ever considered slipping a little something across the border, be it an extra jug of tequila, a pinch or two of dope, or an undeclared sack of oranges, banish this idea immediately. Playing hide-and-seek is a foolish and potentially costly way to end your trip.

3. To simplify matters, have a rough list at hand of your major purchases in Mexico. Again, don't overdo it by listing

every peso. Unless you've spent well beyond the $400-per-person exemption, most agents won't quibble about dutiable goods.

4. What can you bring back to the United States and what is prohibited? The list is long, complex, and constantly changing. Each adult may bring in a quart of liquor, any number of cigarettes (but only 100 cigars), medicines accompanied by a U.S. prescription (or a good excuse), peanuts, garlic, coffee beans, papayas, and almost any food not grown in the United States. In general, don't have citrus fruits, birds, anything of bone or hair or feather, ivory, meat, switchblades, narcotics or hallucinogens, potted plants, or pornography. What does this leave? For endless lists of approved and prohibited items, write to: U.S. Customs Service, Washington, D.C. 20229, or U.S. Department of Agriculture, Federal Building, Hyattsville, MD 20782.

RVs are obviously large enough to hide a considerable amount of contraband. If a customs agent decides to give your rig a closer look, you'll be directed to a large inspection area. Again, this is routine and often random—they haven't necessarily pegged you for a drug smuggler. The usual onceover includes a visual inspection of the vehicle's engine compartment, luggage racks, storage areas, chassis, and interior cupboards. If you stand back and let them do their job, such an inspection can be completed very quickly, often in less than 15 minutes. If you get cranky and combative, however, or lose the keys to a locked closet, the delays can become hours long.

Dope-sniffing dogs are also used on RVs. If you have a pet inside, be sure to advise the agent and dog handler. They may decide to do a visual check, rather than upset your pet.

CHAPTER 3

On the Road

On my first trip to Mexico, four of us crowded into Steve's brand-new Volvo sedan. Volvo prides itself on building a tough car, but overloading and high-speed driving on poor roads soon took care of the suspension and exhaust system, not to mention alignment, tires, motor mounts, and miscellaneous parts torn or rattled away. Erratic maintenance and dirty gas kept the car permanently out of tune, reducing gas mileage to a bad joke. Instead of a car, we needed a Sherman tank on that trip.

Whatever you drive to Mexico, try to strike a reasonable balance between convenience, economy, comfort, and practicality. Careful planning, however, should not be allowed to mushroom into needless and expensive overpreparation. Remember, money equals time and new experiences. The price of a fancy chrome trailer hitch will hire a boat in Mexico for a long jungle river cruise you'll never forget. A one-week trip with lavish gear costs more than a month of camping with improvised equipment. Use self-control; hide your trip money until you're on the road.

Driving

In spite of what you may have heard at the rumor mill, driving in Mexico will not cause you to lose your hair or your sanity. It is a challenge, however, especially for those who are accustomed to the luxurious conditions of the American freeway system. Typical Mexican interstate highways are narrow, two-lane blacktop with meager shoulders. These highways are more or less equivalent to secondary roads in the United States and Canada. I say ''more or less'' because highway budgets in Mexico often don't match maintenance requirements. Asphalt highways take a terrible beating from heavy trucks and intense summer heat. Depending on the weather and local repair crews, a section of highway can be fine one year and in poor condition the next. Potholes will be repaired ''soon'' and narrow bridges replaced ''some day.'' There are freeways in Mexico, but these relatively brief sections of four-lane and specially maintained toll highways are the exception, not the rule.

Whenever I'm discussing Mexico with first-time travelers, the question of safety while driving inevitably comes up. In an average year, I drive between 5,000 and 10,000 miles in Mexico, on everything from Baja back roads to the Mexico City-Toluca Freeway, with a lot of mountains, switchbacks, savannahs, deserts, and unplanned side trips in between. In my experience, safe driving in Mexico boils down to the Four Cs: common sense, caution, courtesy, and constant attention to the road ahead. Drivers who become complacent or impatient, or those who drink behind the wheel, can definitely run into trouble.

By American standards, driving conditions in Mexico can usually be rated fair to difficult. A typical camping trip can include thousands of miles of driving combined with warm temperatures, frequent ups and downs, low-octane gas, and occasional rough road surfaces. Such conditions are challenging but not inherently dangerous or even that difficult, especially for the careful driver.

To avoid undue strain on your vehicle, I strongly suggest that you avoid overloading. Know your vehicle's rated capacity, and do your best to keep loads under this rating. Never push your RV or van to the limit or exceed design capabilities. "Just one more box of groceries and fishing tackle, that's all I ask!" is a plea that must be denied, no ifs, ands, or buts!

Highway grades are often steeper in Mexico than you might expect and mountain curves seem to get tighter as you go south. Good brakes and quick reflexes can't be depended on to compensate for dangerous overloads. When in doubt, leave it out!

Expect to find objects in the highway, especially rocks, bottles, and dead burros. If your vehicle is heavily loaded and unwieldy, quick braking and emergency swerves will be especially hazardous.

Overloading will also lead to overheating of the vehicle's cooling system and excessive wear on brakes, clutch, and running gear.

The following driving tips will help keep you safe:

1. Drive at moderate, conservative speeds, and *expect the unexpected*. I once drove for ten hours in southern Oaxaca without a single distraction—and then I relaxed and hit a single, unexpected pothole in an otherwise unblemished highway. Lowering my guard cost me a busted front shock and a ruptured tire. I rarely drive over 55 mph and I often go 45 or 50 mph.

2. Be prepared to brake at any time. It is not unusual in Mexico to find stalled trucks blocking entire lanes or burros meditating on the centerline. Such situations can occur anywhere, at any time.

3. Beware of fast traffic overtaking and passing you in the left lane. Don't drift into the left lane or use the left lane with-

out checking your rearview mirror carefully. I can't count the number of times I've been unexpectedly passed by cars going over 80 mph.

4. Do not drive at night if you can avoid it. All the hazards of daytime driving will be obscured and complicated by darkness.

5. If you have to drive too fast or too hard to keep to your schedule, change your schedule. Breakdowns—whether in equipment or your humor—inevitably occur when you push things too hard. You can't possibly see all of Mexico in one or two trips, so why not relax and save some of it for the next time?

6. In Mexico, a left-turn signal also means *Siga* (Go ahead, it is safe to pass me). A right-turn signal means *Alto* (Stop or be careful, not safe to pass me). If you are being tailgated, use these signals as a courtesy to the driver behind you.

7. Expect to be tailgated, but don't lose your temper. Insulting or challenging another driver in Mexico can lead to dangerous confrontations. Because turnouts are rare and highway shoulders are narrow, it can be hazardous to move over to allow others to pass. That's okay—Mexican drivers are accustomed to slow trucks.

8. If the highway is constricted by a narrow bridge or disabled vehicle, the standard rule of the road says that the first vehicle to flash its headlights has the right-of-way. When in doubt, apply the brakes.

9. What if an oncoming vehicle flashes its lights at you and the highway seems clear? This signal means there is a road hazard ahead of you. To acknowledge the warning, wave or blink your lights or turn signal in return. In mountainous areas, particularly, this signal can save you and others from unpleasant surprises.

10. American and Canadian auto insurance policies are not valid in Mexico. Buy insurance from an authorized agency at the border before crossing into Mexico. It takes only about 20 minutes.

Cops and Bribes

It is sad but true that the sight of a foreign license plate incites some Mexican traffic cops to invent driving infractions and solicit on-the-spot fines, better known as *mordidas* (bribes). Big RVs and fancier vehicles are especially attractive to crooked cops. In Tijuana, for example, an officer advised an RVer trailing a dune buggy behind his rig that it was "illegal to tow a car in Mexico." Though the gringo knew this wasn't true, he coughed up ten dollars to avoid further hassle.

Some people flatly refuse to pay bribes; others take a more philosophical attitude toward the practice. Keep in mind, too, that when they aren't preying on tourists, the police are pulling the same tricks on fellow Mexicans. Tourists can usually avoid paying unjust "fines" by using one of these tried-and-tested responses:

—Calmly, politely, and persistently refuse to pay. As a last resort, agree to pay only when you've actually gone to the police station and been issued a citation. This bluff is very effective, especially if you don't lose your temper. It is a serious offense to insult a public official or police officer in Mexico. Smile and say, "No, I prefer not to," until your opponent gets the point. Even if you did violate a traffic law, many cops don't want to waste their time on due process; they'd rather turn you loose and find a more willing victim. Don't worry about language barriers. Bribe-seeking cops usually speak English. If they don't, smile and play dumb.

—Never use the term *mordida* (bribe); it offends a crooked cop's sensibilities. "Here's something for sodas," is the preferred explanation for involuntary contributions. A cop in Guanajuato told Steve, "Give me something for beer." Steve successfully checkmated this request with a deadpan, "I wouldn't consider it. I'm an ex-alcoholic."

—A confident, no-nonsense manner will undermine a corrupt cop's resolve much faster than indignation. Rather than engaging in small talk, let your attitude convey, "I have more serious fish to fry.'' After being pulled over near Mexico City for failure to use my turn signal (guilty as charged), I made a businesslike show of jotting down the cop's license number before asking for his name and badge number. ''What for?'' he replied, immediately on the defense. ''So the judge can deduct the money I'm giving you from my fine,'' I replied. Instead of paying him off, I got a police escort to the edge of town and a salute.

—You may be asked to produce your identification and documents. I show my driver's license and *photocopies* of my tourist card and car permit rather than originals, just in case he decides to hold these papers hostage. If the cop goes over your documents with a fine-tooth comb and finds a minor error or invents one, don't cave in. He is a traffic cop, not a customs or immigration official. Major errors are another story; it might be best to pay up.

—Other useful ploys include asking to be taken to the nearest tourism office, or to the mayor's office *(presidencia)*. If you are retired military or associated with any law enforcement agency, flash your I.D. card or wallet badge to invoke ''professional immunity.''

—Don't carry the policy of never paying a bribe too far. If the cop is genuinely belligerent or drunk, for example, I swallow my indignation and reach for my wallet. Hand over a dollar or two; if that isn't enough, he'll be glad to let you know.

—In some cases, a bribe may be ''justified.'' In Valladolid, for example, I wanted to double park in front of a supermarket. I explained this to a traffic cop and was given permission—for about fifty cents.

Back Roads

When facing a very steep grade, up or down, stop and survey the prospects on foot. Downgrades *going in* are upgrades *coming out.* We've run into upgrades that took every spare shoulder to push us over the top. If you can't make a grade, try unloading and/or backing up the grade. Giving up, of course, is the safest choice. I let the decision rest on my burning desire to continue, balanced by my dread of getting badly stuck. If I smell good camping or fishing over the next ridge, we usually hang on and go for it.

Extremely tight switchbacks can be impossible to get around in less than two tries. Have someone block the rear wheels with a large rock or piece of wood before you make the second try. On very steep roads, have someone walk alongside and behind the vehicle, prepared to block the wheels on quick notice. Tell them to watch out for flying gravel and rocks. This type of road is usually found deep in the mountains. Drive with great care. Extra ballast in the rear, either rocks or passengers, may improve traction.

Driving on sand is an interesting and often tense experience. Once you're moving along on top of the sand, it's best to hold the speed steady; don't overreact if you can avoid it. Hitting the brakes or swerving may sink you right down to the frame. Damage is unlikely, but you are definitely stuck. Driving on sand is much like driving on snow. Lug the engine slightly instead of shifting to a lower gear. This prevents spinning the tires, a sure way to bury them in the sand. When you must downshift, do it very gently.

Don't drive on beaches unless you are very confident and have full insurance coverage. We came within minutes of losing Steve's brand-new Volvo to the tide. One second we were flying down the beach, laughing and honking at the seagulls; the next, we were in sand up to the frame, 50 miles from the nearest tow truck. By one of those miracles familiar to Mexico travelers, a nearby rancher produced a World War II vintage Dodge Power Wagon and plucked us out, just as waves were lapping at the tires. Anyone who camps on the beach will certainly spend at least one afternoon helping some foolish motorist dig out of the sand.

Unimproved dirt roads quickly become unimproved

mud slides during the rainy season. Though they may dry quickly and be passable most of the time, even during *las aguas* (rainy season), extra caution should be used. Slides, falling rocks, washouts, and deep unmarked fords are common hazards. This is especially true in the deserts and mountains, where runoff really runs. I always thought Hollywood movies that included monster flash floods were a joke—until I saw one.

When it starts to rain, find a place to wait it out. A delay is better than getting stuck; once you're stuck, you'll be waiting anyway. If you're driving in an arroyo or canyon and can't get out, or if you are definitely stuck, abandon the vehicle and run to high ground.

Never attempt to ford a stream during a rainstorm unless your chances are 100 percent that you'll get safely across. Water that is a foot deep now can easily rise to three feet or more within minutes. I know of one case where a passenger bus was swept away by a flash flood. Your car or pickup would be a chip in comparison.

Stuck Again

When you get stuck, your pathetic call of "Hey? Could ya gimme a hand for a minute?" will ruin a hot afternoon for some obliging soul. Before you go for reinforcements, make a valiant effort with a *shovel,* preferably normal size, but a folding "foxhole" shovel will do, and g*loves* —if you carry two pair your friend can help, too. Stay calm: wheel spinning, mindless shouting, and frenzied fender beating should be used only as a last resort.

The following suggestions can be used one at a time or all together. I prefer the full-scale approach; in the long run, it saves time and energy and avoids worsening the situation with frustrating failures, which tend to soften the ground.

Start by straightening the vehicle's wheels. Keep them straight throughout the entire rescue operation.

Clear any obstructions from in front and in back of all four tires and from under the frame. If one or more tires are in a hole, jack the vehicle up. I always carry a jack pad, a thick square of rough plywood for jacking on soft sand and mud. Rocks make lousy jack pads; they're slippery and therefore very dangerous. When the tire is out of the hole, slip rocks beneath it. Enlarge the hole if necessary before filling it with stones, especially in very loose soil. Branches, grass, fronds, brush, boards, floor mats, and pieces of your nice carpet will also give better traction. In a pinch, use blankets. Be careful while working under a raised vehicle. Jacks usually fail when someone is under them.

When the vehicle is back down on all fours, release air in the tires to about ten pounds of pressure (almost flat). This is too little pressure to drive on, so I hope you didn't forget the tire pump. Now unload passengers and cargo. This is optional, since in some cases the weight increases traction (especially uphill). I'd give a first try at getting unstuck with the extra weight and then jettison the baggage if it doesn't work.

If you've got a tow chain or heavy rope and another vehicle, connect them (bumper to bumper or frame to frame, not to the tie rods, which bend like pretzels). If the nearest solid ground is ahead of you, the first move will be forward, in second gear (or Drive, for automatics). This strains the poor engine but helps prevent overrevving and tire spinning. Tire spinning will get you nowhere. Ease your foot off the clutch and gently press down on the gas. Don't look back; your friends should keep pushing and screaming until you've definitely reached solid ground.

Didn't make it? Try rocking the vehicle back and forth by alternately shifting into first and reverse. The idea is to get a rhythm going, assisted by the weight of the vehicle, to swing you free (forward or backward; at this point either way out is better than staying stuck). A friend at each end can help a great deal.

No luck? Look for large, strong levers—something the size of a fencepost. Have your friends use them under the frame and/or bumper (VW bumpers tend to fall off at this point) as you move the vehicle forward to backward. Don't rock it; you'll hurt the people with the pry bars. Still can't get out? Turn to the Appendix and study some Spanish. You're going to have to wait for more help.

Preparing Your Vehicle

Long-distance driving and camping can take their toll on even the strongest vehicle. With this in mind, some people invest a tremendous amount of time and money in the meticulous preparation of their vehicle, including enough spare parts to stock a certified repair facility. Others take a "wait and see" attitude about predeparture repairs and spares. After all, they say, Mexico is a relatively modern country, with thousands of miles of paved highways, auto parts stores, and trained mechanics.

After driving tens of thousands of miles in Mexico, my own attitude toward vehicle preparation lies somewhere between "go with the flow" and "don't forget the spark plugs and WD 40!" No matter what your attitude is about planning ahead, one thing is certain: breakdowns and jury-rigged repairs always take more time and money than preventive maintenance and spares.

Before You Leave

Whether you're a very conservative Sunday driver or a hell-for-leather type, don't neglect to do the following: (1) a complete tune-up and lubrication, which will help you save money on gas, cut down on wear and tear, and pollute less; and (2) a careful check and test of your vehicle's operation. The costs of preparing for Mexico are often easier to swallow if you consider them as long-term improvements and insurance against vacation-consuming breakdowns. In particular, I "bite the bullet" when it comes to tires, brakes, battery, and shocks.

TIRES AND TUBES

Check the spare, too. We've had consistently miserable luck with recapped tires on Mexican roads, especially on long trips. Heat and chuckholes will murder recaps; try to use real tires if you can afford them. My time-tested rule of thumb is "get the best tires you can afford" for Mexico. The last time I broke this rule, it cost me a $1,000 penalty. It went like this: tires in half-inch sizes are not available in Mexico. Mexican tires come in standard sizes, the most common being 14-, 15-, 16-, and 17-inch. In spite of this, I did not want to buy new wheels for a van with 16.5-inch tires. Instead, I bought a full set of new 16.5-inch tires. I compounded my mistake by buying off-brand tires, on sale for just $50 each. "We'll replace these at the first opportunity," I told Lorena, assuming our new tires would last at least 20,000 miles or more.

Thus began a saga of broken and shredding tires (at 5,000 miles) that ended with broken wheels and, eventually, entirely new sets of both wheels and tires. I not only lost my shirt on the deal, but I spent at least ten full days in tire repair shops throughout Mexico contemplating my sins.

Car tires are plentiful in Mexico, but radial and truck tires are very scarce. Inner tubes are also expensive.

Loosen and then carefully retighten the lug nuts on all four wheels before you leave home, especially if you haven't done this within the past few months. The lug nuts on our van were frozen tight, a discovery I made in the middle of the Sonora Desert when a tire suddenly went flat. I ruined our lug wrench and almost broke my back in a futile attempt to remove the tire.

Lubricate the lug nuts with a bit of heavy grease, or WD 40 motor oil if you'll be near salt water for very long. On most vehicles, a good cleaning of the nut threads with a wire brush will suffice, but some, like our VW van, require careful, light greasing. Check them again for proper tightness after an hour or less of driving.

BRAKES
You'll need and want them, believe me. Check the brake fluid level before you leave and every few days while on the road. Check the condition of the brakes. If they need work, do it before you leave home.

BATTERY
Check the battery frequently. Higher air temperatures in Mexico plus the heat of your engine can dry up a battery in record time. Carry distilled water, improvise a filter, or exorcize crud from ditch water by chanting, ''Pure! Pure! Pure!''

Camping and extended driving will put a considerable strain on your battery. Unless your vehicle's battery is in tiptop condition, give serious thought to buying a new, heavy-duty one. Battery problems have an awful way of turning into expensive alternator-regulator problems. If possible, get a deep-cycle RV or truck battery.

RV batteries cost about twice as much as a regular battery, but they're worth it. Steve's RV battery is still going strong after seven years. Rather than add an additional battery and wiring, Steve modified the battery holder in his van (with the brutal use of a hammer and pliers) to fit the oversized RV battery. ''I can use all of the van's interior lights and the tape deck for at least a week without running the engine,'' he brags, though I noted a handy pair of jumper cables in his tool box.

COOLING SYSTEM
You might want to change the thermostat. Flush the radiator and replace the coolant. Clean air-cooled engines thoroughly, and, when the roads are dusty, clean them again.

STEERING, FRONT-END SUSPENSION
If your tires are wearing unevenly or if the car shimmies or handles oddly, get the front end checked. Improper alignment and balance can eat up new tires before your very eyes, especially on a long trip.

HORN
Mexican drivers use horns like gringos use CB radios. If you want to be heard . . .

HEADLIGHTS
Clean the lenses and consider a set of driving lights for occasions when you violate the Golden Rule and decide to chance driving at night. It's best to attach driving lights permanently to thwart thieves.

WINDSHIELD WIPERS
Poor visibility is said to be a major cause of auto accidents. Having tried driving without wipers on various occasions, I firmly believe it.

DRIVING MIRRORS
Defensive driving is the absolute rule in Mexico. You alone are responsible for your safety. Don't expect other drivers to watch out for you; they're looking out for themselves. Never move out of your lane without checking both rearview and sideview mirrors. If you use truck-type mirrors, be careful— driving on narrow colonial streets in Mexico raises hell with wide mirrors and unsuspecting pedestrians. A friend was struck from behind and seriously injured by a motor homer's mirror in San Miguel de Allende. Folding truck mirrors are almost essential in narrow streets.

Corrosion Prevention

Camping on the beach can lead to serious corrosion problems for your vehicle and equipment, including cameras, metal tent parts, bicycles, cupboard hinges, and RV plumbing and fittings. Before you arrive at the beach, consider having a protective and lubricating *soplete de diesel* (a "puff" or spray of diesel oil) applied to the bottom of your vehicle. This inexpensive service is available at larger Pemex stations, truck stops, and some car washes. It stinks for a while, but the oil should reduce saltwater corrosion.

Your next line of defense against corrosion is to have the vehicle regularly washed with high-pressure soap and water. Again, this service is available at Pemex stations and large car washes.

Last but not least, carry a generous supply of WD 40 and apply it frequently to all exposed hinges, nuts, screw heads, and moving parts. Don't forget lug nuts and roof rack fittings, padlocks, mirror posts, and even the radiator cap.

Any other metal equipment, especially fishing reels, should be regularly washed with warm, soapy water, rinsed, then lubricated. In the jungles of Quintana Roo, I found corrosion on my cameras, even though they were tightly sealed in a metal ammo can. Aluminum tent poles, backpack fittings, and metal fuel canisters are also subject to corrosion.

Spares to Take with You

Although there is a popular belief that *anything* can be found in Mexico City if you look hard enough, don't count on it. In fact, parts for most newer cars and trucks are difficult if not impossible to find in Mexico. For example, Steve lost a considerable amount of his already endangered hair trying to locate brake master cylinders for a 1981 Chevrolet van. When he finally found the much-needed parts in a small shop in Oaxaca, they were triple the stateside price.

Although Mexico manufactures cars, vans, and trucks (including VW, Nissan, Ford, Chrysler, and Dodge) in various familiar sizes and shapes, specific models and parts often don't match non-Mexican vehicles. As Steve says, "Mexican engines seem to be stuck somewhere back in the sixties and seventies, before the proliferation of electronic ignition and pollution control." As a consequence, Mexico's fabled shade tree mechanical geniuses often lack experience with high-tech automotive systems.

The solution to this problem isn't easy. Because I spend so much time in Mexico, I choose to drive older vehicles, preferably VWs, Fords, or Chevrolets (currently, a one-ton '78 Ford van). Newer one-ton and larger vans and trucks also have simpler engines, for which parts are more likely to be available in Mexico.

If your vehicle has electronic ignition, take spare parts (used parts make good spares if they've been tested). Consult with a mechanic or ask the dealership service manager for advice. Experienced mechanics know which parts and systems are most likely to fail on a particular vehicle.

Parts and repairs for air-conditioning systems and automatic transmissions are available erratically in larger Mexican cities. Look in the *Seccion Amarilla* (Yellow Pages) or inquire at a parts store for the local mechanical wizard.

Pollution control devices can stump any mechanic. Again, take parts or consider bypassing the system once you're in Mexico.

Unreliable supplies and distribution of Extra unleaded gasoline have put the brakes on many drivers' plans for Mexico. (See Gas and Oil, below.) What can you do, however, if your engine must burn unleaded gasoline because of pollution control accessories, yet you find yourself in an area of Mexico where unleaded fuel is simply not available? Although burning a few tankfuls of leaded gas probably won't destroy your catalytic converter (check with a mechanic or authorized service dealer to be certain), continued use can cause poor performance and costly problems. Pollution control is not required by law in Mexico. The solution, therefore, is to disable or bypass the pollution control system once you leave the United States. U.S. auto parts stores sell a simple device called a "pollution control" or "catalytic converter" tester. This tester is just a bypass. Install it yourself, or stop at any Mexican muffler or auto repair shop. Don't forget to remove the tester and reconnect the catalytic converter before you return to the United States.

Cars are very expensive in Mexico and even the most beat-up *carcachas* (jalopies) are still chugging away. Used parts are relatively scarce, relatively expensive, and *well used*. The time to buy spares is before you need them, not afterward. (I tell myself this every time I hitch to the nearest parts store.) The following spares should cover average driving anywhere without breaking your budget:

Fan and other belts: Check sizes carefully and take a full set.

Hoses: Carry spares, especially if the hoses are one of a kind.

Motor oil: Take enough for one change or more.

Filters; oil, fuel, and air: Take enough for the trip if they're an odd size or brand. Air filters are especially difficult to find in Mexico.

Brake fluid, transmission fluid

Fuses, bulbs

Fire extinguishers: For cheap insurance, get two!

Flare or reflector: Repairs often take place in the middle of the road in Mexico, especially if there's no shoulder.

Repair manual: Buy a service manual, or at least make clear notes of vital tolerances, gaps, settings, and other routine maintenance specifications. Mexican mechanics will take on any job, regardless of their training and tools (or lack thereof). Many mechanics do not know how to read, so don't expect them to have exact technical information. Adjustments, no matter how critical, are done by ear and intuition. If you've got a VW, buy *How to Keep Your Volkswagen Alive* or *How to Keep Your Rabbit Alive* (Santa Fe, N.M.: John Muir Publications). The former is also available in Spanish. (See Recommended Reading in the Appendix for ordering information.)

Spares for Roadside Repairs

Those who yearn for backcountry adventures should be even better prepared for roadside repairs. A "Damn the torpedoes!" approach can be balanced somewhat by a well-filled toolbox, a spare parts kit, and plenty of reading material for those occasional long waits for assistance. (See Breakdowns and Repairs, below, for information on Mexican government tourist assistance patrols.)

If you must leave your car unattended for any reason, make every effort to find someone to watch it for you. Offer a generous payment; after all, it's cheap insurance against theft or vandalism. Tell them, *"Cuidalo dia y noche, por favor"* (Watch it day and night, please).

I recommend that you carry:

Set of spark plugs, points, and condenser

Fine emery paper for electrical contact cleaning

Feeler gauges for setting the points and valves

Pure alcohol or commercial cleaner for cleaning and drying the distributor on really dusty or wet roads.

Tire and inner tubes: Slow leaks caused by slightly bent wheel rims are beyond most amateurs' abilities to repair. By installing tubes in your tires, you'll avoid this problem. Tubeless recaps are the worst choice for rough roads; when they come apart, it's usually unexpected and irreparable. If you travel deep into the boondocks, carry patching materials— enough for all four tires in case you happen to blunder into a thorn patch. Mexico is the land of the slow leak.

Iron pipe or crowbar: The pipe will extend the leverage of your lug wrench handle. The crowbar is for emergency body work and prying giant limpets off rocks.

Gas: A one-gallon can of spare gas is the minimum. Carry extra gas filters, too. (See Maintenance, below.)

Siphon hose, chamois, funnel for transferring gas.

Water for drinking, filling the radiator, and topping off the battery. If you drive in the desert, especially on bad roads, carry enough water to survive at least three or four days: two quarts per day per person is the minimum. Don't use antifreeze or any other radiator additive if you want to use radiator water for emergency drinking. Don't laugh: almost every year someone dies of thirst in Mexico's deserts.

Tools

Even if you avoid doing your own car repairs, it's wise to carry a basic selection of tools. A friend claims that the tools listed below will repair almost anything in the world, let alone an average car.

Standard screwdrivers, large, medium, and small
Phillips-head screwdriver, medium
Vise Grip pliers, 10-inch
Regular pliers, with wire-cutting jaw
Open end wrenches, metric or standard
Crescent wrench, 10-inch
Jack and lug wrench
Tire pressure gauge (get a good one; cheap gauges are worthless)
Electrical tape and wire
Baling wire
Flashlight
Rags

A *big jack* is next on the list. In fact, carry two jacks—
the one that came with your vehicle and a larger, more stable
jack for quick, middle-of-the-highway tire changes.
Pemex stations often don't have compressed air when
and where you need it. Rather than straining your heart
valves with a hand pump, get an electric one that plugs into
the cigarette lighter, with an automatic shutoff switch. An
electric tire pump is essential for slow leaks or if you're
traveling with kids who want their rafts, soccer balls, and air
mattresses inflated every day. I use a 12-volt minicompressor
from Sears which works like a charm.

Gas and Oil

Gas stations are found along all of Mexico's major highways
and arterials. Look for the big PEMEX sign (*PEtroleos MEX-
icanos*, a government monopoly).

There are just two types of gas: Nova (blue pump,
leaded, about 82 octane, 85 cents a gallon) and Extra (silver
pump, unleaded, about 90 octane, 95 cents a gallon). Diesel
is very common and about 77 cents a gallon.

Uncertainty about the availability of unleaded gasoline
in Mexico has had a serious impact on overland tourism.
Because cars made in Mexico do not require unleaded fuel,
gas stations may not stock Extra. Extra also costs more than
leaded gas and doesn't sell as well to Mexican drivers. In
spite of this, unleaded gasoline is usually (but not always)
available in Pemex stations on Highway 1 in Baja and on the
Pacific coast south to Acapulco. North of Mexico City, Extra
will usually be found along major highways and in large cities. Generally, unleaded gas is not available south of Mexico
City and Acapulco, though there are exceptions. Though the
Mexican government is trying to force more gas stations to
carry unleaded, don't expect to find Extra with any certainty
south of Mexico City or in the Yucatán peninsula. Don't even
bother to look for unleaded in small, rural gas stations.

Off the main roads, you'll have to be satisfied with Nova. It may come out of a battered steel drum, a milk can, or a plastic jug, but at least it's gasoline. When there's no gas station in sight, start looking for crudely lettered signs that say *gasolina*. A couple of dented gas drums outside of a house or *tienda* (small store) probably mean they sell it on the side. Ask anyone, *"¿Donde hay gasolina?"* (Where is there gas?). *"¿No hay gasolina?"* (Isn't there gas?) is also good, especially when accompanied with a smile and a sincere *"¿Por favor?"* Most backyard gasoline costs at least twice as much as it does at the pumps and often even more. It beats running out.

Truck drivers are very helpful and may offer a drain from their own tank. Always offer to pay: *"Muchisimas gracias. ¿Cuanto le debo?"* (Many thanks. How much do I owe you?)

Carry your own siphon hose, neatly rolled up and protected from dirt by a thick plastic bag. Because gas from casual sources may be dirty or contaminated with water, I always try to filter it through a piece of chamois. A good-sized funnel makes filtering much easier. If I suspect water in my gas (likely along the coast or during the rainy season), I also dump a pint or so of pure alcohol (not tequila; it's half water) into the gas tank to help burn off the moisture.

Before buying gas from a barrel, give it a close sniff to make sure it really is gasoline. Mistakes are rare, but all it takes is a few gallons of diesel in a gas-fueled engine to cause dramatic problems. We once got a tank of kerosene. Surprisingly, the car actually ran, though not very well.

Once you've located enough gas to continue your journey, ask if there's more ahead: *"¿Hay gasolina alla?"* (Is there gas there?) Wave your hand vaguely in the direction you're headed and they'll understand. *"¿Esta muy lejos?"* (Is it very far?) Remember that the word *far* can mean just about anything in Mexico, from around the next bend to well over the horizon.

If possible, take enough high-quality engine oil to last

the entire trip. Engine oil and lubricants are widely available in Mexico, but fussier mechanics than I claim that American-made is better. Oil is sold in Pemex stations and auto parts stores, but it's harder to find in the backcountry. Auto parts stores are the best places to look for additives; only the largest Pemex stations carry them.

Antifreeze is difficult to find, so bring extra coolant or buy *lubricante para bomba de agua* (water pump lubricant) to add to your radiator should you have to fill it with plain water. This additive lubricates the water pump and stops oxidation in the cooling system.

Maintenance

Manufacturers' recommendations for various fluid and filter changes are usually based on American highway driving, not Mexican conditions. Read your vehicle's maintenance manual and follow the instructions for extreme conditions. This usually means that routine servicing schedules must be doubled, that is, change the oil and filters every 3,000 miles instead of every 6,000 or 7,000.

I changed the oil in our VW van every 1,500 miles rather than every 3,000. If it looked dirty even sooner, I'd gnash my teeth but go ahead and change it. The same goes for gas filters, air cleaners, oil filters, and whatever else is vital to your machine. If you want to guarantee the long life of your engine, follow these guidelines carefully.

Rough roads can play hell with ignition timing, valve settings, the distributor point gap, hose connections, and so on. I halve the suggested times between tune-ups and valve adjustments. Checking the points more often gives me a chance to clean dust from the distributor and to wipe down the engine. After a really bad stretch of road I check the battery; half the time it's managed to fall over. It also goes dry when I least expect it.

Check your tires often, especially on rocky roads. Gashes and bubbles are potential blowouts. I either change a damaged tire right away or let some air out (down to 50% of normal pressure) and continue with great caution. If the damage isn't too bad, I'll leave the tire on until I get to a repair shop. Don't risk highway driving on a bad tire, however; the consequences of a blowout are just too awful.

Carry at least five spare gallons of gas when exploring back roads, and top off your tank whenever possible. Don't be lazy and put it off.

Drive slowly! Speed combined with unexpected and unmarked rocks and holes will lead to breakdowns and blowouts. Put it in first or second, hang your arm out the window, and enjoy the scenery.

Stop for frequent rests, for the driver, passengers, and the engine. Overheating can be a problem on bad roads, and driver fatigue is dangerous. When you can't go on without great suffering and squabbling, it's past time to stop. Find a reasonable campsite and rest for the night.

Don't drive at night. You're not only exposing yourself to additional driving hazards, but also undoubtedly missing some nice scenery. Nighttime is for campfires, tall tales, and the bogeyman. If you must drive at night, use extreme caution. Watch for livestock, deer, and well-concealed chuckholes. You'll probably see them all.

The lower your vehicle's ground clearance, the slower you must go to avoid problems. A busted oil pan is a disaster anywhere, but 100 miles into the Sierra Madre, it's a downright depressing development. One impatient gringo spent ten days camped next to his car, waiting for parts. Low-slung vehicles can make it over very lousy roads but only with extra care.

Breakdowns and Repairs

As part of a national program to encourage RV tourism, the Mexican government has increased the number of ''Green

Angel'' tourist-assistance trucks on the country's highways. These trucks are equipped with radios, first-aid kits, spare parts, and gasoline. Some, but not all, of the drivers speak English. Green Angel patrols are arranged to cover all major highways at least twice a day. In reality, they may pass by more or less frequently, depending on their work load.

Lorena and I have been helped by Green Angels on several occasions. In every case, we found them to be extremely helpful and courteous. They do not accept gratuities, but you will be asked to fill out a report form. In the Yucatán, a Green Angel driver flagged down two semi trucks when our wrenches wouldn't loosen the lug nuts on our van's rear wheel.

''Do you have a bar that would loosen these nuts?'' the Green Angel asked the truck driver. The man hopped down from the cab with a big grin on his face and dove into his tool compartment. ''Listen,'' he said, ''I've got a bar here that would loosen the Devil's nuts!''

It is the custom in Mexico to help motorists who have broken down. Like many other visitors, I've been helped by Good Samaritans with everything from flat tires to an empty gas tank. On one memorable occasion in the middle of the Sonoran desert, two ranchers crawled under our VW van in their best clothes and jury-rigged a broken clutch cable. They then escorted us over 100 miles to a garage, declining any payment. Better yet, the mechanic replaced our damaged clutch with parts from his own VW, invited us to dinner, and let us camp in his front yard. We were back on the road the next morning. Total bill: $25. Stories such as this are common among travelers in Mexico.

Should you need a *mecanico* (mechanic), look for signs announcing *Taller Mecanico* or *Taller Automotriz* or for groups of obviously disabled cars, patiently waiting their turn for repairs. Flat tires are restored to life at a *Vulcanizadora*, *Llanteria*, or *Desponchador* (a ''depuncturer'').

Unless you're driving an oddball vehicle or one too complicated for a shade tree genius, repairs and servicing will be relatively easy to find. The farther you travel from highways and cities, the fewer and farther between any services will be, but with good maintenance and common sense you should have no trouble.

Steve and Tina were exploring the remote mountains and back roads of Guerrero in search of folk art when their van developed a sudden and serious ignition problem. As Steve put it, "This region of Mexico isn't convenient to anything, much less a Chevrolet dealership." By the time they finally limped into a village on a wing and a prayer, Steve had resigned himself to a major delay and change of plans. Their luck improved, however, when a man claiming to be a mechanic offered to look under the hood. "I'm not exaggerating," Steve reported. "This guy didn't have anything but a screwdriver and a pair of old Vise-Grips, yet he immediately diagnosed the problem as the electronic ignition."

After telling Steve to remain calm, the mechanic tore into the remains of a much older Chevrolet engine that was lying in the weeds behind his house. "The chances of finding the right part were worse than 16 billion to one," Steve said, "but sure enough." Not only were they back on the road within an hour but the entire job, including parts and labor, was under $10.

Getting Parts from the United States

In the event of a major breakdown, parts can sometimes be shipped by air to Mexico. This is definitely a hassle, but with enough long-distance (and expensive) phone calls and helpful friends, it can be done. Our friend Eve Muir telephoned her son, Curly, from Manzanillo with an urgent request: "Get me a head gasket for my new Toyota van, as *pronto* as possible!"

Curly rushed to an auto parts store and from there to the Los Angeles airport, where he convinced a departing Good Samaritan to hand-carry the gasket to Mexico. The agreeable but slightly puzzled vacationer was told, "When you get to Manzanillo, look for a lady wearing a red carnation." Within one day, Eve had the gasket in hand.

Steve shanghaied a friend as an impromptu courier for a Chevrolet axle, but the "friend in need" prize goes to Patti Kilpatrick, who hand-carried four 16-inch wheels for our Ford van on an overnight flight from Seattle to Cancún.

Patti's arrival at the *aduana* (customs) in Mexico City drew a crowd and raised an important point: because car parts are restricted imports, subject to substantial duties in Mexico, you may be told that the part cannot be allowed into the country without special paperwork. The customs agent may say, for example, "We need proof that the vehicle is broken down and parts are not available in Mexico."

If this happens, remain calm, but be prepared to plead for mercy. In virtually every case I know of, including Steve's axle and Patti's outrageous cargo of wheels, the customs agents finally allowed the parts into the country. *Warning:* Don't offer a bribe until you've exhausted every other means, including flattery, tears, and impassioned appeals to a higher power.

Mailing auto parts to Mexico is slow and just too uncertain to recommend. When all else fails, you may have to jump on a bus or plane and fetch the part yourself.

The Trip Home

Once your trip is about over, consider a front-end alignment. Not all shops have the necessary tools or experience to do this job, so ask a large car dealer or tire dealer for advice. Aligning the front end and balancing the tires can save a great deal of wear on the trip home.

We once ventured over a road so awful that it barely qualified as a burro trail. After 75 bone-cracking miles, our VW van developed a tendency to go wherever it pleased, rather than where it was pointed. One look under the front end was enough; a steering arm was bent almost double. We wobbled into a typical Mexican auto taller and explained the situation to the *maestro* (master mechanic, boss).

"Do you have a chain?" he asked. I dug it out.

"Park it right there," he said, pointing to a huge post that supported the entire roof of his shop. Several assistants stood under the roof, taking advantage of the shade. The maestro quickly wrapped the chain around the post and hooked the other end to the steering rod.

"Put it in reverse and back up," he ordered, joining the others in the shade.

I shrugged. Fate had evidently decreed that I pull this shop down on their heads. At the first tentative pressure the post groaned, then a heavy shudder rattled the roof and walls. The mechanic and his friends looked up apprehensively.

"*Otra vez, mas recio!*" (Again, harder!) the maestro called. I obediently popped the clutch. Mouths gaped as the entire shop leaned drunkenly toward the van. "Harder! Harder!" he urged. Just as the roof rafters began to pop and splinter, showering many years' accumulation of bird droppings into the shop below, he yelled, "Okay!" The job was done.

Total cost: 50 cents. "It was your chain," the maestro explained. "I just supervised." As we drove away, I avoided looking at the new angle of his shop.

CHAPTER 4

Food, Health, and Services

Food

I consider eating well to be one of the greatest pleasures of camping and traveling in Mexico. There's nothing quite like a tropical sunrise followed by a glass of fresh squeezed orange juice and an exotic fruit salad—or a cup of café puro, huevos rancheros, and a platter of just-baked sweet rolls.

Although Mexico is known far and wide for the quality and variety of its cuisine, many RV campers are downright paranoid about food. More than a few people head to Mexico with bulging cupboards, convinced that the only way to stay healthy south of the border is to eat only ''real American'' food, canned, packaged, dried, and preserved. Talk about bringing coals to Newcastle; I've met campers in Mexico who brought a winter's supply of canned chickens and coffee from home.

Mexico exports over two billion dollars worth of agricultural products to the United States every year, including lettuce, tomatoes, beef, seafood, grapes, melons, and other produce. Americans eat food from Mexico far more often than they realize.

Warnings that fresh foods should be cooked or completely peeled before eating are usually based on myths that human waste (night soil) is used as fertilizer. This is false. Mexican farmers do use modern chemical fertilizers, herbicides, and pesticides, however. I always wash fresh food, at home or in Mexico, to remove chemical residues and ordinary dirt. I don't wash bananas, for example, because they are very easy to peel, but if I'm going to squeeze fruit for juice, I wash it well. Relax—Mexico's fruit and produce are of far better quality and flavor than most of what we get at home.

Campers will rarely have trouble finding everything they need in the way of food, but you may not find everything you want. And when I'm camping, I want (and need) extra virgin olive oil for salad dressings, dark sesame oil for stir-frying *gambas* (jumbo prawns), gourmet popcorn, Chinese mustard, granola, brown rice, whole wheat flour, peanut butter, tamari sauce, ginger root, dried cherries, dark chocolate, smoked almonds—the list goes on, according to the size of one's appetite, cupboards, and RV, not to mention the limits of one's budget. In other words, take the goodies and buy everything else in Mexico, as you travel. After all, shopping in Mexico's wonderful markets and neighborhood stores is one of the best parts of the adventure.

Where to Buy Food

ALONG THE ROAD
I love Mexico's roadside fruit stands and food vendors. Lorena and I will stop at the slightest temptation, such as a sign tacked to a farmer's hut advertising *miel de abeja* (bee's honey) or *elotes* (fresh corn). These are golden opportunities, not only to buy and eat local treats but to meet people on a one-to-one basis. Once you've tucked a homegrown papaya or a bunch of bananas into your bag, just ask, "*¿Qué más hay?*" (What else is there?) You might get a shrug for an

answer—or an invitation to check out the family garden and orchard for something that interests you. Nothing breaks the ice quicker than expressing friendly curiosity. When I asked a Baja farmer selling cheeses from his front door, "What is this tree? Can the fruit be eaten?" he loaded me down with grapefruitlike samples, then threw in a squash and a handful of dried figs for good measure. By the time we'd toured his goat pens and admired the family hog, our brief stop to buy a cheese had turned into a real visit and a memorable experience.

Among my favorite roadside attractions are stands selling *pollos rostizados* (roast chickens). I'll buy a whole barbecued chicken in the morning and put it directly into the ice chest for lunch or dinner.

When we're on the road, Lorena and I watch carefully for bakeries and tortilla factories. Look for lines of women holding buckets and towels (to carry their fresh tortillas in), or just sniff the air for the unforgettable aroma of roasting corn. Wrap the tortillas in a cloth and eat as soon as possible. Corn tortillas should not be stored in a plastic bag for more than several hours or they'll go sour. (If you find tortillas boring, smear them with your secret stash of peanut butter.)

TIENDAS AND SUPERMARKETS
Although some RV parks will have small *tiendas* (stores) on the premises, you'll have more fun and find better bargains by shopping in town, or in neighborhood stores. Supermarkets are common in larger Mexican towns. Fortunately for campers, most packaged foods are offered in a range of sizes, including very small. Cooking oil, for example, comes in tiny cans and bottles, just about enough for one meal.

Mexican supermarkets are excellent sources of dried and lightweight prepared foods. Campers can find interesting and tasty bargains by touring the shelves. Look for instant refried beans, instant soups and potatoes, dried meat, fish and shrimp, quick desserts and cake mixes.

Alpura 2000 is a typical "super pasteurized" whole milk. It can be found on supermarket shelves in squat paper cartons that do not require refrigeration. Alpura is said to last up to six months (unopened). This makes it an excellent camping food, though once the carton is opened, the milk should be handled as if it were regular milk.

In markets and small tiendas, most food is still sold "in bulk." When you buy a pound of onions, a dozen eggs, or a bunch of grapes, your purchase will be dropped into a thin plastic bag, a twist of newspaper, or a cheap cardboard box. Be prepared by carrying your own shopping bag, Mexican-style, and transferring your purchases into sturdier containers once you're "home."

Foods are sold by weight and volume, kilogramas and litros (2.2 pounds and 1.1 quarts). The most commonly used fractions of these amounts are:

medio kilo	1.1 pounds
cuarto de kilo	0.55 pound
medio litro	0.55 quart (close to a pint)
cuarto de litro	0.27 quart (close to a cup)

Many foods are sold by the gram: "*Dame cien gramos de arroz, por favor*" (Give me one hundred grams of rice, please). It takes practice to learn how many grams of beans are equivalent to the familiar packages you are used to buying at home. When in doubt, buy less, especially of fresh foods that may spoil.

Loose foods are also sold by the *mano* (handful), *montón* (mound, pile), and *pieza* (piece). Eggs, for example, may be sold *por pieza* (by the piece, individually) or *por kilo* (by the kilo; also *por peso*, by weight).

Bartering over the price of food is not too common in larger marketplaces. In most cases, the vendor will prefer to give you a bit more food rather than take a bit less money.

CONASUPO AND MOBILE TIENDAS

Conasupo (the name of a government agency) stores usually sell below the normal price, especially for staples. Tourists are welcome to shop in the Conasupo, but if the stock is very limited, don't clean out all the goodies (such as canned juices). Local people can't compete with your buying power, and if you take everything, they'll go without until the store is restocked.

In Baja, the Yucatán peninsula, and other remote areas of Mexico, you may see food shops-on-wheels, usually a broken down pickup truck stuffed to the rafters with fresh produce, cooking oil, tortilla flour, hard candies, candles, eggs, and other staples. Some trucks sell fresh meat, ice, and cheese. By all means, make use of their services. Most of these trucks have regular routes and timetables. We've camped in places where the driver was happy to include us on his round, and literally brought our groceries to the door of our van. On the Michoacán coast, one man was kind enough to fill out his own limited stock by taking our shopping list into town and buying on special order.

The people who live along Mexico's rivers, lagoons, and remote seacoasts are also served by an irregular fleet of freight canoes and supply boats. While kayaking north of La Paz, in lower Baja California, Lorena and I lucked on one of these small floating stores. It had been weeks since we'd last seen groceries of any type, and fresh foods were just a mouth-watering memory. Once the crew of this 50-foot ''tramp'' got over the shock of two sunburned gringos frantically chasing them down in a kayak, they seemed to delight in waving delicacies under our noses. Before our shopping spree was over, we'd packed our Klepper with cooking oil, beans, flour, eggs, fresh jalapeño chilis, and even a sack of red, ripe tomatoes. The final treat was presented to us with great ceremony by the captain—a two-pound brick of homemade panocha, a sticky concoction of crude cane sugar and fruit that made my sweet tooth sing.

When shopping in remote areas, keep in mind that prices are usually higher than in the cities due to scarcity and the cost of transportation. If something seems outrageously expensive, don't complain; it won't do you any good and may cause hard feelings.

Types of Food

MEAT AND POULTRY

Supermarkets and *carnicerias* (meat markets) have both packaged and fresh cuts of beef, pork, and chicken. Dedicated carnivores often find meat difficult to come by, however, while camping in the backcountry. Small villages rarely have refrigeration, and most campesinos rely on a weekly or monthly slaughtering of a pig or steer for fresh meat. In between times, they eat dried meat or chicken or do without.

Meat will be sold early in the morning, generally before 10:00 a.m. Look for a red flag, the usual "fresh meat" signal. Get there ahead of the rush or you'll have to be satisfied with snouts and elbows. Poultry is sold live, though in most cases you can ask the seller to do the dirty deed, including plucking, for a reasonable fee. Mexicans love chicken heads and feet, so give them away if you don't use them yourself.

CHEESE

I eat lots of cheese while camping and often don't have any way to refrigerate it. Buy a large block of *queso de chihuahua* (a very popular cheddarlike cheese) and wrap it well in several layers of paper or clean cotton cloth (cheesecloth was invented for this purpose). When you want a piece of cheese, carefully shave off any mold—which won't hurt you but tastes funky. Remember, the moldy outside layer is protection for the cheese, so only trim it off the piece to be used. If the weather is warm, the cheese will exude water and natural oils. This is part of the aging process and actually improves the flavor. A block of mild cheese will gradually turn sharp, though I usually eat it up before this happens. Carefully wrapped cheese that is kept well aired and away from prowling dogs and rodents will last for weeks, even in warm weather.

SNACKS

The best place to buy snack foods (salami, sausages, cheeses, economy-sized bags and cans of nuts, canned meats and seafoods, candy bars by the box, instant soups, etc.) in Mexico is a large supermarket and in stores and stalls that sell sweets, nuts, and dried fruits in bulk. Shop around; the prices can vary quite a lot. Packaged dried fruit, for example, is expensive in small bags, but if you find a store that sells it *suelto* (loose, in bulk), the cost will be much lower.

Try homemade Mexican sweets before you stock up on prepackaged candies and confections. Ates are fruit jellies, molded into rolls and large bricks. They are very tasty and inexpensive. Nuts and seeds are mixed with brown sugar or honey and prepared similar to peanut brittle. Look for them in the market or in candy shops. You'll usually get a sample taste if you ask with a smile, *"¿Se puede probarlo, por favor?"* (May I try it, please?).

For a lot more on food in Mexico, including candies, nuts, and typical confections, see *The People's Guide to Mexico.*

FRUITS AND VEGETABLES

Though early mangoes and other fruits are sometimes eaten green, Mexicans prefer well-ripened fruit and produce. Because of this, fresh foods are picked at the last possible moment and do not keep for long periods. To reduce spoilage, it is customary to shop often and avoid overbuying.

Fresh food is rarely treated with preservatives in Mexico, and many gringos don't recognize a banana or mango that has been allowed to ripen naturally, rather than under controlled artificial means. A natural ripe banana is usually spotted brown or black and is not only still good inside but incredibly sweet and flavorful. Taste it before you toss them into the garbage bucket.

If you are heading into a remote area and want to stock up on food in advance, select your fresh produce with special care. First and simplest, buy some produce that is ripe and ready to eat and some that is still green or hard. By buying both ripe and unripe produce, you should be able to cover your needs for at least a full week in one shopping trip.

Cabbages and cucumbers are classic long-lasting foods. Buy the best you can find and reject any that have started to spoil or are very ripe. Limes with thin hard skins and oranges with thin skins (very difficult to peel) last far longer than thick, easily peeled varieties. Thin-skinned oranges are usually called *naranjas para jugo* (oranges for juice).

To soften limes that have formed a very hard skin, drop them into boiling water for one minute. You can also roast them quickly right in the coals of a fire. You won't believe how juicy they'll be.

Lorena and I made a long boat trip on the spur of the moment, with almost no time at all to shop or gather food carefully. I bought a gunny sack near the marketplace and grabbed whatever looked good and not too perishable: onions, garlic, potatoes, limes, cabbage, cooking oil, salt, bananas, and honey. A typical meal (breakfast, lunch, or dinner) would be fresh fish cooked on a stick, chopped cabbage with lime juice dressing, and a potato or onion baked in the fire. By the end of the trip, our taste buds were as sensitive as a cat's whiskers. A simple variation such as a tablespoon of minced onion in the cabbage salad was noticed and really appreciated. One meal was just broiled fish followed by roast bananas and melted honey. Ambrosia!

Food Storage

There's nothing quite like dipping into the food larder at the end of a long, hungry day to find that the tomatoes and bananas have gotten together with the peanuts and garlic to make a strange and disgusting sauce. Food spoilage is a constant problem while camping, especially if the weather is warm and refrigeration just a dream.

Keep your food in sight, not hidden away where it will be forgotten until it starts to reek. Lorena and I carry fresh foods in baskets, one or two with lids or cloth covers to keep flies off the bananas and tomatoes. A typical meal or snack begins with ''What's left in the baskets?''

Spoilage caused by natural bacteria on the surface of produce can be delayed for a considerable time by simply washing the food in a cleansing bath of *yodo* (iodine) or bleach (see Staying Healthy, below) to kill anything in the water or on the produce. For good measure, increase the dose used for purifying drinking water by 50 to 100 percent depending on how dirty the produce looks. (This is the same procedure, by the way, that you should use for all produce, regardless of whether you want to store it or use it immediately.) Soak the food for at least half an hour, then remove and drain until completely dry. Don't rinse it off; what little purification agent remains will also help retard spoilage and will have a negligible, if any, effect on the flavor of the food.

Now wrap the individual pieces of produce in paper, taking care not to bruise or break the skin. Newspaper works fine, but don't use plastic, aluminum foil, or other impermeable wrappings. The food has to breathe. Plastic bags can be used for food storage inside a refrigerator, but at room temperature, they actually speed up spoilage by trapping moisture, heat, and bacteria. Arrange the wrapped food in a basket or box and store in a dark place, or at least in the shade.

If you are unable to purify the food first, try the wrapping method anyway. Check all the produce daily, using up any that is ripe or shows signs of spoilage. Under ideal conditions, a green tomato will keep for weeks. Cucumbers, chayotes, onions, limes, cabbage, and other fairly durable fruits and vegetables will also last a surprisingly long time.

Store food for immediate use in baskets or boxes that have good air circulation. In humid weather, you may have to dry your food in the sun every morning to avoid rapid spoilage from condensation and dew. Line the container with paper or cloth, not plastic.

Health

Health precautions actually take little time and pay great dividends in terms of how enjoyable your trip is. The secret to staying healthy while camping in Mexico is quite simple: pay attention to what you're doing to yourself and imagine the consequences if you get sick. I once casually accepted the offer of a "quick trip around the bay" with some friends who wanted to catch a *sierra* for lunch. I was fresh from the States, sporting a typical gringo pallor. I jumped at the chance for a boat ride in the sun. Two hours later, when I crawled back onto the beach, I had a sunburn that forced me to hide in the shade for the next three weeks. If I had simply grabbed my pants and a shirt instead of going out in shorts, I would have saved weeks of discomfort, not to mention untold lost hours of fishing and diving.

When preparing for a camping trip, especially one into a remote area, I always indulge in a brief bout of "creative paranoia" to help plan my health kit. What if the bugs are vicious? Pack another bottle of repellent. What if my skin is too pale? Another tube of sunscreen. What if the water is especially suspicious? Don't forget the water purifying pump. These, in fact, are the three most common camping health hazards. An amazing number of people shrug off the possible discomfort of biting insects, sunburn, and *turista* (diarrhea) with a bland, "Ah, don't worry about it!" that quickly turns into a cry for help when they find themselves swatting mosquitoes or crouching behind a thorn bush half the night.

Medical assistance is readily available in Mexico, and

anyone who stays close to the tourist circuit (trailer parks, campgrounds, motels, popular beaches, etc.) should have no problem finding professional care and medicines should they be needed.

Easy Does It

Don't let your memories of Mexico be nothing but a blur of campgrounds, bus stations, poorly lighted restaurants, and ear-splitting hangovers. If the old cliche, "I have to go back to work to rest up from my vacation" applies to your current style of camping and traveling, you're pushing far too hard. The secret to avoiding a coronary or even a bad muscle cramp is to take it easy. Don't sprint to the top of the Temple of the Sun until you've had time to adjust to a new climate, new foods, and a different style of daily living.

Lorena claims that being slightly out of shape is actually an advantage. While hiking, for example, one's body cries out for rest stops. These are ideal opportunities to appreciate small things: a wild fuchsia in bloom beside the trail, the good taste of a fresh brewed cup of coffee, the shy questions of a passing campesino family. These small and seemingly insignificant images will combine with hundreds more to form the mood and memories of your trip.

Stay Healthy

Campers in Mexico often find themselves in places where supplies of food and water are less than reliable or sanitary. Think of this as a challenge, not as a threat, and you'll find that staying healthy can be surprisingly easy.

The following suggestions about health in Mexico represent long years of hands-on research. Some of these tips are backed by sound medical advice; others are based on less scientific sources such as hard-earned personal experience, common sense, and the practical realities of travel and camping. The point is that these suggestions really work, if you follow them carefully and even religiously. If you're as religious as I am, however, you'll undoubtedly backslide on occasion. Do your best; none of these precautions takes much time or energy, especially after they've become a part of your normal daily routine. Follow these guidelines as if they were commandments, however, and you'll drastically reduce your chances of getting sick while traveling.

Memorize this list and study the rest of the chapter carefully. A much more detailed discussion of health and food can also be found in *The People's Guide to Mexico.*

- Use Pepto Bismol as a diarrhea preventative.
- Drink bottled beverages and purified water.
- Go easy on alcohol, especially at high altitudes.
- Buy a water purifying pump and use it regularly.
- Eat regularly and moderately while traveling; don't "pig out."
- Avoid foods that are greasy or too-heavily spiced for your taste.
- Avoid eating red meat whenever possible.
- Avoid street food.
- Wash, rinse, or peel food whenever possible, but don't lie awake at night worrying about it.
- Wash your hands at least three times a day.
- Don't get sunburned.
- Don't get overtired. Rest often and learn to enjoy siestas.

Filter or purify all drinking water. I sometimes get lazy and drink some fairly awful water. I sometimes get awfully sick, too. It doesn't really take much to purify your water and to protect your health. Guzzling dubious water isn't a sign of bravery in the face of the amoeba; it's just plain foolish.

Small water purifying units for campers remove microorganisms and some noxious chemicals. Using one is easy and avoids the terrible taste of water-purifying tablets and drops.

Boiling also purifies water, but contrary to what most people believe, it takes time—at least 30 minutes of boiling at sea level and at least 45 minutes at 7,000 feet. This is a lot of boiling and a lot of fuel. (A pressure cooker would probably reduce these times by one-half.)

Water purification tablets (called hidroclonazone in Mexico) are convenient but taste terrible. Let pill-treated water stand for at least 30 minutes before drinking. Liquid bleach can be used instead of tablets: 8 to 10 drops per quart of water, then allow to stand for 30 minutes or more. If you purify one bucket of water at a time and leave it uncovered for several hours, much of the bleach flavor will go away.

Iodine (yodo) is the most common water purifying agent in Mexico. It is sold in *farmacias*. The usual dose is five to seven drops per quart of water. New products are now appearing, both in farmacias and supermarkets. The best we've tried, Elibac and Microdine, have almost no flavor and take only a few drops per liter of water. Ask for *gotas para purificar agua* (drops for purifying water) or *pastillas para purificar agua* (pills for purifying water). Remember, if you can't find anything else, use plain blanqueador (bleach).

Powdered scorpions, chia and 7-Up, camomile and "dog tea," acidophilus, papaya seeds, dried apricot pits—when it comes to upset stomachs, nausea, and diarrhea, I've tried most everything. As a firm believer in the value of medicinal plants and home remedies, I'm sorry to announce that Pepto Bismol beats them all. In fact, my experience with Pepto Bismol indicates that taking the stuff in moderate doses, during and even after traveling, can dramatically reduce stomach problems.

But I don't like Pepto's cloying pink taste and I don't like to pour it repeatedly into my stomach. As a result, I compromise by taking about half of the manufacturer's recommended dosage (1 tablespoon three to four times a day). I start my Pepto program a few days before leaving home, and I continue taking it once or twice a day for about two weeks. If my stomach shows no sign of rebellion in that time, I put the Pepto on standby and keep it close at hand in the event of sudden turmoil after a meal of barbecued pork tacos smothered in green chili sauce.

Because your body has to readjust to every major change in location, your stomach may also be upset by going home. To avoid this, take Pepto Bismol at the end of your trip and continue taking it for two or three days after your return.

Pepto Bismol liquid is widely available in Mexican farmacias but chewable tablets are not. For some reason, Mexican Pepto Bismol tastes slightly different from that made in the United States.

Lime juice and garlic have proven antibacterial qualities. Both have been used by Mexicans for centuries as disinfectants. Lime juice will purify water, but I'd add enough to make it taste like limeade just to be sure. Water treated with lime juice makes terrible coffee.

Squeeze lime juice liberally over fresh and cooked foods; it's one "medicine" that tastes really good. Lorena and I rarely suffer stomach troubles while traveling and camping, even in areas where sanitation is very poor. We attribute this to a little luck and a lot of lime juice and garlic.

Purify all fruits and vegetables. Forget that old cliché about purifying only food that can't be peeled; *do it all,* even the oranges. Any food can get dirty, and contamination can easily find its way from peeling to hand to mouth. Keep a bucket or large sturdy plastic bag on hand. When you've finished a marketing trip, put your fresh fruits and vegetables into the container, cover them with water, and add enough pills, bleach (cheapest), or yodo to purify both the water and the food. Add a bit extra for good luck. Leave the food in this bath for at least half an hour. When the food has been well soaked, remove from the bath and drain until dry. Don't rinse it; the rinse water itself may be impure. This simple operation will do more to protect your health than a suitcase stuffed with modern medicines.

If water is scarce, use seawater or put the food into a

plastic bag with just enough water to coat everything well. Add enough purifier to make a strong solution.

Try to avoid as best you can any unpasteurized or uncooked dairy products. Notice that I said "try." Raw milk and cheeses, especially the very common *queso del rancho* (white cakes of homemade cheese) are considered special treats in the backcountry of Mexico. I often find myself eating raw dairy products and hoping for the best. Raw milk and cheese aren't always hazardous, of course, but you're safer without them.

Raw dairy products should be cooked well before eating. To sterilize raw milk, bring it slowly to a boil, stirring frequently to avoid scorching, then allow to cool. Mexicans generally boil milk twice, which is doubly safe.

Queso de Chihuahua and queso de Oaxaca style cheeses are almost always pasteurized. Fresh carton milk, dried pasteurized milk (Nido/Nestle), and super pasteurized carton milk are safe and very common.

Go very easy on fried and greasy street foods, baked goods, chilis, green fruits, and local moonshine and homemade beverages. Hell, you say, what does that leave, tortillas and Coca-Cola? These foods don't have to be passed over entirely, just take it very easy until your body has adjusted to Mexico. People who forage at random and without self-control often suffer indigestion and frequent bouts of turista. After you've become more familiar with Mexican foods and new flavors, you can begin sampling with less risk of a sudden revolt from your stomach.

Use liberal amounts of soap and water on your dishes and yourself. Some people seem to think that camping means living like Neanderthals, without benefit of soap and simple hygiene. In areas where water is scarce, even the most fastidious campers may be lax when it comes time to wash their dishes or hands. Either attitude can lead to health problems. It is important to take special care in washing up.

At least once a week, put all of your dishes and utensils through a purifying ritual: fill one bucket with hot soapy water, another with a mixture of water and one-quarter cup of plain bleach, and a third bucket with clean rinse water (purified). Run the dishes through this cycle until they're spotless. If water is really scarce, keep a bucket of bleach and water to use for casual rinsing of cups, forks, and not-so-dirty plates and bowls. This purifying rinse temporarily takes the place of a full-scale soap wash.

For your hands, keep a bucket or tin can of soapy water in a convenient spot and insist that everyone use it at least a couple of times a day, especially after trips to the outhouse and before handling food. You'll feel better by not being grubby and substantially reduce the risk of health problems, especially hepatitis.

Clean minor wounds, insect bites, and infections often. It is far easier to prevent infections than to cure them.

Health Care and Medicines

Doctors and dentists are usually easy to locate in Mexico, and excellent hospitals can be found in larger cities. Most people, however, rely heavily on the local farmacia for both medical advice and medicines. Drugs of all sorts are dispensed without prescriptions and injections are often given on the spot.

In the country, medical care is unreliable. Small towns and villages may boast of a *clinica,* but the staff will be small and often unqualified to do more than dispense aspirins and antibiotics (greatly overused in Mexico). The Cruz Roja (Red Cross) has emergency facilities in many small towns; look for road signs that show a red cross and telephone number. Some can be reached by CB radio.

Curanderas (healers), *brujas* (witches), and *espiritualistas* (spiritualists) are very commonly consulted by poorer people in Mexico. They may even honor a healer with the title *doctor de campo* (country doctor). Don't laugh; many are highly skilled in the use of medicinal plants, folk remedies, healing massage, and the setting of broken bones. The farther you go into the backcountry, the more you'll find local people depending on traditional methods of healing. I've been fed some strange brews and potions, but not too surprisingly, these remedies often worked just as well as—or even better than—standard medications.

What should you do if you need a doctor? First, and most important, ask yourself, as calmly as possible, do I really need to see a doctor? Am I overreacting or just plain scared? Don't be embarrassed; when you feel lousy, everything tends to look a lot worse than it really is. Calm down, have a cup of soothing tea, and give yourself time to relax before heading to town. Often a good night's sleep or holding someone's hand will do the trick. Combine a stomachache and a sunburn with a case of diarrhea and many people automatically head for the hospital. If it's close by, that's fine, but if you're out in the sticks, you'll probably find that you can get over this temporary crisis by taking it easy and treating yourself.

Still feel rotten? Don't hesitate to seek a doctor if you really feel you can't handle the situation.

I once got sick on a long hike and spent a week in a very hospitable village being cared for by a family who made room for me in their small house. It was a strange time; I didn't feel like talking very much and just laid in bed, listening and watching the people around me. I soon got better, due in large part to loving care and lots of herb tea. In the end, I was glad it had happened in a village rather than in an impersonal city or lonely hotel room.

Services

Pure Water

Look for signs in town that say *Agua Purificada* or for trucks and hand carts bearing large five-gallon glass *garrafones* of purified water. If you want your own garrafone, a (sometimes) refundable deposit is required; otherwise, just have them empty the bottles into your containers. No other water, no matter where it comes from or whoever swears that it is pure, can be trusted absolutely. Always ask, *"¿Se puede tomar el agua?"* when using water from a tap or hose. If the water cannot be drunk, most people will say so quite emphatically. When in doubt, don't drink it without purifying first.

Ice

Some of my most vivid memories of camping in Mexico involve searching for ice. Like most such ordinary chores, finding ice in Mexico is seldom a cut-and-dried experience. In most cases, locating the ice dealer gives you a chance to practice both Spanish and patience. "Go down this street until you see a big wet spot. The building next to it is the *fabrica de hielo*. Knock on the door and you'll be served. *¿Me entiendes?* (Do you understand?)"

The most common source of block ice is the *fabrica de hielo* (ice plant). My rule of thumb is that if a Mexican town is large enough to have two gas stations, it probably has an ice plant. When in doubt, ask, *"¿Donde esta la fabrica de hielo, por favor?"* (Where is the ice plant, please?) It could be anywhere, from downtown to an outlying suburb. Considerable time can be saved by hiring a cab. Either follow the cab driver to the ice plant or go with him and load your ice chest into the trunk of his car.

Ice plants sell to beer and soda dealers, independent ice vendors, fish buyers, raspada (shaved ice snow cone) vendors, cantinas, restaurants, and individuals. Any of these can, and sometimes will, sell ice to you. Your best bet is to buy from trucks or from beer and soda agencies (called *agencia, sub-agencia,* or *deposito de cerveza*). Ice is commonly delivered in the morning. If you see a dripping truck, don't be shy about flagging it down or approaching the driver. I always open with, *"¿Me hace el favor de venderme un poquito de hielo, por favor?''* (Will you do me the favor of selling me a little bit of ice, please?) If you're temporarily tongue-tied, a smile and "please" will work wonders.

In Oaxaca, the ice man appeared like clockwork in front of the main city market every morning at 8:30. For a modest tip, he or an assistant was happy to lug a block of ice to my van, and to trim it for the ice chest.

Learn to watch for *"Hielo''* signs. You never quite know where it will appear. In Palenque, for example, ice is sold in a doctor's office near the bus station.

Cubitos de hielo, ice cubes, are commonly sold by the bag in supermarkets, gas stations, liquor stores and beer agencies, and some RV parks. Cubitos cost more than block ice and don't last as long, but you'll probably use them often. Unless ice cubes are obviously homemade, they are probably made from purified water. If the bag doesn't say, ask the clerk, *"¿Son de agua pura?''* (Are these from pure water?) The answer, of course, will be *"Sí.''*

Paletas are frozen, flavored ice on a stick. Neighborhood paleta dealers often sell plain, bagged ice in paleta-sized pieces. This ice is seldom made from pure water.

Bulk ice is sold in standard-size blocks or fractions. A full block is a *marqueta, barra,* or *bloque.* It takes two boys or a strong man to lift one. The average ice chest will hold un *cuarto* (a quarter) or perhaps un *medio* (a half). If you want even less, ask for un *octavo* (an eighth). Most dealers will carefully trim the ice to fit your ice chest. If overenthusiastic kids do the job, however, you may have a punctured ice chest. When done with care, I usually offer a modest tip or a soda. Block ice is rarely made from pure water.

Hieleras, ice chests, are sold in supermarkets, hardware stores and sporting goods shops, and liquor stores. Most Mexican ice chests are made of lightweight, fragile styrofoam. These coolers can be quickly reinforced and repaired with a liberal wrapping of duct tape. Insulated jugs are not commonly available.

Public Baths

Baños publicos (public baths) are located near the market-place, in some gas stations, trailer parks, and dirty factory districts. For a very reasonable charge you can have a long shower or both a steam bath *(baño de vapor)* and shower *(baño de regadera)*. Soap and towels are extra; bring your own if you wish. Their soap may be very harsh and their towels very tiny.

Laundry

True self-service laundromats are rare in Mexico, but towns of any size will have at least one *lavanderia automatica* (automatic laundry). These laundromats are staffed, not self-service, and customers cannot do their own washing and drying. All the same, the service is usually good and reasonably quick. If you drop your clothing off in the morning, most lavanderias will have it finished by evening. Always ask, however, just to be sure. A tip to the attendant for good service will be appreciated. Prices tend to be equivalent or higher than do-it-yourself laundromats in the United States.

Fuels

PROPANE
Propane is simply called *gas;* look for signs and large storage tanks on the side of the highway, especially on the outskirts of fair-sized towns and cities. Campers who spend long periods in one area may want to rent large propane tanks from the local gas dealer. This frees you from having to make numerous trips for a refill.

KEROSENE
Petroleo (kerosene) usually can be purchased in small stores or from government pumps near the market. In areas where the sale of petroleo is tightly controlled by the government (for

some reason), you must buy it at authorized Expendios or under the counter. By asking discreetly, *"¿No hay petroleo?"* (Isn't there any kerosene?), you should eventually locate a source.

WHITE GAS

You may find *gasolina blanca* (white gas) in drugstores (sold by the cup), hardware stores, the odd gas station or two, and tailor shops (for removing spots). But don't count on white gas to be there when you need it, especially in rural areas.

Exchanging Money

Tourists have several choices when they wish to change their dollars into pesos. Cash and traveler's checks can be exchanged in banks, money exchange houses *(casas de cambio)*, hotels, restaurants, and shops. Banks give the best rates, though some shopkeepers offer high exchange rates as a means of attracting customers. Money exchange houses offer slightly lower rates than banks and keep more convenient hours.

Normal Mexican banking hours are 9:00 a.m. to 1:30 p.m., Monday through Friday. Money exchange services, however, are much more limited, usually from 10:30 a.m. to 12:00 noon. Some banks post notices in the lobby giving the daily peso/dollar exchange rate and their money changing hours.

DEVALUATION

The Mexican economy has taken a terrible beating in recent years. Peso exchange rates have plummeted and inflation has soared. What does high finance have to do with your next trip to Mazatlán or Mexico City? Actually, the peso's problems tend to work in your favor. Prices in Mexico, *outside of the most popular beachside tourist resorts*, are now lower than we've seen since the early 1970s. The traveler who visits Mexico *People's Guide*-style will find that devaluation of the peso has created great bargains in food, lodging, transportation, and souvenir shopping.

NOTES ON MONEY
• If there is a rapid devaluation while you're in Mexico, don't get nervous. Although banks may close for a few days while they sort things out, it won't be long before they resume business as usual.

• As a precaution, I always carry at least $50 to $100 in U.S. currency to tide me over.

• Buy a money belt and use it religiously. Purchase a well-known brand of *American* traveler's checks.

• If you have credit cards, especially Visa, MasterCard, or American Express, take them, too.

• Personal checks are virtually impossible to cash or spend in Mexico.

• A current passport is not required for travel to Mexico, but it is without doubt the best identification you can have for any banking transaction.

• U.S. dollars are commonly used in Baja, although it's best to have some pesos too.

• For extended trips, ask your banker about bank-to-bank transfers.

Telephones

If you must call home, by all means call collect or it will cost an arm and a leg. Look for *Larga Distancia* signs. Small businesses, especially restaurants, serve as long distance suboffices.

The day rate, the most expensive rate for calls, is from 7:00 a.m. to 7:00 p.m. Monday through Saturday and from 5:00 p.m. until midnight on Sunday. The cheapest rate is 11:00 p.m. to 7:00 a.m. Monday through Saturday, and from midnight to 7:00 a.m. on Sunday.

Write out the following information and give it to the operator:

Por cobrar (collect) or *Pago aqui* (I'll pay here)
A quien contesta (station-to-station)

City
State
Country
Area code and number
De (from): your name

A charge for services rendered is normal and if the call isn't completed and the operator tried very hard, this charge can be fairly high (a few dollars). Credit cards may or may not be accepted.

Post Office

Postal service in Mexico is notoriously erratic. In small towns and villages, it can be downright ridiculous. In one village near our camp the postmistress was illiterate; she relied on neighbors to decipher addresses and to complete postal forms.
Post offices are open from 9:00 a.m. to 1:00 p.m. and, after a break for siesta, from 3:00 p.m. to 6:00 p.m. on weekdays. Saturday hours are 8:00 a.m. to 12:00 noon for mailing letters only. These hours vary, so don't be shocked if the post office is open on Sunday or closed on a Monday.
Send all letters and postcards *por avion* (by airmail). Ask anyone writing to you from outside of Mexico to write the same on the envelope. Most travelers receive mail at Lista de Correos (General Delivery). Tell your friends to write the address and name very clearly. It should look like this:

Abe Lincoln
Lista de Correos
San Patricio, Jalisco (city and state)
Mexico

Go to the post office and ask to see the Lista or just say, "*¿Hay una carta para (name) por favor?*" Write the name on a slip of paper to avoid confusion.

For information on packages, certified mail, change of address, and other postal mysteries, see *The People's Guide to Mexico.*

Telegraph

The *Telegrafos* may be close to the post office—or it may be across town. Working hours are often longer than those of the post office. The fastest service is *urgente.* Telegrams can be received at a specific address, at the telegraph office, *Lista de Telegrafos* (most common), or at the post office, Lista de Correos.

Money can be wired to Mexico as *giro* (money order) and will be paid at the office in pesos. Giros are reasonably fast, but don't hold your breath; delays of ten days are not unusual.

CHAPTER 5

Beyond Trailer Parks

Camping in Mexico is different in many ways from camping in the United States and Canada. Many Mexicans live all of their lives on a scale that we would consider "camping." Chopping firewood, hauling buckets of water, and sleeping on mats or hard cots are all part of the normal daily routine for millions of people. Most Mexicans, especially campesinos, find it difficult to understand why rich people, *and we are rich by their standards*, deliberately regress from luxury to "roughing it."

Camping, therefore, is an unusual activity, something to be curious about. This curiosity makes "getting away from it all" next to impossible. The farther you venture from cities and tourist areas, the more interesting you become to the local people. Your arrival in a remote area will not go unnoticed. People—curious, questioning, staring—seem to be everywhere. You're mistaken if you think that all of those interesting natives are just going to stand there like natural rock formations while you point and take photographs. You'll find, instead, that the interest is mutual. They'll soon be outstaring you and even taking *your* picture.

Finding a Campsite

Trading information is one of the most useful and reliable ways I know of to simplify the search for the perfect campsite. All travelers have their favorite spots, their private visions of Shangri-La at the end of a long dirt road. Some campers guard their favorite places with a degree of secrecy that would delight the CIA; others freely pass information along to anyone willing to ask. But people may differ about the meaning of ''perfect.'' I've heard some of the best (in my opinion) camping areas in Mexico described as ''bug infested,'' ''having absolutely no food or water,'' or ''really not very interesting.''

When talking with another traveler about campsites, frame your questions around your particular interests. If the mosquitoes are bad, how's the fishing? I can put up with a lot of scratching and blood donations if the bass are biting, too. Is food available? What kinds? Lorena and I often live for months on the standard Mexican staples of beans, tomatoes, onions, chilis, eggs, and tortillas. Other people can handle about two days of this diet before they abandon Paradise for access to a supermarket.

Warning: There is a rare breed of camper who can endure anything when one major requirement is met. We talked to three young men who had just returned from what they swore was the mythical Perfect Beach. They hardly looked like they'd been in the Garden of Eden; they were emaciated, terribly sunburned, and seemed to suffer some type of group delirium. They completed each other's thoughts, just like Huey, Dewey, and Louie.

I started off the questioning by asking the obvious: ''How was the food at this beach?''

''It was really awful and expensive!'' they said in unison, shaking their heads in disgust as they went on to describe the diet of greasy fried bananas and watery beans they lived on. I asked about the weather.

''Too hot to. . . ''

". . . sleep and really. . ."

". . . humid."

They told of the lack of shade, the brackish drinking water, and the scorching sun. What about insects?

"Giant mosquitoes and. . . "

". . . clouds of no-see-'ums and. . . "

". . . huge horseflies and scorpions!"

They lifted their shirts to reveal scars, welts, sores, and infected swellings. Mosquitoes bit swimmers half a mile from shore. Well then, how were the local people?

"Nobody there. . . "

". . . except for some. . . "

". . . really mean cops!"

"Then what the hell were you doing there for six months?" I finally yelled.

"The surfing there is. . . "

"AWESOME!"

Good campsites are not always obvious. Lorena and I were sitting in a small open-air restaurant on the Pacific coast near San Blas, speculating on possible camping places nearby. Because it had been an especially tiring day, half of it spent driving in low gear on a hot, dusty road, we decided to ask the owner for advice rather than explore.

"A place to camp?" she said, staring vaguely off into the distance as if we'd just ordered oysters Rockefeller. "Well, I'm not really sure," she muttered, "but if we move these chairs. . . and that table. . . "

Five minutes later I carefully eased the van into the space she'd cleared behind the jukebox. A few late evening diners gave us rather odd looks as we prepared for bed in the center of the restaurant, but we were otherwise ignored. Once the jukebox had been unplugged, we spent a very pleasant night.

In the morning our "landlady" graciously refused payment and invited us to return whenever we were in the area.

Another good way to find a campsite is to grab your compass and your pith helmet and explore. Don't fall into the habit of passing up any spot that doesn't meet all of your requirements. Once you've stopped long enough to do some additional exploring on foot, you'll often find that there's more to a place than first meets the eye. Lorena and I once spent a week camped next to a high stone wall surrounding an ancient cemetery in northeastern Mexico. What we'd chosen out of desperation at the end of a hard day's traveling turned out to be the best campsite for miles around. It was within easy walking distance (easy coffin-carrying distance) of a village, convenient to a large network of interesting mountain trails, quiet during the daytime, and dead quiet at night.

Friends of ours stumbled on a beautiful, secluded campsite overlooking a small beach. There was just one minor problem: the site could only be reached by a narrow, mile-long footpath and they were traveling in a van. Rather than pass the place by, however, they came up with an ingenious solution. First, they went to the nearest village and found a shade tree auto mechanic who was happy to keep their van behind his shop for a small fee. Then they tracked down a farmer who "leased" them a pack burro to carry their gear out to the campsite. Whenever they hiked into the village for food and water, the animal was waiting patiently to haul everything back for them.

Campers traveling by public transportation or hitching often find themselves moving from one town to the next, making little contact with the countryside. This makes finding a campsite especially difficult. The solution is to leave your luggage at a hotel, trailer park, restaurant, or bus baggage room and explore on foot, by local bus, or by taxi. You will quickly save the few dollars you spend on being driven to a campsite by *coche* (cab) by cooking your own meals and not paying for a room.

Asking Mexicans for advice on campsites seldom pays off. Because few Mexican campesinos camp, they find it difficult to understand what you're looking for. It's usually simpler to find a reasonable spot and then ask for permission to use it.

Don't open your conversation with the landowner by bluntly asking, "Can we camp here?" This is too abrupt and doesn't give them a reasonable opportunity to size you up. Mexicans are very hospitable to strangers, especially gringos, but they prefer to avoid head-on questions and answers.

Start with the customary and very necessary polite greeting, comments on the weather and so on. When the ice is broken, ask, "*¿Se puede acampar aqui?*" (Can one camp here?) or better yet, "*¿Por favor, pudieramos pasar la noche aqui?*" (Please, may we pass the night here?) The word *acampar*, to camp, may be as strange to them as tap dancing. If they look startled or dubious, I add, "*Tenemos todo. Cobijas, comida, y cama.*" (We have everything. Blankets, food, and bed.) This clarifies that you only want a place to camp, not a bed and meals.

Ask for permission even if you're sure it doesn't really matter that much. How can a rancher object if you occupy a few square yards of a vast hacienda? That's not the point; you are asking for two reasons: to be polite (which, once again, is extremely important in Mexico) and to advise people of what you are doing there.

If, by any chance, you are told that you cannot camp, don't argue. There's nothing to be gained. You might be sitting in the middle of someone's cattle rustling operation or on the spot where their grandfather saw Pancho Villa's ghost. Thank them for their trouble and continue on your way.

In many cases, there won't be anyone around to ask permission of. Don't worry; you'll have company before too long. When someone asks, "*¿Que hacen aqui?*" (What are you doing here?) the obvious answer is "*Pasando la noche. ¿Esta bien?*" (Spending the night. Is it okay?) Rather than being treated like a dangerous weirdo or told to get moving, you'll probably get a smile and an offhand, "Why not?" An old man once asked us why we parked in the middle of a dusty field in the hot sun, when there were fine shade trees a short distance away.

"*La barda,*" I answered simply. "The fence."

He reached into his pocket, pulled out a pair of much-used wire cutters, and proceeded to snip through the barbed wire strands, pulling them aside. "*Pasa*" (Go ahead), he said, graciously waving us toward the trees. After I drove the van through the hole in the fence, he twisted the wires back together. "Just do the same thing when you leave," he said, continuing on down the road.

Beauty or Comfort?

Once you find an area you like, the decision of exactly where to park the RV or pitch the tent comes up. The more people there are in your group, the more difficult this final selection can be.

Everyone wants a campsite that is both beautiful and comfortable. Unfortunately, the most comfortable places are not always the most aesthetically pleasing. You may find your group torn between camping in a grove of trees, with lots of shade and places to hang hammocks, or on the beach with beautiful sunsets and the sound of the surf. I advise you to choose in favor of the most comfortable location. You'll be able enjoy everything much more: sleeping, the weather, the food, and the view. If you have to stake your sleeping bag down to keep from sliding over a cliff, the fabulous sunrises and sunsets will soon begin to pale in comparison to a good night's sleep.

Camping on the beach means sand. Sand can drive you crazy. It will soon be in your hair, food, clothes, crotch, books, and toothbrush. Beaches also mean salt mist from the spray of waves and the wind blowing over the sea. The mist makes things feel damp and slightly greasy and salty. Avoid this by camping back from the beach if possible. You'll be amazed at how much easier and more enjoyable your camp life will be.

Camping away from the beach often means, however, that you lose cooling breezes that keep the temperature down and act as a barrier against insects. Lorena and I have camped on a number of beaches that were unlivable unless we set up right on the edge of the water. Trees and brush, no matter how skimpy, are favorite mosquito haunts even on cool windy days.

Protection from the sun is very important, for both comfort and health. When I first began camping in Mexico, I spent a lot of time underneath coconut palms, loafing in the shade without a care in the world. I was oblivious to the danger until a large green coconut fell one night, narrowly missing my head but knocking some sense into it. On calm nights, when there isn't the slightest breeze to disturb them, you'll hear the palms shedding their heavy nuts. The thudding impacts will give you an idea of what they can do to a human skull or the roof of a car. Fronds that are brown and obviously dead also have the disturbing habit of falling unexpectedly. One missed us by inches on a quiet afternoon, splattering into the middle of our camp kitchen, destroying our lunch and a great deal of pottery.

Another potentially dangerous tree, the manzanillo, is found on the Pacific coast. It is quite large, offers excellent shade, and bears a distinctive fruit that resembles a small green apple. The fruit and the sap of the manzanillo are mildly poisonous. If you break off one of these ''apples,'' you'll notice a milky white fluid exuding from both the stem and fruit. This fluid will raise blisters on your skin and tongue if you taste it, as I did. The tree occasionally drips its poisonous sap onto the ground. Woe to anyone underneath.

Huts, Houses, and *Jacales*

On beaches where palm-thatched huts and sun shelters (*palapas, ramadas*) are built to accommodate Christmas and Easter crowds, traditional times for Mexicans to flock to the sea, you can often just move into an empty one during the long off-season. Depending on how energetic and businesslike the owner is, you may or may not be asked to pay rent. Bartering over the price, in a polite respectful manner, is almost expected. If the rent asked is very high (as is the case during holiday periods) and you don't want to pay it, just go somewhere else. I've seen a disturbing number of gringo campers who seemed to think that they had a *right* to use a palapa, rather than an obligation to pay rent when asked to. In most cases, the owners of these huts actually have to pay taxes on them, in addition to the not inconsiderable expense of building and maintaining them. Be cooperative rather than *chocoso* (aggravating), and it will benefit those who follow you.

Abandoned huts and shacks (*choza, jacal*) are uncommon, but you may occasionally come across one that can be used as a camp. Farmers who tend *milpas* (cornfields) a good distance from home will erect shelters, or even small houses, in the vicinity of their fields. When not in use as a dwelling, they often double as *bodegas* (storerooms) for corn, fodder, or tools. If you find one, use it with respect and take great care to avoid burning it down or otherwise damaging the contents. Campesinos do not like to camp in the open, and will often direct hikers to shelters such as these. If you're lucky, the fleas will have hitched a ride on a passing dog.

Beaches

Although Mexican beaches are all legally owned by the federal government, many tourists mistakenly believe that this allows unlimited public use and access. This isn't true: many beaches are leased, controlled by *ejidos* (cooperatives), or managed by a *concesionario* (concessionaire). You may be asked to pay a nominal rent, especially if you're building a lavish camp or hut. If the price isn't reasonable and can't be lowered, it's best to move on rather than hassle over it. Even if you win the battle, you may well spoil things for the next camper who comes along.

Food and Water

A good camping place will hopefully have access to food and water. Long trips for a few tomatoes and a canteen of water tend to get longer and less enjoyable, even though the campsite itself is otherwise ideal. If water isn't readily available, you may decide to dig for it, but few campers will have the time or energy to plant a vegetable garden (though I've seen a few who have).

Since you'll save money and eat better by living on fresh rather than canned foods, you'll want to be able to buy the basics: eggs, tomatoes, onions, beans, rice, bananas, salt, and cooking oil. Local people provide good examples of how to live on what's readily available. Ask them if they can sell you fruits, vegetables, and eggs from their own homes. In isolated areas, it may take a week or more to establish good contacts. Allow for this by carrying sufficient food, booze, and water to avoid running out completely.

Depending on local supplies has advantages other than convenience. Casual requests for a few eggs can lead to the most interesting and unusual side trips. You notice, for example, that a farmer has a few beehives in his back yard. *"¿Hay miel?"* (Is there honey?) you ask, and before you know it, you're following him to his brother-in-law's rancho to see if his hives are producing. Along the way, the farmer suddenly plunges into the bushes and emerges a few seconds later, hands filled with a strange bittersweet berry. At the relative's rancho, there is no honey but how about some fine fresh goat's cheese? How about a bowl of beans and a few tortillas? How about going hunting tonight? How about. . . . ?

The more remote your campsite, the less you'll want to depend on tedious and time-consuming trips to town for supplies. This is especially true when camping with a vehicle. Running into the store for an onion takes half a day or more and a tank of gas. Those are expensive onions. The solution is simple to describe but often not so simple to do. It requires a change in your attitude toward your vehicle and some very careful shopping.

First of all, prepare for long periods away from stores by making detailed lists of what you eat and drink. Don't forget things like cigarettes and vermouth; when you can't have a smoke or evening martini, you'll be back behind the wheel, barreling toward town. Lorena and I have a master list that ranges from spices and potatoes to midnight snacks and matches. When we stock up, we use the list (if I haven't forgotten it at camp) as a reminder, adjusting the quantities according to where we're camping and for how long.

Your second line of defense against trips to town is to learn how to stretch what you've got to the maximum or just plain do without. This rather obvious measure can have curious side effects. Stretching supplies teaches that you can get along quite well on a lot less than you'd have thought. A friend who spent several weeks holed up on a remote beach told me, "I didn't really appreciate onions until I found myself using every bit, including the outer skin for soup stocks." When the bananas get black and mushy, you won't just toss them into the garbage; you'll dig out the flour and make a delicious loaf of banana bread.

In many popular camping areas, people get together to make communal supply trips. I like to take a local person with me, not only to give them a ride but to take advantage of their knowledge of where to shop and how much to pay for things. A guide can save hours of searching for things like purple sewing thread, size 29 huaraches and all the other odds and ends that make these trips so . . . interesting.

One morning a fellow gringo camper asked for a lift to town. As we passed another camp on the way out, a voice called, "Get some *bolillos* (bread rolls)! Get lots!"

"How many is 'lots'?" our passenger cried.

There was a moment of hesitation. "All they got!"

When Lorena and I returned from a long foray into the market, we found our friend sitting in the back of the van, surrounded by bulging flour sacks stuffed with *bolillos*. There weren't just a lot of bolillos, there were several hundred, all freshly baked, without preservatives.

"Boy, oh boy, are those folks gonna be happy!" he chortled.

He is still remembered as the Bolillo Kid and the camping area is called Bolillo Flats.

Being offered gifts of food by local people is common, especially in areas where few gringos or other campers have visited. Campesinos are quite generous, though they can often ill-afford to give things away. If there is any doubt in your mind whether something is being offered as a gift or is for sale, quietly ask, "*¿Cuanto le debo?*" (How much do I owe you?) or "*¿Que se le ofrece?*" (What can I offer?) The standard refusal of payment is a negligent wave of the hand or a simple "*Nada*" (Nothing). Don't push it; you'll offend them by insisting on paying. A sincere "Thank you" is sufficient, or you might offer a small gift in return.

Privacy

Unless you camp in RV parks and organized campgrounds, your camping trip will turn into a "people" trip. There are ways, fortunately, to increase your privacy without hiding inside a tent or camping on the edge of an active volcano.

Children are the worst intruders. To avoid them, camp a long way from the nearest village or ranch. This certainly won't eliminate their visiting, but it will keep the smaller and less adventurous away. Large kids are notoriously difficult to avoid, and if they have to walk five hot dusty miles to see you (which they will do), they'll probably make a day of it.

Avoid camping near trails, us ally the major travel routes for local people. Don't camp near obviously popular swimming holes. Half-used bars of soap, discarded scrubbers, and picne. garbage near an inviting pool of water are sure indications that weekends and evenings will find it full of people.

After you've chosen a campsite, you can expect visitors within hours. On the coast and in the lower mountain areas, people are generally more open with strangers than are the Indians of the high mountains. You can expect them to stare. Silent staring can be unnerving (to say the least), especially if you're alone or don't speak Spanish. Paranoia may have you packing up and heading to a city unless you understand—and try to accept—the reasons for this mute intrusion.

Natural curiosity is obviously part of the reason that people want to stare at you. You look funny. Your hair is weird, your clothes are strange, your vehicle and all of your possessions are wonderful to look at, and you talk and act like no normal person in the village. Curiosity itself isn't difficult to understand, but the open staring, pointing, and excited talking over everything you unpack or do can be infuriating, and for some, quite frightening. Why do they do it? How can they be so blatant and unembarrassed? The answer is that they have no feeling of each man's house being his castle and no concept of being rude or impolite merely because they are observing what you are doing in your house, that is, your car, RV, or tent.

You will probably notice that this open curiosity doesn't normally reach the point where visitors will walk uninvited into your camp or actually handle your things. When you want someone to "come in," you'll usually have to invite them (women are especially shy). It's as if invisible boundaries marked off the area of your camp from the general community.

This attitude can best be understood by visiting one of your curious visitor's homes. Communal activity isn't restricted to work in the fields. The same people who sat 20 feet from your van for hours on end will crowd around the house you're visiting, hanging on every word of conversation between you and your hosts.

You'll inevitably have people around camp at mealtimes. I personally find it difficult to eat in front of a staring crowd. Remember, however, that your guests do not feel embarrassed by eating in front of others. This, too, is just another aspect of village life.

When the food supply or budget is limited, sharing a meal. with 10 or 15 others could lead to a food crisis in your camp. We often invite Mexican visitors to eat, however, and they almost always politely refuse or accept only a token bite as a gesture of appreciation. It's the other tourists who eat you out of house and home.

Maintaining normal activities (eating, reading, writing, lying around in your underwear) can be difficult with a group of people looking on, but it can be done. Present a rather unexciting appearance and don't do anything hilarious or unexpected. Your visitors will eventually drift away or at least relax the intensity of their stares. Keep high interest items such as radios, tape recorders, cameras, fishing and diving gear, and tools out of sight. This will greatly reduce onlookers' interest once they have recovered from the initial shock of your presence. If you decide to do an engine tune-up, however, you'll undoubtedly have them on the edges of their seats, if not right in the engine compartment with you, for the entire fascinating procedure, no matter how long it may take.

Once you've accepted the fact that there are going to be people around, take advantage of their curiosity to satisfy your own curiosity about them. I've found that there's no better way to get into an area than to select some likely looking person and suggest that I'd like to do something: go fishing, bird-watching, exploring, collecting water, or gathering firewood. The response is almost automatically enthusiastic. This quickly changes the relationship from frustrated curiosity about you to a desire to demonstrate something that they can do, whether it's climbing a coco palm or leading you to an interesting ruin. By doing this, you'll soon have real friends among your guests. Rather than feeling a slight sense of dread at their visits, you'll begin to look forward to them.

Where to Camp

Camping becomes much easier in Mexico once you realize that almost any place can be a campsite. Although your mode of travel will affect your choice to a certain degree, most of the places described here will do just as well for backpackers as van nomads and motor homers.

Note for motorists: No matter where you camp, park with the assumption that your trusty vehicle will have either a flat tire or a dead battery in the morning. Better safe than sorry, especially if it means jacking the vehicle up in sand or pushing it backward onto the highway. The simple precaution of parking the vehicle so that it points in the direction you plan to leave can greatly simplify a push start. Flat tires in Mexico's backcountry are as inevitable as hangovers after a fiesta, so park on level, solid ground whenever you have the chance.

Trailer Parks and Campgrounds

Although trailer parks are relatively common on major highways and around popular tourist towns (usually right on the outskirts), they are few and far between elsewhere. Look for road signs that show a picture of a small house trailer or the words *Parque de Trayler, Trailer Parque, Casas Rodantes, Campamento* (campground), *Remolques* (trailers), or any other combination of English and Spanish that may have struck the management as appropriate. My favorite, one that has puzzled Mexicans and gringos alike, is *Trailer Parque y Cabanas de Tio Tom de Mark Twang.* It's hard to pass up a place with a name like that.

Motels and Hotels

As the number of motor campers to Mexico increases each year, more hotel and motel owners are offering informal camping spaces, hookups, and even tent sites. In fact, virtually any

modest motel or hotel will be open to the idea of allowing vehicle campers to spend the night. Just ask, *"¿Se puede pasar la
noche en el camper?"* or *"¿Hay lugar par camper?"* (May one
spend the night in a camper? Is there space for a camper? In
this case, "camper" is usually understood to refer to a camper
van or RV.)

In some hotels you'll get nothing more than a place to
park; in others you'll be allowed the use of all the facilities,
including bathrooms, swimming pool, and restaurant. If temporary hookups are available, it often helps to have your own
power cords and hose.

Don't be surprised if the rates for camping in a vehicle
aren't much lower than the cost of taking a room. This is very
common, especially if the rate includes any hookups or
showering privileges. Instead of complaining, take the room
and use it for bathing, relaxing, or sorting your gear.

In towns, I prefer to look for a larger hotel that has fallen
on hard times, one with plenty of room in the central patio
to park long-forgotten carriages and horse-drawn wagons. In
one hotel of this type, the desk clerk agreed that the decaying patio was even more comfortable than the decaying rooms
and let us camp for the night, providing we didn't build a
camp fire or hang our laundry in plain view.

National Parks

Camping facilities within Mexican parks, reserves, and
national monuments are quite limited. Many are closed to the
public at night, and camping is *prohibido.* If you are told that
you can't camp, it is often possible to make a "special arrangement." This means you pay the guard or caretaker to forget
that you are there.

Archaeological Sites

These used to be favored campsites, for very good reasons.
Archaeological sites are interesting to visit, especially at the

crack of dawn or during the full moon when camera-toting, children-dragging tourists are safe in their hotels. And the sites are often near water or a prominent hill.

Recently, however, the government has been cracking down on camping in or near ruins, not without justification. Vandalism, theft, and amateur efforts to make midnight archaeological discoveries really irritate authorities and authentic archaeologists. It is also particularly exasperating for the police to have people in various states of "nonordinary reality" tripping around, over, and off pyramids, temples, and tombs. It may be illuminating to play Mayan priest at the full moon, but the caretakers and police never seem to appreciate what you're doing.

Camping is still allowed in some sites, but in general it is either officially prohibited or really frowned on—which means you may or may not be run out in the middle of the night, depending on the local attitude and your behavior.

Wide Spots

In previous years, before Mexico's traffic and population boom, I often camped beside highways and major arterials without a second thought—unless it was a groan every time a truck or bus driver gave me a friendly honk in the middle of the night. Things have changed, however, and I no longer recommend wide spots for camping. Traffic has not only increased on Mexico's highways but so has the hazard of being hassled in the middle of the night by cops, drunks, or cruising teenagers. If you find yourself too tired, lost, or otherwise unable to continue driving, it is best to park away from the highway and out of public view. As the saying goes, out of sight, out of mind. Whenever we need an emergency camping place, Lorena and I will look for an isolated country lane or the driveway into a rancho. Don't be timid, either, about asking if you can park near someone's house. Mexicans are very sympathetic to travelers who need a place to spend the night. Parking your van or RV in a stranger's front yard might seem odd at first, but believe me, it's safe. This type of camping is also a great way to meet people and overcome your shyness with Mexicans.

Side Roads

All side roads lead to that mythical Perfect Camping Spot, or at least it seems as if they should. Of the hundreds that I've followed, most led to sand traps, mudholes, ranches, and towns. Unlike secondary roads in the United States, which seem to go everywhere and nowhere in particular, almost without exception, Mexican side roads lead to a group of houses or a small town. If you block the road, even though you'd swear it's a long-abandoned trail, you can almost count on being blasted out of bed by someone leaning impatiently on the horn of a bus or truck.

The Desert

Weary travelers may reach the desperation point and say, "Hell, let's just pull off into the desert!" And there they remain, stuck in sand or dust, until help comes along. The desert is occasionally made of rocks, but more often of something softer. In winter, when rain is extremely rare, the ground dries out quite hard in some spots and quite soft and dusty in others. During the rainy season, it may be surprisingly soft, even after a light sprinkle.

Always check the ground directly in line with where you're moving the vehicle before leaving the road. Once off the road, don't get carried away and race a quarter of a mile onto the desert just because the ground is solid; it may suddenly change to a sand trap.

Among the worst hazards of driving in the desert are cactus spines and thorns. They are all over the ground and will play hell with your tires.

Dams

We rate *presas* (dams) as choice camping areas. Keep your eyes peeled for signs; many dams and reservoirs are poorly marked, even on major highways. Hundreds of dams have been built around the country, and there are more to come as the government fights a chronic shortage of surface water.

Don't pass up a sign for a presa just because you can't see something on the order of the Grand Coulee or an obvious lake. In the desert, for example, dams are often hidden in narrow canyons. One of our favorites is near the edge of a vast barren plain, one of the most unappetizing camping areas imaginable. But tucked deep inside the foothills there's a stream shaded by ancient mesquite trees which drains a large artificial lake. The water is full of fat bass and attracts a wide variety of birds and wildlife. Most dams have the added attraction of large, flat spaces to camp on, the result of excavations and earth-moving during their construction.

Hot Springs and Spas

There's nothing quite like camping with natural hot water to bathe and relax in. Mexico has thousands of hot springs and spas, some developed centuries ago by Spanish colonists, others just bubbling out of the earth in a completely natural state.

Look for *aguas termales, aguas medicinales, aguas calientes, ojo de agua* (''eye of water'' also means spring or pool), *balneario* (bathing spot, not always hot water), or *atotonilco*, an Indian word often given to villages or ranches located on or near hot springs.

Some spas have been developed to the point where you might not want to camp near them, especially on weekends when the crowds flood in. In most cases, however, a large developed hot spring won't be the only one around. Smaller springs serve campesinos and their families at a fraction of the price of fancier facilities. There probably won't be an organized campground, so just ask for permission to camp.

Backpackers should keep their ears open for mention of hot springs. We've often been directed to hot water while walking in the backcountry. After a hard day on the trail, the pleasure of a hot bath is indescribable.

Bridges

At one or both ends of many bridges you may see the remains of a road leading to the old bridge or ferry landing. These roads are often quite indistinct, particularly at night. They are good emergency camping places, especially as many lead right to the water's edge.

Quarries and Dirt Pits

Dirt pits are found along most Mexican highways, especially if they are new or recently repaired. Be very careful when driving into one of these places; some are soft, and some have huge holes and trenches that you could easily fall into at night. If it has been raining, send someone ahead to check the firmness of the ground, but don't forget that a human foot may not make a dent where a heavy RV would sink.

Friends of ours almost lost their van when the wife walked ahead into an old excavation. What looked and felt like wet grass turned out to be a bog covered with a very thick layer of floating weeds. It took a passing team of oxen and a large gang of men to save their van from sinking.

Dumps

I personally rate camping in dumps over all other desperation campsites. Unlike dumps in the United States, full of rotting food and rats, Mexican dumps are usually dry and pest-free. This is undoubtedly because few Mexicans throw away food.

Dumps are often just flat areas close to the road, easily spotted by swirling heaps of discarded plastic. Not AAA-approved but very convenient. Dumps are also excellent places for bird-watching.

Cemeteries

Don't drive right into the cemetery, but don't make yourself conspicuous by attempting to hide. Park openly near an entrance and you won't arouse suspicions of grave robbery. I enjoy a early morning tour of the graves and have never met with any resentment or hostility from caretakers or visitors. Cemeteries are quiet, peaceful places with very few curious children hanging around, especially after dark.

Schoolyards and Soccer Fields

You may be driven by desperation to stop near a town or village. The edge of a schoolyard has the advantages of being reasonably level and away from noisy cantinas and drunks. The big disadvantage, however, is that schoolyards, playing fields, and soccer fields are frequented by packs of children and there's no place to answer a call of nature. Don't park in front of the goal posts of a soccer field or you might block an early morning game (as we did).

Parking Lots

Camping in an *estacionamiento* (parking lot) might seem odd, but it can make a good overnight site. Unless the lot has an overnight guard, however, you'll probably be locked in with the cars, taco carts, and buses. Larger private parking lots have a *velador* (watchman), a grungy bathroom, and perhaps even electricity. I've seldom met the owner of a parking lot who wasn't willing to strike a good bargain for a temporary parking/camping combination.

If you want to get an early start, don't allow your vehicle to be blocked in by others. Lorena and I once had to delay our departure for three hours because a careless client had neglected to leave his keys with the attendant. The problem was finally solved Mexican fashion, by grabbing half a dozen passing men and asking them to carry the keyless car to another spot.

Gas Stations and Tire and Mechanic Shops

You can try this, but it doesn't always work. Buy some gas and then ask the attendant if you can park behind the station for the night. Noisy, bright, and smelly— but better than nothing.

Mexico's highways have busy sidelines of *vulcanizadoras* (vulcanizers, tire repairs) and *taller mecanicos* (mechanic shops). The usual flat fixer or mechanic lives with his family in the back of the shop and is more or less always on call. Even if you don't have a slow leak or a worrisome engine knock, these roadside shops make good (though sometimes noisy) overnight parking places. Again, offer to pay for parking and if it isn't accepted, return the favor with a cup of coffee or a small, token gift.

Police Station

Some people seem to think the police (being public servants) should know of good camping places and make a point of going to the station to ask where they can park. The usual answers seem to be: (1) a motel, (2) a parking lot, or (3) nowhere, get out of town. But there is a sneaky way to avoid actually going to the station while still enjoying its protection. (I don't recommend this if you look very weird.) Find the police station and then park on the street, just around the corner. The logic to this is that criminals and drunks won't be lurking close by. I prefer the cemetery or a good dump.

Streets and Businesses

If camping in the countryside makes you too nervous for comfort, try parking on a well-lighted city street or in front of a friendly, all-night business. If there is a cop around, ask for permission to spend the night and offer a donation to the policeman's ball. You'll probably get a secure place to park as well as your own security guard.

Because of the usual problem of urban crime, I don't recommend camping on the streets of large cities. When in doubt, pick a "better" neighborhood or park beside a business that has an all-night watchman. You can enlist the watchman's help by pointing to your eye, then to your vehicle, and offering a tip.

Public Buildings

In small towns and villages, especially remote ones, you may be allowed or invited to sleep in the school, jail, town hall, or other communal building. I've tried them all, and what they lack in comfort is more than made up for in hospitality. In one case, however, Lorena and I accidentally stirred up a hornet's nest by accepting a young schoolteacher's offer of a bed on the classroom floor. We had just begun to lay out our sleeping bags when the teacher began apologizing profusely for embarrassing us, but the truth was, he'd overstepped his authority and had to withdraw the offer.

We had been hiking for several hours and were extremely tired. Even the bricks looked tempting. Could we sleep in front of the school? No, he said, that would offend the town elders, since it would appear that they were being inhospitable. The problem, in fact, was that the townspeople had built the school without federal assistance but the teacher was a federal employee, not a local man. Did we understand?

Sure, sure. But where could we sleep?

Four hours later, after a town meeting, we were invited

by the elders to sleep on the porch of the school, satisfying all factions. Once this minor problem had been resolved, the elders kept us awake half the night asking eager questions about our *tierra* (homeland).

Pipeline Access Roads

Mexico's booming petroleum and natural gas industry has spawned a number of pipelines, some hundreds of miles long. During their construction, access roads are bulldozed for heavy equipment and maintenance crews. These narrow dirt roads are poorly marked, but you'll soon learn to recognize the coded signs and the word PEMEX, for Petroleos Mexicanos, the government oil monopoly. Some pipeline roads cross private property, but if you carefully close cattle gates, you probably won't bother anyone by camping.

Microwave Stations

There are hundreds of *microondas* towers (also called *estación de microondas*), most located on top of mountains or large hills. These are federally operated relay stations for television and communications. Since the towers and their relay transmitters are deliberately built on the highest ground, they make fine campsites. Most are reached by cobblestone roads, narrow and often quite steep. Think twice before attempting one of these roads in an extra-large or underpowered vehicle.

Microondas stations are not usually staffed, so you probably won't find anyone around to ask permission to camp. Please keep in mind, however, that they are government property. If campers are suspected of vandalism or mischief (like climbing the tower to howl at the moon), they will undoubtedly be closed to the public.

Where Not to Camp

Moonshine and Marijuana, Heroin and *Sindicatos*

When traveling in the backcountry, be receptive to discreet warnings about places that may not be safe to camp or hike. A Mexican warned us repeatedly about leaving the trail in one area, insisting, ''There is nothing interesting in the bottom of these canyons.'' With a little persistence, I learned that there was something very interesting in those shady hollows: a lucrative and very illegal series of mescal stills cranking out tax-free moonshine.

Remote fields of marijuana or opium poppies are often jealously guarded by armed farmers. These fields are quite well hidden, especially after the considerable success of the Mexican/American drug eradication programs of the past few years. If you should stumble on a field of dope, turn around quickly and leave. It takes foolish persistence to find these fields, and the problem will rarely arise for even the most adventurous camper.

Although drugs can be cultivated almost anywhere, the state of Sinaloa is considered the opium and heroin capital of Mexico. I know a number of gringos who have hiked in the mountains of Sinaloa without problems, but I cannot recommend it unless you travel with a local guide. This area is also frequently embroiled in disputes between farmers and *latifundistas* (big landowners, agribusiness). If you camp there, keep your ear to the ground and your mouth shut on the subjects of dope and politics.

The state of Guerrero is somewhat notorious in Mexico, both for dope cultivation and the traditional resistance of its people to domination by the federal government. A schoolteacher who protests inhumanly low wages, for example, will be branded a ''guerrilla'' and hounded into the mountains. I and many friends have camped in the state of Guerrero and thoroughly enjoyed it. Once again, your own awareness and attitude will be your best protection against potential trouble.

Borders

Other potentially "dangerous" areas are borders between the United States and Mexico and Mexico and Guatemala. The border patrols of all three countries will be curious about anyone camping, hiking, or boating very close to the boundary line. Bureaucrats take borders seriously, so you'd better humor them and observe the law carefully. With continued political violence in Guatemala, that border always attracts attention from both Mexican and Guatemalan authorities. Have your papers in order, and don't stray from one country into another.

PART **II**

Campground Directory

CHAPTER 6

How to Use the Directory

Ratings

In preparing this directory, Steve Rogers and I made a pact to take objectivity with a grain of salt. One of our biggest complaints with other publications is their detached, tourist-brochure style. We vowed to make this directory an outspoken and personal guide to camping in Mexico, not a bland and boring list of four-star recommendations. When we like a campground, we'll tell you so in no uncertain terms. If we don't care for a place, however, we may save space by not listing it at all—or say a few words in spite of a double thumbs-down to point out some noteworthy feature such as low price, convenient location, or unusually friendly management.

Although we avoid objectivity, we have done our best to be both fair and accurate when describing a campground or service. The establishments we've listed include many of our personal favorites, but we've also noted campgrounds that appeal to tastes other than our own. As you'll soon realize, our preferences run to free camping on undeveloped beaches, down-home, Mexican-style campgrounds, and old-fashioned trailer parks. Though we occasionally camp in neatly groomed, American-style RV parks, we feel less in touch with Mexico in these places. At the same time, we recognize that many travelers sleep better when their rig is parked on a concrete pad, with full hookups and an alert *velador* (night watchman).

Although we were tempted to use the familiar rating system of one to five stars, we soon discovered that many of our listings refused to fit into such convenient categories. After all, how do you compare a relaxed Mexican spa campground with a modern, full-service RV park in Ensenada? What the spa might lack in facilities is more than compensated for by its wonderful setting, hospitable caretakers, abundant hot water, and ridiculously low price. Do we give the spa one star for cleanliness, three stars for "atmosphere," or four stars for "effort"? As long as we're comparing papayas to pineapples, how do we rate the RV park, with its cable TV connections, laundromat, and spic-and-span showers?

Our solution to the ratings puzzle is simple: rather than devise some complex formula for awarding stars, we'll give you the same sort of recommendations we'd give any other friend—our personal, sometimes quirky impressions of each campground we've visited. Once you visit a place, rate it according to your own likes and dislikes by scribbling stars in the margins of the book. As you travel, compare your impressions of the campgrounds and attractions you visit with our descriptions. Before you know it, you'll soon be able to read between the lines of this directory and tailor your selections to your own tastes.

As you look over the directory, you'll see an occasional parrot in the margin. We've made a few exceptions to our "no stars" policy by marking special campgrounds and attractions with a parrot. We haven't given them out lightly. Our criteria for granting a parrot include everything from natural beauty to *ambiente*, a difficult-to-define quality of "good feeling" that sets one campground apart from another. For example, we've awarded parrots to Agua Azul (Chiapas) for its breathtakingly beautiful waterfalls and pools and to Lago Dorado KDA campground near San Miguel de Allende (Guanajuato) for its relaxing location, impeccable grounds, and very helpful management.

Price Codes

Because of fluctuations in the rate of exchange from U.S. dollars to Mexican pesos, we've coded each campground's prices according to the following system:

$	Cheap: less than $5.00 U.S.
$$	Moderate: $5.00 to $8.00
$$$	High: $8.00 and above

These price categories are based on overnight rates for one vehicle with two persons and basic hookups. Most parks fall into the middle price range, but a substantial number of rustic campgrounds still cost less than $2.00 or $3.00 per night per family. Full-service RV parks commonly charge $8.00 or $10.00, but only a few parks we visited were more than $11.00 or $12.00 a night. Additional charges for children or extra adults run about 10 to 20 percent per person. Some parks also charge more for air-conditioners, extra-large rigs, laundry, or boat storage.

I'm sorry to say that fancier American-style RV parks seldom welcome tent campers with open arms and may even prohibit tenting. If they are allowed, tent campers may pay as much as vehicle campers. As one American park manager in Baja told Steve, ''You pay for the space, not what you put on it.''

In more relaxed parks, especially those catering to families, Mexicans, and international van campers, tents are given a good discount. Van and tent campers can often save money by asking if there is a discount for camping without hookups. Electricity is expensive in Mexico and low-budget campgrounds may charge a premium for *luz* (light, power).

In general, rates for campgrounds in Mexico tend to be lower in the southern regions of the country and higher in the north. Most campgrounds give discounts for stays of several days, and 10 to 20 percent monthly discounts are common. Some parks, especially those in Baja and the northern Pacific coast, offer annual rates, leases, and even time-share ownership of spaces.

Local and state parks, spas, and other undeveloped campgrounds usually charge fees for admission to the grounds. There may also be additional modest fees for parking, rest rooms, and overnight camping. To complicate bookkeeping, these fees are charged ''per person.'' The total fees for a family rarely add up to more than a few dollars at most, but to avoid time-consuming misunderstandings, be sure to keep track of all the flimsy, tissue paper receipts you'll be given.

How fast will rates go up in Mexico? By the time you take this book south, you may find that our ''moderate'' rate of $5.00 to $8.00 a night has increased from $6.00 to $9.00 or slightly higher. After tracking prices over the past several years, however, I don't expect campground prices to increase appreciably. Many campgrounds fix their prices to the American dollar, not the peso. You can expect a modest annual increase in dollar costs, regardless of the fluctuations of the peso. If there is a major devaluation of the peso, however, prices should decrease significantly for at least a few months, until inflation catches up again. (In parks that charge dollar prices, of course, the client does not get the benefit of a devaluation of the peso.)

Types of Campgrounds

''Mexican-style'' is a broad term that we use for more relaxed campgrounds and RV parks. ''American-style'' parks with services apparently identical to Mexican-style campgrounds can be worlds apart in atmosphere, not to mention reliability, cleanliness, and attention to detail. Though I personally prefer the fair prices and easygoing nature of most Mexican-style parks, their facilities may include less-than-perfect plumbing and on again-off again electricity.

American-style parks (including those owned and operated by Mexicans) do their best to imitate RV facilities in the United States. Cement pads, laundromats, swimming pools, satellite TV, game rooms, and other luxuries not typical of Mexico are important features in these parks. They also go to great expense to offer 24-hour-a-day hot water and electrical power. Although crime is seldom a problem in Mexican campgrounds, many American-style parks have serious security fences, night watchmen, and street lights. As you'd expect, such facilities and services come at a price—though compared to similar places in the United States, most RVers consider Mexico's most expensive parks to be a bargain.

I have a few general complaints about some of the American-style RV parks I've visited in Mexico. First and most distressing, they tend to isolate travelers from Mexico. Their facilities are enviable, but only the most affluent Mexicans can afford to use them. This not only guarantees that English will be the campground's official language but it also increases a sense of aloofness from the local people and culture. Though Mexico is very safe for visitors, I've heard nervous RVers warning each other not to camp outside of "safe" RV parks for fear of being robbed and looted in broad daylight. These attitudes are only reinforced by the circle-the-wagons atmosphere created by cyclone fences, armed guards, and halogen street lights. A desire for security is natural, but when it reaches the point of distrusting "outsiders" in general, we have to wonder, "Why visit Mexico at all?"

On the other side of the coin, spas, picnic grounds, *balnearios* (swimming areas), local parks, and other typical Mexican recreation and camping areas seldom offer more than rustic services. They're also very cheap—just don't expect much more (and sometimes less) than an outhouse, an outside water tap, and a thatched shelter or two. For those willing to venture just slightly off the beaten track, however, these informal campgrounds can be wonderful places to meet local people and practice speaking Spanish. At the same time, you'll discover some of the best hidden natural attractions in Mexico.

Directions and Distances

No two maps or guidebooks agree on the distance between any two points in Mexico. The distances we've given are usually our own odometer readings, backed up with map measurements. Since your own odometer doesn't exactly match mine or Steve's, you'll want to allow for a margin of error, even on relatively short distances. We've done our best to keep our distance measurements in miles, but in some cases we've cited highway kilometer markers. On some highways, the *kilometraje* (kilometer distance) is measured from the state line or international border. In other cases, kilometers are marked off from the state capital, the largest city, or the center of Mexico City.

Carry a compass and consult it frequently. I have a dashboard compass and a key chain compass for a backup. When in doubt, trust the compass, not your sense of direction.

Road maps of Mexico do not always show every place we've mentioned in the directory. With this in mind, we've oriented our directions to the nearest significant city, town, and highway. I strongly recommend that you visit tourist offices to ask for local maps and suggestions on good camping places. Some of Mexico's finest camping and natural areas are known only to local people. Though you'll occasionally strike out when exploring on your own, the rewards of the search are usually more than worth the effort.

This directory is meant to supplement other guidebooks and maps, not replace them. Backpackers will obviously have to keep their reference material to a minimum (use razor blades and staple loose pages into booklets), but drivers can carry a small library. In describing cities, for example, I've kept remarks and descriptions as brief as possible, preferring to use the space for highway reports. Use this directory in combination with one or more supplemental guidebooks and you'll get a good overall picture.

CHAPTER 7

A Geography Lesson

Mexico is a very large country, covering over 760,000 square miles, an area about one-fifth the size of the United States or Canada. It includes two major peninsulas (Baja and Yucatán) and over 6,000 miles of shoreline. In cross section, Mexico's topography is a rollercoaster of mountain ranges and canyons. Most of the country is above 3,000 feet high, but several individual peaks soar over 17,000 feet. Contrasts in climates are as dramatic as the topography, varying from deserts so arid they may see no rain for years at a time to eternally drenched tropical rain forests.

There are four distinct temperature zones within the country, from the low, humid southern *tierra caliente* (hot land) to temperate, cold, and even *helada* (frozen). Though much of the country is dry and cactus studded, there are vast pine and oak forests, lowland savannahs, immense wetlands, lagoons, jungles, and deserts of several types. When such factors as climate, altitude, vegetation and topography are all shuffled together, the country is revealed as a collection of more than 50 distinct regions, a complex geographic jigsaw puzzle that defies a simple description.

Travelers will find that Mexico's diversity not only translates into sudden and dramatic changes in scenery, temperature, and camping conditions but it also affects the people. In Oaxaca, for example, the customs, daily lives, and language of highland Mixtec Indians are quite different from the Zapotecs of the central valleys or the mixed-blood mestizos of the coastal fishing communities. Though their differences are as obvious as those between Americans and Chinese, these diverse groups are separated by only a few hours' travel.

An understanding of Mexico's unusually varied climate, geography, cultures, and camping conditions is important for trip planning, especially if your concept of the country is a vague, never-ending desert "south of the border." To begin, think of Mexico not as a single country but as a group of loosely connected regions.

For our purposes, I'll divide Mexico into seven regions:

Baja Peninsula
Pacific Coast
Central (Colonial) Highlands
Northern
Southern Highlands
Gulf Coast
Yucatán Peninsula

Look at a map of Mexico and get a rough idea of each region's boundaries. Before we discuss particular quirks of climate and geography, let's note a few characteristic conditions of Mexico as a whole.

Higher altitudes mean *cooler temperatures.* Mexico is made up of highlands and lowlands, with steep, narrow transitions between the two. In summer, the highlands are temperate and the lowlands are quite hot. In winter, the lowlands become temperate and the highlands surprisingly cool, especially at night. For example, at an elevation of 5,000 feet, Guadalajara's climate is often described as "eternal spring" or "Mediterranean." At 7,000 feet, however, nighttime temperatures in winter will occasionally drop into the 30s around

Climate

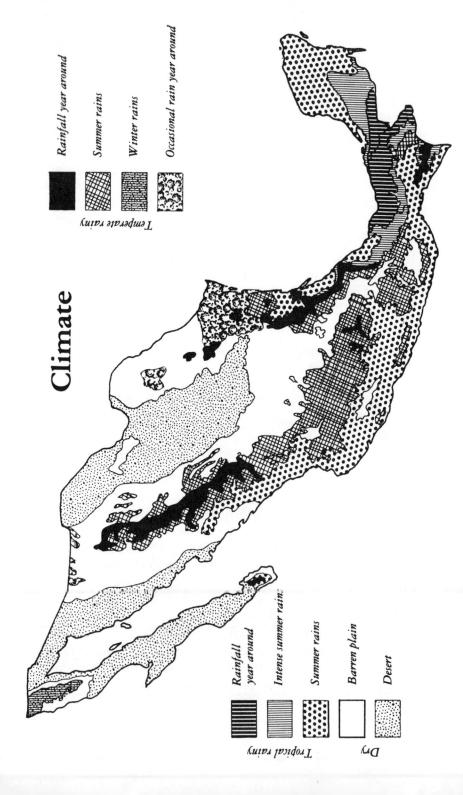

Temperate rainy
- ■ Rainfall year around
- ▨ Summer rains
- ▤ Winter rains
- ▦ Occasional rain year around

Tropical rainy
- ▬ Rainfall year around
- ▤ Intense summer rain
- ▦ Summer rains

Dry
- □ Barren plain
- ▒ Desert

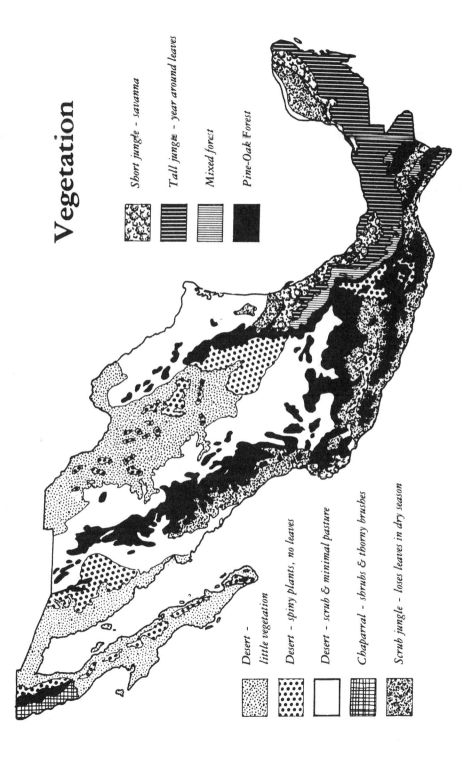

Vegetation

Short jungle - savanna

Tall jungle - year around leaves

Mixed forest

Pine-Oak Forest

Desert - little vegetation

Desert - spiny plants, no leaves

Desert - scrub & minimal pasture

Chaparral - shrubs & thorny brushes

Scrub jungle - loses leaves in dry season

Mountain Ranges

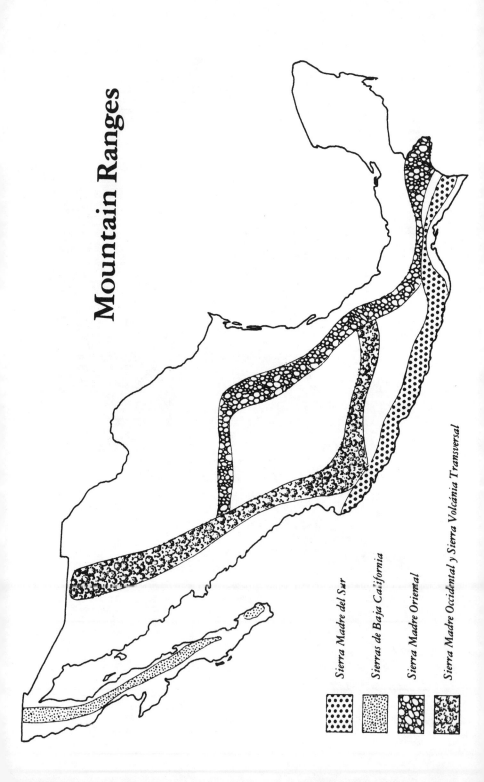

Sierra Madre del Sur

Sierras de Baja California

Sierra Madre Oriental

Sierra Madre Occidental y Sierra Volcánia Transversal

Mexico City. In summer, Mexico City's altitude holds daytime temperatures to the 70s and 80s.
In winter, temperatures go from cool in the north to hot in the south. Northern and eastern Mexico are strongly influenced by winter weather systems from the United States and Canada. Cooling effects are commonly felt as far south as Mexico City, with occasional heavy snows in Chihuahua and the north-central mountains. These same storms will affect the Pacific beaches as far south as Guaymas and Mazatlán, though Puerto Vallarta is usually reliably warm. Depending on your luck, the entire Baja peninsula can be quite cool in January and February.

Eastern Mexico, including most of the Yucatán peninsula and the entire Gulf of Mexico, is swept by winter *nortes* (northers) from the American Midwest. The Gulf of Mexico is also the country's wettest region. The gulf's ''dry'' season is never entirely dry. It comes in late winter and lasts only a few months.

Roughly speaking, the warmest winter weather is on the Pacific coast south of Manzanillo, including Ixtapa-Zihuatanejo, Acapulco, Puerto Escondido, Huatulco, and Salina Cruz.

Summers are rainy and winters are dry. Mexico's rainy season is from mid-May through October, but, in fact, it seldom rains significantly until late summer. In our experience, mid-August through mid-October is the wettest time of year. During *las aguas* (rainy season, ''the waters''), most tourists find that the lowlands are too hot and humid for comfort. In the desert, rain will be very infrequent and the temperature will be quite high.

Except for wetter tropical areas and the Gulf of Mexico, summer rains are usually brief but intense. A typical rain will come in the afternoon or at night and be followed by clear or partly cloudy skies. The rainy season is a particularly beautiful time in Mexico, but it definitely complicates camping. When the rainy season is approaching, select a campsite that won't be inundated or made unlivable. Anticipate that a lot of rain, even for a short time, can turn a creek into a river and a pond into a lake.

If your camp centers around a vehicle, you'll want to be especially careful where it's parked. This doesn't just mean preventing it from being washed away. Park where you won't be isolated by the first heavy rain. Be sure there is some way to get to an all-weather road once the rains begin.

The dry season, *las sequias*, begins in late October but doesn't really show its effects on vegetation until mid-winter. The end of the dry season is often the hottest time of year. The month of May can be especially warm in the dry central highlands, southern Mexico, and Yucatán. But May can also be perfect on the Pacific beaches from Manzanillo to Mazatlán and in Baja.

The hurricane season is summer and autumn. Although hurricanes have hit as late as December, the greatest chance of a *ciclon* is from late summer to mid-autumn. Hurricane Gilbert, one of the most destructive storms in history, struck Mexico in mid-September 1988. Because they usually coincide with the hot summer "low season," very few campers will be concerned with hurricanes. When hurricanes do hit or even pass close to Mexico, they bring torrential rainfall to a significant portion of the country. Unless you read Mexican daily newspapers, don't expect much, if any, warning of a hurricane.

By comparing these descriptions with a map and the table of temperatures and rainfall, you should note several trends. The most important is also the most obvious: the best time of year to go camping in Mexico is during the cooler dry season (October to May). In fact, my favorite period is from mid-October, when the rainy season ends and the temperatures quickly moderate, through January and February. The sky and vegetation have been thoroughly washed, the harvests are in, and the weather tends to be very settled. Of course, springtime is also very pleasant, especially on the

Temperature

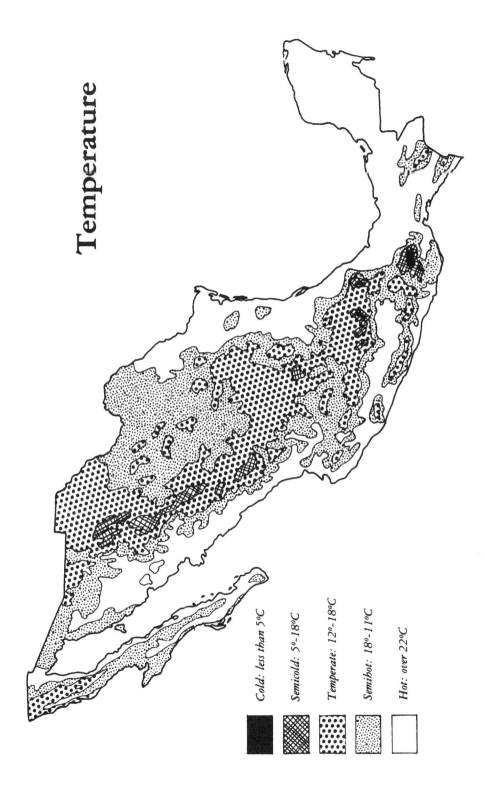

Cold: less than 5°C

Semicold: 5°–18°C

Temperate: 12°–18°C

Semihot: 18°–11°C

Hot: over 22°C

Rainfall

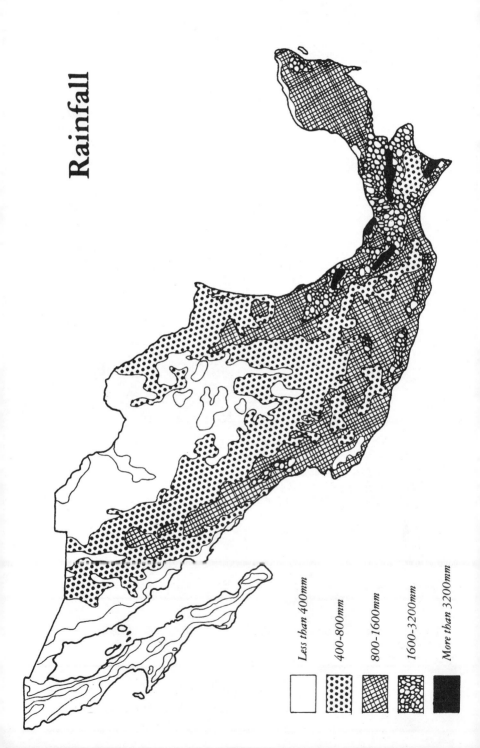

Less than 400mm

400-800mm

800-1600mm

1600-3200mm

More than 3200mm

ANNUAL AVERAGE TEMPERATURES AND RAINFALL

Altitude		Jan T*	Jan R*	Feb T	Feb R	March T	March R	April T	April R	May T	May R	June T	June R	July T	July R	Aug T	Aug R	Sept T	Sept R	Oct T	Oct R	Nov T	Nov R	Dec T	Dec R
Acapulco, Gro.	23	78	0.4	78	0.0	79	0.0	80	0.0	83	12.	83	17.	83	8.6	83	9.8	82	14.	82	6.7	81	1.2	79	0.4
Aguascalientes, Ags.	6258	55	0.5	58	0.2	63	0.1	68	0.1	72	0.7	70	4.8	69	5.8	67	4.1	67	3.6	66	1.3	64	0.7	56	0.6
Apatzingán, Mich.	2237	78	.16	80	.28	84	.06	86	.04	90	.56	88	3.5	84	7.4	82	6.8	83	6.6	83	1.8	81	.32	78	.63
Campeche, Camp.	26	72	0.7	74	0.4	77	0.5	79	0.2	81	1.7	81	6.1	80	7.0	81	6.7	81	5.7	80	3.4	76	1.2	74	1.2
Chetumal, Q. Roo	13	73	3.0	75	.86	77	1.1	80	1.2	81	5.5	82	7.0	82	5.1	82	4.2	81	5.5	79	8.4	75	3.4	75	3.7
Chihuahua, Chih.	4690	49	0.1	52	0.2	59	0.3	65	0.3	74	0.4	79	1.0	77	3.1	75	3.7	72	3.7	65	1.4	56	0.3	49	0.8
Chilpancingo, Gro.	3800	66	0.1	67	0.2	70	0.1	72	0.2	73	2.0	70	6.0	70	7.0	69	6.6	69	6.2	70	3.1	69	0.9	67	0.0
Cd. Obregón, Son.	131	65	.27	68	.20	72	.06	77	.16	81	0.0	90	.07	93	.27	93	1.8	91	1.7	85	.57	75	1.7	67	.51
Cd. Victoria, Tamps.	1053	60	1.4	64	1.0	70	0.8	76	1.5	79	5.0	81	4.8	81	4.1	82	2.7	79	7.9	74	4.3	67	1.7	60	0.6
Colima, Col.	1657	72	0.5	72	0.3	74	0.0	77	0.0	79	0.3	79	5.7	78	7.7	78	7.2	77	7.7	78	3.1	76	0.9	73	1.3
Cordoba, Ver.	3049	61	1.8	63	1.5	67	1.5	62	2.2	73	4.3	72	13.	70	15.	70	16.	70	18.	68	9.1	65	3.7	63	2.1
Creel, Chih.	7724	41	1.9	41	.31	42	.59	50	.55	55	1.1	63	5.3	63	5.3	61	5.5	59	1.1	54	2.6	44	1.3	39	1.8
Cuernavaca, Mor.	5000	65	0.1	67	0.2	70	0.3	72	0.3	74	2.1	70	7.8	68	8.6	68	8.7	68	9.7	68	3.1	67	0.3	66	0.1
Culiacn, Sin.	216	67	0.4	69	0.4	71	0.2	74	0.0	79	0.1	83	1.2	83	5.8	82	6.8	82	4.6	80	1.6	73	0.4	67	2.1
Durango, Dgo.	6209	53	0.5	56	0.4	60	0.0	65	0.1	69	0.5	62	2.4	69	4.9	69	3.6	67	4.0	64	1.2	58	0.6	54	0.7
Fortín, Ver.	3326	61	1.9	64	1.5	67	1.6	70	2.1	72	5.0	71	14.	71	15.	70	16.	70	18.	69	8.5	64	3.5	62	2.4
Guadalajara, Jal.	5220	58	0.7	61	0.2	65	0.1	70	0.0	72	0.7	71	7.6	69	10.	68	7.9	67	7.0	65	2.1	61	0.8	59	0.8
Guanajuato, Gto.	6835	57	0.5	60	0.3	64	0.2	68	0.2	71	1.1	68	5.4	67	6.6	66	5.5	65	6.0	63	2.0	60	0.7	59	0.6
Guaymas, Son.		64	0.3	66	0.2	69	0.2	73	0.1	73	0.1	84	0.0	87	1.8	87	3.0	86	2.1	81	0.4	72	0.4	65	1.1
Hermosillo, Son.	638	60	0.1	63	0.6	68	0.2	73	0.1	79	0.1	88	0.1	90	2.8	88	3.3	87	2.5	79	1.6	70	0.2	60	1.0
Ixtapan la Sal, Mex.	6349	84	0.6	67	0.5	70	0.3	72	1.2	75	2.3	73	6.4	68	7.3	68	11.	69	9.5	67	0.6	66	0.6	66	0.3
Jalapa, Ver.	4540	58	2.1	60	2.1	63	2.1	67	2.3	68	4.7	67	12.	66	8.5	66	8.0	65	11.	64	5.1	60	2.8	52	1.9
La Paz, B.C.	59	64	.13	68	.45	71	.03	74	0.0	79	0.0	81	0.0	88	.25	88	1.6	85	2.0	80	.37	72	.54	60	1.3
León, Gto.	6180	58	0.5	61	0.2	66	0.2	70	0.1	73	0.9	71	4.3	68	6.6	68	5.5	68	5.2	66	1.5	61	0.7	60	0.5
Manzanillo, Col.		75	0.9	74	0.5	74	0.0	76	0.0	79	0.1	81	0.9	83	5.4	83	7.4	81	15.	81	5.0	79	0.7	77	2.1
Mazatlán, Sin.	3	67	0.5	67	0.4	67	0.1	70	0.0	75	0.0	79	1.1	81	6.6	81	9.6	81	10.	79	2.4	74	0.5	69	1.7
Merida, Yuc.	30	73	1.2	74	0.6	78	0.8	81	1.0	82	3.2	81	5.9	81	5.5	81	5.1	81	6.0	79	4.0	75	1.2	74	1.2
México, D.F.	7240	54	0.2	56	0.3	61	0.4	63	0.5	65	0.2	63	4.2	61	4.9	61	4.1	60	4.6	59	1.3	58	0.6	54	0.3
Monterrey, N.L.	1749	59	0.8	62	0.9	68	0.6	74	1.1	78	1.7	81	3.3	81	2.9	82	2.5	78	8.1	72	4.3	63	1.0	57	0.9
Morelia, Mich.	6234	57	0.5	60	0.3	64	0.3	69	0.3	69	1.7	67	5.2	65	8.4	64	6.4	64	6.2	63	2.3	60	0.8	58	0.2
Oaxaca, Oax.	5068	63	0.1	66	0.1	70	0.4	72	1.0	73	2.4	71	4.9	70	5.3	68	5.9			65	0.3	64	0.4		
Orizaba, Ver.	4079	59	1.8	61	1.6	64	1.8	68	1.9	70	5.3	68	14.	67	15.	67	18.	67	13.	66	5.1	63	3.9	66	2.1
Pachuca, Hgo.	7999	53	0.3	54	0.2	56	0.3	61	0.5	60	1.3	60	2.8	59	2.3	59	2.1	59	3.1	56	1.9	54	0.8	55	0.2
Patzcuaro, Mich.	7180	57	0.8	56	0.5	61	0.3	64	0.3	66	1.4	62	4.6	62	6.5	63	7.9	63	9.8	63	9.5	58	3.1	55	0.9
Progreso, Yuc.	46	73	1.3	74	.67	76	.59	80	.70	79	2.1	80	2.9	80	1.8	80	1.8	80	2.1	79	2.7	76	.80	74	1.0
Puebla, Pue.	7200	54	0.2	60	0.2	62	0.5	65	0.5	66	2.0	64	6.2	63	5.4	63	5.8	62	7.4	61	2.2	58	0.8	54	0.2
Queretaro, Qro.	6160	57	0.4	60	0.1	64	0.2	68	0.5	70	1.1	69	3.7	67	3.4	66	4.8			63	1.3	61	0.6	59	0.5
Sn. Cristóbal L. C., Chis.	7087	54	0.3	55	0.0	57	0.4	60	1.4	60	5.1	60	10.	60	5.6	60	6.3	60	9.9	59	4.3	57	0.5	55	0.6
San Jose Purúa, Mich.	6335	57	0.7	60	0.6	63	0.3	67	0.3	70	0.2	71	6.3	70	7.1	69	6.6	68	7.0	65	2.5	64	0.8	60	2.5
San Luis Potosi, S.L.P.	6157	55	0.5	59	0.2	63	0.1	67	1.6	71	1.2	67	3.4	65	3.7	65	3.4			63	0.7	59	0.7	55	0.6
Tampico, Tamps.	39	65	2.1	68	0.9	71	0.5	77	0.4	80	2.0	82	7.9	82	5.8	82	5.9	81	13.	78	7.0	72	2.2	67	1.7
Tapachula, Chis.	551	77	.28	78	.24	80	1.2	81	2.6	81	9.6	81	13.	77	18.	77	16.	77	17.	77	18.	76	3.4	77	.45
Taxco, Gro.	5500	66	0.0	69	0.2	72	0.4	75	0.9	74	2.5	70	8.1	69	7.6	68	7.5	69	3.5	69	3.5	68	1.0		
Tehuacán, Pue.	5509	60	0.1	62	0.1	65	0.1	68	0.8	70	2.6	69	3.7	68	2.8	68	2.2	68	4.7	65	1.1	62	0.1	61	0.3
Tehuantepec, Oax.	328	58	1.5	66	0.2	69	0.3	72	1.4	74	3.6	72	6.5	70	4.9	71	3.2	69	8.5	68	3.6	67	1.5	66	0.6
Tepic, Nay.	3000	63	1.2	63	0.8	65	0.0	70	0.0	71	0.1	74	6.8	74	14.	74	12.	74	8.1	73	8.0	70	0.3	64	2.1
Tlaxcala, Tlax.	7500	49	0.4	57	0.1	61	0.3	67	0.4	64	2.9	63	5.3	61	5.5	61	5.4	60	1.9	58	0.3	57	0.1		
Toluca, Mex.	8712	49	0.4	52	0.0	54	0.4	57	1.1	59	2.0	58	5.3	56	3.6	56	5.7	56	6.0	54	2.0	52	0.8	50	0.3
Torreon, Coah.	3720	54	0.5	60	0.2	66	0.2	74	0.2	81	0.1	80	1.8	80	2.2	81	1.9	80	2.3	70	1.6	58	1.7		
Tuxpan, Ver.		67	1.6	80	.70	72	1.0	78	1.2	80	2.1	80	8.0	80	7.0	83	6.6	83	6.2	78	8.9	72	2.1	78	1.5
Tuxtla Gutierrez, Chis.	1759	71	0.7	73	0.4	77	0.5	80	2.2	81	1.7	78	6.1	77	6.7	78	6.5	81	5.7	80	3.4	73	.16	74	.25
Uruapan, Mich.	5500	61	0.6	65	.86	68	0.8	69	1.0	70	2.4	72	13.	71	11.	70	16.	69	16.	68	7.1	64	1.5	61	1.2
Valladolid, Yuc.	72	70	2.5	73	1.0	77	1.0	80	3.0	81	4.7	80	6.0	80	7.3	81	7.1	80	7.7	79	5.7	75	1.9	72	2.2
Villahermosa, Tab.	33	72	5.1	75	3.9	70	1.8	80	1.8	83	3.5	83	8.0	80	7.0	83	6.6	83	6.2	80	11.	76	5.6	73	7.1
Zacatecas, Zac.	8187	49	0.4	51	0.2	54	0.1	59	0.1	62	0.9	61	2.1	57	3.5	58	2.3	57	3.0	56	0.9	52	0.6	50	0.5

* T = Temperature in °F, R = Rainfall in inches. Altitudes are in feet.

Pacific coast. Then again, May is wonderful in Mulege and June is ideal in. . .

There are two weather oddities, however, that are "somewhat" predictable. The first comes in late July or early August (usually) and is called *la canicula*, loosely, "dog days." This is a period of a few weeks when normal summer rains stop and are replaced by hot and dry weather. The other side of the weather coin comes in early January, when it suddenly rains in the middle of the dry season.

Study the temperature/rainfall chart and maps. Remember: averages are a combination of highs and lows and 90 degrees might not sound too bad until you find that it really means 100 or more in the middle of the afternoon. Once again, if you make a mistake, just move until you find an area that is agreeable.

CHAPTER 8

Baja California

Imagine a narrow, sparsely populated desert island almost a thousand miles in length, cut off from the rest of the world until the mid-1970s. Now connect the north end of this island to California with a single two-lane highway and the south end to Mexico with a few small vehicle/passenger ferries. This, along with a mere handful of towns, thousands of miles of beaches, and seemingly endless deserts, is Baja California. Until it was opened to overland tourism by the Transpeninsular Highway, Baja was a vast, exclusive reserve for well-heeled American sportsmen and off-road driving buffs. Fly-in resorts catered to celebrity anglers, the wealthy, and fanatical fishermen.

Baja now has been opened to the rest of us. Judging from the numbers of tourists who visit the peninsula every year, it is clearly living up to its reputation as an outdoor paradise. Several factors make Baja particularly attractive to campers. Free camping and off-the-beaten-track hideouts abound. Thanks to its sparse population and widely scattered small towns, campers who wish can find true privacy and solitude in Baja. When you do meet people in the backcountry, they tend to be shy, circumspect, and very courteous. You'll usually be left alone or visited only occasionally, even when camping near ranches or settlements.

In fact, Baja's popularity is due in great part to the character of its people. Most campers, including me, feel much safer here than at home. Crime is so low that Steve says even the cops are mellow. With the nagging exception of a few gas stations, thefts are very uncommon. As in mainland Mexico, the vast majority of people have "old-fashioned" values of honesty and hospitality.

Baja's Pacific shore includes several huge, seafood-rich lagoon systems and hundreds of miles of empty beaches. In addition to beachcombing, surf fishing, and birding, campers can observe the annual winter migration of hundreds of gray whales from the Bering Sea to Magdalena Bay and Scammon's Lagoon.

On the east coast of the peninsula, the Gulf of California, also known as the Sea of Cortez or Vermillion Sea, has some of the best fishing, kayaking, and beach camping in the world. Because the Sea of Cortez has little or no surf, it is ideal for small boats and sailboarding. Snorkeling and scuba diving are also very good, especially in the southern "Los Cabos" (Capes) region.

Although most of Baja is quite arid, there are dramatic variations in landscape and vegetation from one area to another. The west coast, for example, is considerably cooler and more moist than the eastern shore, along the Sea of Cortez. In winter, heavy snows blanket the northern peaks and chilly winds sweep across the upper portions of the peninsula. Wind, in fact, is the region's greatest drawback. Though the fishing and diving are excellent in late summer, much of Baja is too warm for comfort at this time of year.

Driving

In spite of its reputation as four-wheel-drive heaven, highway driving is often easier in Baja than in mainland Mexico.

The peninsula's major highway, Mex 1, is typical Mexican two-lane, narrow, patched, and very slim in the shoulders. It is subject to seasonal storm damage, flash floods, bridge washouts, and minor rockfalls. *Vados* (dips) can be filled by flash floods and shallow rain runoff. Always slow down for vados, even if it isn't raining. A cloudburst 20 miles away can fill the vado ahead of you. A friend witnessed a tragedy in Baja one winter when an impatient motorist tried to cross a rain-swollen vado in a pickup truck. The current tipped the truck onto its side, drowning the driver. Even dry vados often collect sand and debris.

First-time travelers are often disappointed to find that their meticulous preparations for rough, Baja 1000-style driving conditions are largely unnecessary. Unless you'll definitely be plunging off the map and into rugged back areas, don't bother to drape your vehicle with spare tires and gas cans. I regret to say that painting ''Baja or Bust'' across your fender is also unnecessary and may actually attract good-natured ridicule. In fact, the majority of campers in Baja today drive standard RVs, vans, pickups, and passenger cars. For better or worse, the days when Baja was open only to 4x4s, dune buggies, and all-terrain desert rats is long past. Like many people, Lorena and I regularly explore Baja's better dirt roads and desert tracks. Although we take precautions when going ''off-road'' in a standard vehicle, including plenty of water, we've seldom felt the need, and only occasionally the desire, for a special, off-road rig.

Even before the asphalt had cooled on the final stretches of Mex 1, Lorena and I were eagerly exploring the peninsula. Our ''RV'' or ''Road-weary Vehicle'' was a chocolate brown '59 Ford station wagon with overload springs. I was so impressed with the word ''overload'' that I couldn't resist taking a full roof rack and a 12-foot plywood sailboat with the hull of an icebreaker. Although the newly paved highway was as smooth as a billiard table, the lure of off-road travel proved irresistible. In less than ten miles of backcountry exploration, the Ford's muffler was reduced to twisted junk and the shocks were as loose as pogo sticks. My innovative bellyflopping technique for crossing sandy arroyos also took its toll, flattening and reducing the gas tank to less than seven gallons capacity. Fortunately, I had planned ahead and packed a spare can—a one-gallon white gas container with a leaky spout. Lorena described that memorable trip as "the Baja 1000 meets the Beverly Hillbillies."

Once you leave the pavement behind, expect to find lots of washboard, sand, ruts, and even mud. Well-traveled dirt and gravel secondary roads are safe for virtually any vehicle, and you can spend weeks exploring these in your van or RV. The next category down—unimproved roads, ranch tracks, bulldozer trails, and the like—clearly separates the sheep from the 4x4s and all-terrain goats. We once attempted to climb a loose, rocky hill in a heavily loaded VW van. We not only had to unload the van and portage hundreds of pounds of gear, food, tools, and bedding on foot but in trying to back out, we also dropped the van into a sand trap. It took several dune buggies and half a day to rescue us.

Traveling off-road in Baja can be exciting, challenging, rewarding, and dangerous. It is ridiculously easy to get lost or stuck, break a tire, puncture the radiator, and so on. Unless you're well prepared, stick to the main roads, and until you're experienced, always travel off-road in company with another vehicle.

As in the rest of Mexico, there is one simple rule for night driving in Baja: *Don't!*

Baja lore is rich with running-out-of-gas stories. In fact, gasoline is almost always available, though it may not be as plentiful as you might wish. Gas stations sometimes run out, especially if thirsty RV caravans are passing through or the delivery truck has been delayed.

Baja Campgrounds

Nothing demonstrates the strong economic bonds between Mexico and the United States quite so vividly as the lively twice-daily cross-border commute. This is a civics lesson I would choose to avoid, however, especially if I was at the helm of a large RV. To reduce wear and tear on your nerves, plan to cross the border at "slack tide": mid-morning, early afternoon, or early evening.

Our usual border crossing routine includes about two hours on the United States side of the border for a last-minute shopping spree, a final tank-up of high-octane gasoline, and a "wish you were here" phone call to family and friends. We also make a brief stop to buy insurance (just watch for billboard advertisements) and exchange dollars into pesos. Money exchange rates at the border are often the best you'll ever find.

If you're heading into mainland Mexico, you can get car papers and tourist cards at Sonoita (southeast of Tijuana). Allow another hour for red tape and a Mexican customs inspection. Travelers who go south of Ensenada into the Baja peninsula are only required to have a validated tourist card, not "car papers" (vehicle importation permit; see chap. 2, Red Tape). If you plan to cross from Baja to the mainland on a ferry, you'll pick up your car papers in Santa Rosalia, La Paz, or Cabo San Lucas.

After so much anticipation and nervous excitement, crossing the border can often be anticlimactic. "Are we really here? Is this it? Old Mexico?" Once the initial shock (and relief) has worn off, your instinct will probably be to head south as fast as possible. Resist the temptation; there are lots of comfortable campgrounds close to the border.

By the time you've crossed into Mexico, you probably deserve a rest. Make your first day an easy one—start looking for a place to spend the night. Too many overeager travelers find themselves driving after dark rather than enjoying the sunset or a relaxing shower. Remember the cardinal rule: don't drive at night.

Mexico's border towns have come a long way from their days as notorious "boys' towns" of honky-tonks, tattoo parlors, and bordellos. Tijuana, for example, is one of Mexico's most prosperous and fastest-growing cities. The town's supermarkets, shopping malls, museums, restaurants, and nightclubs attract hundreds of thousands of tourists every year. As a duty-free port, "TJ" also has some of the country's best bargains in pottery, leather goods, hand-loomed blankets, silver jewelry, and other handicrafts.

Tijuana to Ensenada (70 miles): You have a choice of two highways from the border, both of which provide views of the ocean. The old coastal highway, Mex 1, is interesting but congested and slow (follow signs for Rosarito Beach via the Libre [Free] highway). Passengers tend to enjoy this busy route more than drivers. The newer toll highway, Mex 1D, is faster, easier, and safer to drive—and also quite scenic. Mex 1D begins in Tijuana and ends on the north side of Ensenada. Follow signs for Ensenada Toll (Cuota).

As you might expect, camping is limited in Tijuana, and most people skip south to Rosarito Beach or Ensenada. There are several RV parks in Rosarito Beach, a popular rest and retirement community for Californians. Unfortunately, most of these parks are crowded with resident campers. Overnight spaces can be very difficult to find. Overnight rates in full-service parks near the border also tend to be higher than average for Mexico.

To simplify matters, go directly to Ensenada, or if it's late, to a large KOA campground conveniently located between Tijuana and Ensenada.

KOA Kampamento Rosarito ($$$) is 14 miles south of Tijuana. Take Mex 1D, the cuota (toll) highway, or the old free road to the San Antonio Shores exit. Watch, too, for KOA signs to guide you. Cross the freeway and climb a cobbled lane into the campground. It's steep, but large rigs can make it.

This is a large, comfortable, well-managed campground with attractive lawns, flowers, and trees. Unlike some parking lot-style campgrounds, this park manages to provide all the modern conveniences without sacrificing its pleasant *ambiente*. After "TJ's" hectic traffic, you'll enjoy the relaxing hillside view of the Pacific Ocean. There is also beach access just half a mile walk from the campground. The ad-

ministrador (manager), David Molina M., is very friendly and speaks English fluently. If you don't yet have Mexican auto insurance, you can buy it here.

Facilities and Services: There are 200 spaces, 100 with full hookups. Tenting is also available, and there are eleven clean bathrooms, generous amounts of hot water, ice, tables, and a coin laundry. There is a small store and a children's playground.

Free camping near Tijuana is very scarce. Your best bet is to watch for other campers south of Rosarito Beach, especially on side roads leading to the beach from the old coastal highway. This stretch is popular with surfers. If there's free camping to be had, they'll find it first. Look for boogie boards and mind-bending music.

Steve reports that campers were overnighting near the ocean at Km 34-35 and farther south at Km 52 on the old highway.

Ensenada: This is your last chance for supermarkets, nightlife, and souvenir-hunting expeditions before heading deeper into Baja. Steve and Tina found that handicrafts and leather goods were cheaper in Ensenada than any other resort, second only to Tijuana as Baja's "best bargain." Like many people, we find Ensenada easier to cope with than the traffic and crowds in Tijuana.

This busy port and resort city has a number of RV parks, including many residential campgrounds. Our recommendations are all on the south end of town.

Ensenada Bypass: This is easier than it sounds, especially if you use a compass instead of a street map. To bypass Ensenada from the north, just follow Mex 1D as it branches right and then curves around the port, eventually rejoining Mex 1, the Transpeninsular Highway. This is straightforward, except for one distraction: when Mex 1D enters Ensenada, its name changes, first to Costera Boulevard, then to Lazaro Cardenas Boulevard, then to Sangines, then again to Calle Delante, which mercifully meets with Mex 1. If your head is spinning at the final intersection, don't forget to turn south. Clear enough? If not, just follow any large street south until you find Mex 1. Some of the maps I've used are even more confused about these names than you are.

If you are coming into town from Tijuana on the free highway, you're already on Mex 1. Don't be confused; as Mex 1 doglegs through Ensenada, it follows Avenida Juarez to Avenida Reforma, which eventually becomes Ejercito Nacional. Finally, about a mile south of town, Mex 1 assumes its final identity as the Transpeninsular Highway—sometimes known as the La Paz Highway. When in doubt, follow signs south to San Quintin.

Campo Playa RV Park ($$): From Mex 1D, follow Costero Boulevard south until it turns inland and becomes Sangines. Turn left at the huge Tecate beer sign across from Kiki's Restaurant. If you're heading south on old Mex 1, turn right (west) on Sangines. Look for the Gigante supermarket on the southwest corner of the intersection.

The Campo Playa (Beach Camp) is by no means the fanciest place around, but it's easy to locate, inexpensive, and nicely landscaped. The name, however, is wishful thinking: the park is separated from the beach by a couple of busy streets. If you're willing to dodge traffic, locals say that halibut and corvina can be caught off the rocks and jetties. Be sure to have a valid Mexican fishing license; Ensenada's "fish cops" don't fool around. Horses can also be rented at the beach, but swimming conditions are less than appetizing.

Facilities and Services: There are 65 spaces, most with full hookups, and a few pull-through spaces for long rigs. Tenting is also available. The management is friendly and English-speaking. The park offers clean bathrooms, bottled pure water, Ping-Pong, and free cable TV. In addition to several nearby restaurants, there's a laundry one block north and a large supermarket, Gigante, a few blocks to the east, at the corner of Mex 1 and Sangines. If you haven't yet shopped in a Mexican supermercado, try this one.

Hermosa Beach RV Park ($$): Follow the directions given above to Sangines Street, then turn south on Dr. Pedro Loyola Street and follow signs to the park. If you're coming through Ensenada on old Mex 1, turn right (west) on Sangines at the Pemex gas station and Gigante supermarket. Look for a giant letter "G" on the store. Go west on Sangines, then left (south) on Dr. Pedro Loyola. Don't be put off by the neighborhood—warehouses, fish packing plants, and junkyards. Steve's favorite is Yonke Cheap.

Hermosa Beach RV Park was still under construction during our visit. At the rate the American manager was working, it will undoubtedly shape up nicely. He was very proud of the park's 18,000-gallon water tank and heavy duty power hookups. Steve, always in search of a bargain, was more impressed by the park's moderate price and beachside location.

Facilities and Services: There are 40 overnight spaces with full hookups. Rigs to 40 feet, but no pull-throughs can be accommodated. There are no tent sites. Tables and a laundromat are in the works.

Several miles south of Ensenada you'll see signs for El Faro Beach, Corona Beach, and Estero Beach, all located on Todos Santos Bay. This area and the cheap campgrounds on the road to Punta Banda (described later) would be my choice for peace, quiet, and enjoyable beaches.

El Faro Beach Trailer Park ($$) has a few overnight beach spaces that include bathroom privileges in the adjacent hotel. "I'll sound like Midnight the Cat before this is over," Steve says, "but this beach is nice."

⭐ *Estero Beach Trailer Park ($$$):* This "high end" RV park has everything from a boat ramp and deep sea fishing charters to horseback riding and tennis courts. The park is associated with the Estero Beach Hotel, so you've got access to the restaurant, bar, small museum, and pricey boutiques—your last chance to pick up a Rolex or a piece of Bavarian porcelain.

Facilities and Services: The park is landscaped and has 40 attractive, large spaces with hookups. As you might have guessed, tents are not allowed. There is no laundry or pool. The beach makes up for it, however, and the bathrooms are "super." For Palm Springs-style camping, this park's rates are quite fair.

Cheap Camping ($): If you're looking for quiet, laid-back surroundings and bargain prices, try Punta Banda. About 10.5 miles south of downtown Ensenada, just north of Maneadero, take a paved side road west from Mex 1 to Punta Banda (12.5 miles). La Bufadora, a natural ocean blowhole at the end of this side road, is also worthy of a visit.

In addition to a pleasant, scenic drive, you'll find several inexpensive beachside campgrounds along this road. These camps are owned by local *ejidos* (agricultural cooperatives). The "amenities" are usually limited to an outhouse and a panoramic view of the sea. With their rustic facilities and low rates, these campgrounds are the next best thing to free camping.

San Carlos Hot Springs: About two miles north of the turnoff to Punta Banda (and approximately eight miles south of Ensenada), a dirt road goes east 12 miles to San Carlos hot springs. This road is rough and should be driven carefully. You may or may not make it in a car, depending on your clearance. We did it in a Ford station wagon, but it was an experience I'd rather not repeat.

The hot springs is set in a secluded desert canyon. There

is a rustic resort, shade, good bird-watching, hiking, and wonderful stargazing. The water isn't scalding, but all in all, Lorena and I thoroughly enjoyed our time here. A popular weekend spot for Mexican families, but otherwise almost deserted.

Immigration Checkpoint: About a mile south of the village of Maneadero, you'll come to a small Mexican immigration checkpoint. Be prepared to stop, although the checkpoint seems to be open or closed according to bureaucratic whim. This is where you'll show your tourist card and proof of citizenship. If you don't have either, you could be told to return to the border. The officials here can issue a tourist card, but they tend to be very grumpy. Try to think of something to cheer them up.

Leaving Maneadero, the highway climbs and twists through low mountains (or hills if you're from the West) to Santo Tomás, the home of Baja's best-known winery.

El Palomar ($$): Thirty-two miles south of Ensenada on Mex 1, the small roadside campground and balneario (spa or swimming place) is set in a very productive olive grove. In fact, the ground beneath the trees is sometimes littered with ripe olives. Steve and his daughter, Churpa, usually manage to gather up a gallon of olives before the engine has cooled on their van. Steve stuffs the olives into a large jar, adds half a pound of table salt, and then tops it up with fresh water. After aging the olives for three weeks and tasting them frequently, he and Churpa vie for any that are left. I won't dispute Steve's claim that El Palomar's olives "taste like they came from a Greek delicatessen," but if his recipe is too salty for you, soak the cured olives overnight in fresh water before eating.

Olives are not only an important part of El Palomar's atmosphere, they've also entered Steve's family lore. Churpa has been camping in this park since she was born, and at ten years of age, she's still creating her magnum opus, a novel called *The Olive Factory*. The characters include the inventive but rather prickly Cactus Ear Mouse and Rain Over the Bridge, a rodent real estate magnate with cactus homes throughout Mexico.

El Palomar's special, laid-back charm is reminiscent of a 1940s resort, complete with lukewarm showers, less-than-perfect landscaping, and an amiable caretaker/manager called Nieto (Grandson). If, for example, you should arrive after dark and find the entrance to the park closed with a chain, Nieto will open it up for you. Just look for him across the highway, in the Pemex station. Or, if the showers run cold, dash back to the Pemex and ask Nieto to fire up the water heater.

Facilities and Services: There are 16 spaces with hookups but no pull-throughs. The entrance is a steep downgrade that drivers of large or underpowered rigs might want to scout on foot. In addition to the olives, El Palomar has a playground, a restaurant, and a store with an erratic selection of food, seashells, and ceremonial masks. The swimming pool is filled between Easter and mid-November. On weekends and holidays, it is often filled with vacationing Mexican families.

Once you've passed the Maneadero checkpoint, you'll be tempted again to put the pedal to the metal and plunge as deep into Baja as possible. I do my best to resist this headlong style of travel by stopping frequently for wave watching and walks in the desert. You won't see the best of Baja through your bug-blurred windshield. Instead of rushing, prolong the pleasure of your trip by taking frequent rest stops to brew a pot of fresh coffee, photograph a cactus, or just kick a few rocks. Before you know it, you'll be relaxed and enjoying that famous ''Baja feeling.''

Free Camping: Although the highway runs inland between Maneadero and Camalu (95 miles south of Ensenada), several side roads reach a beautiful and often overlooked coast. The beaches here can be chilly and fog-bound in winter, but they provide good camping, fishing, and exploring.

About five miles south of Colonet, a good road goes east to San Telmo, penetrating Baja's highest mountain range, the Sierra San Pedro Martir National Park. With peaks up to 10,000 feet, you can expect deep snow in winter at higher elevations. There is an observatory in the mountains, resort-style ranches, and lots of opportunities for hiking, exploring, rock climbing, and rough road driving. For a detailed guide to this area, read *Camping and Climbing in Baja* by John Robinson (see Recommended Reading).

Colonia Guerrero, 105 miles from Ensenada, is easily confused with Guerrero Negro, over 200 miles to the south. Most travelers go through Colonia Guerrero without a sideways glance. I consider it a great place to stay overnight and to catch my breath with some therapeutic beachcombing and surf fishing. Besides angling for corvina, halibut, and perch, you might be lucky enough to fill your plate with Pismo clams or *mejillon* (mussels).

There are two noteworthy RV parks in Colonia Guerrero, both reasonably priced, quite comfortable, and close to the highway. To reach either park, turn west, toward the ocean, on a dirt road one mile south of Colonia Guerrero. (The turnoff is just north of the butane tanks.) Tortillas, ice, groceries, beer, and other basic supplies and services are available in town.

Meson Don Pepe ($): The first park you'll come to, Meson Don Pepe, is attractively landscaped with trees and flowers. This campground has fewer services than the nearby Posada Don Diego, but Don Pepe's is prettier, slightly cheaper, and has a pleasant Mexican flavor. There are picnic tables, grills, good showers, and a restaurant. In fact, the restaurants in both parks are given high marks by Tom Miller, the voracious author of *Eating Your Way Through Baja* and other Baja guidebooks. Tom rates Don Pepe's lobster "superb."

Facilities and Services: There are 15 full hookup spaces, 10 with water and power, a dump station, tables, a watchman, and bathrooms. If you've already gotten into the vacation spirit and read every Stephen King novel in sight, there is a book exchange. Don Pepe's is to be commended for discounting already fair prices for tent campers and those who don't use hookups. The annual rates at this park are low enough to turn Scrooge into a snowbird.

Posada Don Diego ($$): Just down the road from Don Pepe's, this friendly, well-run park has a couple of noteworthy services. Personal checks can be cashed with proper identification, and mail is sent daily to the United States by private plane. There is a restaurant, coin-op washers (no dryers), and a curio shop with books on Mexico. Credit cards, except American Express, are accepted.

Facilities and Services: There are 100 spaces, 40 with all hookups, and rigs up to 40 feet can be accommodated. Tenting is available. The bathrooms have lots of hot water, and the restaurant is great.

San Quintín (120 miles south of Ensenada): Don't judge this area by the sprawling commercial zone you'll see along the highway. San Quintín's attractions are to the west, on the shores and protected waters of Bahia San Quintín. In fact, this is one of the most popular spots in northern Baja, with excellent fishing, clamming, birding, and off-road exploring.

Although free camping on San Quintín Bay and along the beach south to El Rosario can be very good, the selection of RV parks is quite limited.

Cielito Lindo Motel and RV Park: Eight miles south of San Quintín, turn west on the road to San Quintín Bay and go 3.5 miles. Though the motel is still functioning, we found that this beachfront RV park had been trashed by a severe storm and evidently abandoned. (If Cielito Lindo campground gets back on its feet, please let us know.)

Honey's RV Park ($$): Ten miles south of San Quintín, follow a good dirt road west for one mile. If the park gate is closed, open it yourself. This park is located on a sandy beach that inspires thoughts of fishing. Though the campground is new and decidedly bleak, if the recently planted banana trees and flowering shrubs are as enthusiastic as Juan and Honey, the park's hard-working owners, the landscape will improve rapidly. Electricity hadn't yet been installed, but there was an abundant supply of fresh water. Juan says, "We specialize in clean rest rooms and hot showers." They also offer hospitality and a contagious "can do" optimism. Honey's is well worth a look.

Facilities and Rates: There are 27 spaces with water and sewer but no power (as of this writing) or shade. There is space for up to 200 rigs, a laundry lady on call, and supplies in nearby San Quintín.

Free Camping: Between San Quintín and El Rosario, the highway offers tantalizing views of the beach and ocean before turning inland for a considerable distance. Lorena and I inevitably yield to temptation and camp at the end of a side road, usually near El Socorro or El Pabellon. Don't be surprised if early rising Mexican *pescadores* (fishermen) pass by your camp on their way to and from work. It's not only a good chance to share a cup of coffee and practice your Spanish but you'll probably get a bargain on a fish.

El Rosario is your best bet (and probably last chance) for both unleaded gas and groceries until Guerrero Negro. There is a gas station at each end of town, but only the southern station has an unleaded pump. Steve still rants about the incredible buy he got in the supermarket here on fresh abalone. By the way, if you need fresh bread or amazing fossilized seashells, the local bakery sells both.

Catavina: This classic transpeninsular tourist outpost is nothing but a wide spot in the highway with a hotel, a trailer park, and a more-or-less abandoned gas station, surrounded by a melancholy landscape of rock, cactus, and thorny shrub. If you are traveling with a VCR, do not watch old Alfred Hitchcock movies or Twilight Zone reruns in Catavina.

When Baja's Transpeninsular Highway was completed in 1973, someone in a high government office conjured up the brilliant idea of installing paradores (rest stops, RV parks) at unlikely intervals along the route. After bulldozing the desert to within an inch of its life, these parts were paved, surrounded by kangaroo-proof wire fences, and opened for business. Oddly enough, something about the concentration camp atmosphere didn't appeal to tourists. Within a few years, the wind and weeds took over these forbidding boondoggles. Recently, a few *paradores* have been rehabilitated by local ejidos and private optimists.

Parque Natural Desierto Central Trailer Park ($): At Catavina, 76 miles south of El Rosario, this former government park is not as grand as the name (which refers to the region's beautiful natural rock and cactus gardens). There are 66 spaces with water and power. There are also bathrooms, showers, and an abundance of desert plants. Steve says, "This place is fine for overnight, but I sure as hell wouldn't want to live here."

If you're too tired to cook, the nearby Hotel La Pinta has a better-than-nothing restaurant.

The huge Pemex station across from the Pinta Hotel was closed tight during Steve's last visit. The Extra pump at the Pinta was also dry. Cross your fingers, but don't count on Catavina for fuel.

Parador Punta Prieta ($): This semiabandoned government RV park is located on Mex 1, at the turnoff to Bahia de Los Angeles, 65 miles south of Catavina. Steve and family joined several other campers here for the night. The park has no water or power, but in the morning, a young boy collected the trash and flushed the toilets with buckets of water. This self-appointed caretaker charged each party one dollar, which seems a fair price for his services.

Los Angeles Bay: It's about 40 miles on a paved road from Parador Punta Prieta to this beautiful bay on the Sea of Cortez. There is excellent free beach camping on the north side of Bahia de Los Angeles. It's also a good kayaking area, but be very careful of fierce and sudden winds. Regular gas is usually available.

Back on Highway 1, gasoline is usually available in the village of Punta Prieta, 8.5 miles south of Parador Punta Prieta. Gas is also sold at Villa Jesus Maria, 59 miles south of the junction to Los Angeles Bay. If the power is out—and it usually is—the gas pump (regular only) has to be cranked by hand.

Free Camping: South of Punta Prieta you'll have several opportunities to follow side roads to good beach camping, surfing, and fishing.

Guerrero Negro: ''Black Warrior'' is famous for its gray whales, salt mines, and empty, endless beaches. The land tends to be flat and windswept, somewhat like Kansas with cactus. Fortunately, the fishing, clamming, and beachcombing are all very good.

Extra gasoline should be available at the Pinta Hotel at the 28th Parallel and at the Pemex in town. Services, basic supplies, restaurants, and motels are all available in Guerrero Negro, but RV parks are very scarce.

Trailer Park Benito Juarez ($$): This park is on the main highway, just past the Hotel Pinta and the not-easily-missed 28th Parallel monument, said to represent an eagle but more often mistaken for the world's largest tuning fork. This is also the state line. Bird watchers should look for an osprey nest on a signpost near the monument.

Benito Juarez campground is another ex-government parador that has been "rejuvenated" by a local ejido. It is stark but adequate.

Facilities and Rates: There are 60 spaces with full hookups, clean bathrooms, and showers. No tents.

Free Camping: Guerrero Negro can be surprisingly cold, especially if you're sleeping outside. To escape the fog, Lorena and I often camp between Guerrero Negro and San Ignacio in one of several flat spots bulldozed in the desert during highway construction. The air is drier here, and we found these "quarries" to be comfortable and private. Watch closely. They're easy to miss.

San Ignacio: This small colonial-era village and palm-shaded oasis is located midway across the peninsula on Mex 1. San Ignacio is famous for its Spanish mission and ancient Indian rock paintings. The area tends to be overlooked by travelers eager to take the plunge in the Sea of Cortez.

I learned to appreciate San Ignacio the hard way. While hurrying to begin a long-delayed kayaking expedition in La Paz, my brother Rob and I blew the engine in our VW van about two hours west of town. We crawled into San Ignacio on two cylinders and a prayer, then coasted directly into the junkyard across from the Pemex station. It took a full week to get back on the road, including a marathon bus trip to San Diego with the engine in a cardboard box. During that week, Rob and I camped out in the junkyard with the broken glass, busted tires, and wrecked, dust-covered cars, swatting flies and choking on the fumes from an eternally smoldering pile of garbage.

Once the shock of our situation had worn off, we spent our free time exploring the village and surrounding hills, bird-watching, swimming, collecting *datiles* (dates), identifying plants, and visiting with other travelers. Every afternoon we'd hike into the village, buy a handful of dried dates and figs, and then check out the evening "action" around the tiny plaza. Thanks to these relaxing distractions and the unselfish kindnesses extended to us by the junkyard owner and his family, we actually enjoyed the experience.

Parador San Ignacio ($): This on-again, off-again ex-government campground is located behind the Pemex station, along Mex 1 west of San Ignacio. When it is open, this park gets a lot of noise from the gas station. During a recent visit, the water was running, but the bathroom plumbing had failed miserably. At four dollars a night, this rates as emergency camping only.

Cheap Camping($): Much more pleasant surroundings can be found in one of the rustic campgrounds along the paved side road leading from Mex 1 to San Ignacio. About a mile from the main highway, on your left, you'll see an unnamed camp with a sign, Camping-RV Park $2. The facilities are crude, but how often do you get to camp in a grove of date palms?

Calendario Trailer Park ($): Just beyond the campground described above, the road to San Ignacio takes a sharp turn to the left. Watch for signs at this corner, but if you don't see them, follow a narrow dirt road to your right. (This road can be a real squeeze for larger vehicles.)

If you're burned out on deserts or suffering a case of white-line fever, **Calendario** comes as a welcome refuge. This campground has one very special feature: a clear, shockingly cool spring-fed pond surrounded by date palms and dense cane brakes. This is a great place to swim, bird-watch and swat mosquitoes. You won't find much in the way of services, but the combination of shade, swimming, and quiet sleeping makes this one of my favorite camps in Baja. Like most such hideouts in Mexico, I've also met some interesting characters here, from old-timer desert rats and peso-pinching snowbirds to vacationing African safari guides. The price is right, too.

Santa Rosalia: This small but busy mining town on the Sea of Cortez doesn't have many "tourist attractions," but I always enjoy stretching my legs here. Other than a few restaurants, bakeries, and food stores, Santa Rosalia's biggest draw is an unusual corrugated iron church, designed by Eiffel and prefabricated in France. The Frances, a restored wooden hotel on a bluff overlooking the town, is also an interesting local landmark and a good example of French colonial architecture.

There are ferry connections to Guaymas on the Mexican mainland. Because of mining operations, the waterfront is not very attractive.

Free Camping: The highway from San Ignacio meets the Sea of Cortez at the bottom of a steep grade north of Santa Rosalia. There is good camping on a rocky beach, and a road leads to beaches farther north.

San Lucas RV Park ($): Nine miles south of Santa Rosalia, turn east off Mex 1 and go about a mile to the campground. Located on a beautiful, palm-shaded cove, this no-frills campground has most everything a serious fisherman needs to be happy, namely, a boat ramp, hot showers, and a good-smelling restaurant. In fact, with its sun-faded thatched roofs, San Lucas feels more like a genuine Baja fishing camp than an RV park. The regulars here are more impressed by the sharpness of your hooks and the originality of your lies than the size of your rig.

Santa Rosalia's beaches tend to be rocky and quite windy. This campground is fortunate to be on a protected bay, with hard-packed sand for easier boat launching. The yellowtail fishing is said to be best in December, January, and February.

Facilities and Services: There are 18 beachfront spaces with water only (no power) and a dump station. Though it is small, the manager says this park has adequate parking for caravans.

Santa Rosalia to Loreto: Your greatest driving challenge along this coast is to watch the road ahead rather than the mouth-watering views of the Sea of Cortez. This is it, the fabled ''Vermillion Sea,'' one of the world's finest fishing, diving, boating, and camping areas. Considering how far you've come by now, your reaction to this feast of natural wonders should be an uncontrollable urge to stop at the first possible beach and make camp.

Side roads to the Sea of Cortez are limited, however, especially for large RVs and low clearance vehicles. Don't let your enthusiasm overcome common sense. Once a road turns bad in Baja, it can usually be counted on to get much worse. I recall one excited driver who "bridged" a deep, narrow dip in a rocky road with his oversized motor home. It took a lot of shovel work, pry bars, borrowed jacks, and a rented tractor to free his RV. What had begun as a carefree search for the beach at the end of the rainbow turned into a costly and time-consuming lesson in backroad driving tactics: when in doubt, back out.

Punta Chivato Campground ($): Turn east off Mex 1 about 25 miles south of Santa Rosalia, at Km 156. Avoid the old, lousy road 20 miles south of Santa Rosalia. The newer road is gravel and quite passable, but be prepared for 18-plus miles of classic, screw-loosening, denture-rattling Baja *permanente* (washboard).

The jackhammer trip into Punta Chivato tends to discourage overnighters, but if you're looking for peace, quiet, and beautiful beaches, this place is hard to beat. Fishing is good for dorado, yellowtail, and bonita. There is room for camping on several small crescent beaches as well as shelling and safe swimming. (Note: Punta Chivato is privately owned; there is no free beach camping.)

Facilities and Services: In traditional Baja style, it's first-come, first-serve for everything at Punta Chivato, including the campsites, outhouses, cold showers, and communal water tap. Just to remind you that you've reached the real Baja, a sign in the middle of camp says, "Eugene, Oregon—1760 miles" and "U.S. border—620 miles." There is a dump station near the airstrip.

The last time Steve camped at Punta Chivato, a stubborn north wind prevented him from going fishing. The seafood situation became so desperate, in fact, that he was forced to ransack his cupboards to make canned clam spaghetti. Here he was, in the land of mesquite, grilled lobster, buttery sea bass, and exquisite broiled tuna, guiltily reaching for a can opener! Despondent, Steve was just heating a skillet when a local fisherman dropped by. Pointing to a cracked plastic bucket between his feet, the man asked shyly, would it be possible that perhaps ... *someone* might buy a kilo of freshly shucked scallops for four dollars? It is said that Steve's joyous reply could be heard as far away as Mulege.

Mulege: Like most towns in Baja, Mulege strikes the first-time visitor as surprisingly small. In fact, this busy little town provides shopping and services to a wide area, including ranchers, farmers, and fishermen, plus a steadily growing population of resident RVers, campers, kayakers, sailboarders, and miscellaneous tourists. Mulege has food, ice, restaurants, hotels, a laundromat, car parts, and a limited selection of etceteras. Local fishing and diving are good, and the beaches north and south of town are among the best in Baja. Concepción Bay, just to the south, has some of the finest camping and boating in Mexico.

Free Camping: Free beach camping near Mulege is very limited. The value of waterfront property is skyrocketing along this coast, and almost every landowner charges at least a minimal fee for camping. Don't be surprised—or indignant—if someone pops up in the middle of nowhere and charges you a dollar or two for the use of a beach. It's better to pay graciously than to risk returning next year to find a locked gate.

Cheap Camping ($): Mulege's main street becomes an unpaved lane that goes two miles east to Sombrerito, a *playa publica* (public beach) at the mouth of the river. Though this "campground" is just an open area at the end of the road, it is quite popular with van campers. For a modest fee, you get a place to camp and a beautiful sunrise, but there are no facilities or services.

Mulege does its best to distract passing RVers from more publicized resorts in Loreto and Los Cabos. There are four RV parks along the short, shallow, palm-shaded Mulege River on the southern edge of town, all within easy walking and biking distance. Although our personal preference is to camp farther afield, Mulege's campgrounds are very popular with RV residents. Most, if not all, of the larger parks offer special annual rental rates and long-term leases.

From Mulege to the south:

Jorge's: It was closed for sewer installation when Steve dropped by, but it should be open by now.

Pancho's ($$): Though it isn't quite as nice as the other parks, Pancho's is the cheapest. Pancho's steep, curved driveway may have something to do with his price; scout it carefully if you're driving a big rig.

Facilities and Services: There are 40 spaces with full hookups.

Huerta Saucedo RV Park ($$): Half a mile south of the Mulege river bridge, this park is on the south shore of the river. ''The Orchard'' is very roomy, pleasant, and nicely shaded. There are abundant date palms as well as plantings of orange, mango, lime, and fig trees. Most of the park's spaces are designed for long-stay RVers and leaseholders, but twenty full hookup spaces are reserved for overnighters. Fishermen will appreciate the camp's boat launch on the river and a convenient fish cleaning station. According to the management, the camp's water is safe to drink.

Villa Maria Isabel RV Park ($$): Less than two miles south of the Mulege bridge, on the east side of the highway, this park is excellent. It has everything from potable drinking water to tasteful landscaping, a swimming pool, a boat launch, and a dump station. The management is very friendly and will arrange fishing charters. The camp also has a barbecue area. If your fishing trip is successful, the staff will cook your catch on request. Better yet, the park actually has its own bakery. Steve reports that the oven has become a shrine for pizza-starved campers. Facilities and Services: There are 25 full hookup spaces. This exceptional park merits special thanks for welcoming tent campers at budget rates.

Bahia de la Concepción: According to my statistics, anyone who spends more than a week at Concepción Bay is invariably hooked on Baja for life. In fact, it is a fantastic natural playground for swimming, snorkeling, camping, boating, or just loafing in the sun, pretending to fish. What it lacks in modern conveniences is more than compensated for by the bay's smooth, curving beaches and tempting, clear water. More than a few travelers bound for Cabo San Lucas and points south find themselves distracted by Concepción's easy-going atmosphere and irresistible beauty.

Cheap Camping ($): Playa Santispac, 13 miles south of Mulege, is a locally famous and much-photographed *playa publica* (public beach). For a modest fee, you'll have the use of small thatched palapa sunshades, outhouses, trash cans, and a very basic restaurant. There is no fresh water, however, so bring your own.

Santispac is a large beach, but it is popular and often crowded. But the swimming is great, the boating is fantastic, and the other campers are down-to-earth and very friendly.

Cheap public camping beaches are also found at Rancho El Coyote, 17 miles south of Mulege, and at El Requeson, 27 miles south.

There are also a few privately operated campgrounds along the western shore of the bay. The usual charge is less than five dollars a night. Facilities vary from rustic and funky to primitive. Forget about hot showers and power; in most of these camps, you'll be lucky to find an outhouse. The sand and sun are very bright here, and other than occasional palapas and ramadas (thatched or improvised shelters), you'll have to provide your own shade. You'll also have to depend on Mulege for food, water, and services.

RV Park El Coyote ($$): On Bahia de la Concepción, at Km 108, this park has almost everything the other bay camps don't, including drinking water, showers, and flush toilets. Besides having shade—a rare feature in such arid country— the beach here is prettier than average, even by Baja's high standards.

Facilities and Rates: There are some beachfront sites, but others are half price. The park offers water only, no power or sewer hookups. There is good access for big rigs, a restaurant, and a small *tienda* (store).

Mulege to Loreto: Just south of Mulege, the highway snakes along the convoluted eastern shore of Bahia de la Concepción, providing 25 miles of eye-popping views. Be careful; good pull-offs are few and far between. Give your attention to the tight curves and slow traffic. Be especially alert if you're driving a large RV. It's unfortunate, but this road just isn't made for Sunday-style driving and sightseeing. For your own safety, don't stop on the highway to take photographs or otherwise block the flow of traffic.

Once you're beyond the bay, the only side road of interest goes to the west, to Comondu and the Pacific Ocean. This is an unpaved alternate route to Villa Insurgentes and La Paz, and unless you'll be returning to Mulege, you'll have to slip Loreto if you take this detour. After feasting your eyes on Bahia de la Concepción, missing Loreto is like skipping dessert.

Loreto: This relaxed, palm-shaded town has been teetering on the edge of a tourist boom for several years. Loreto's natural resources are impressive: excellent fishing, diving, and small boating around Isla Carmen; hiking, hunting, and exploring in the raw, rugged Sierra de la Giganta; miles of untouched beaches; abundant pure water; and a sunny, dry climate. Combine these attractions with nearby Puerto Escondido—perhaps the finest natural harbor on the Sea of Cortez—and the town's friendly, laid-back population, and you've got a developer's dream.

Almost in spite of itself, however, Loreto remains a small, easygoing town where conversation seems to focus on fishing and the price of mangoes, rather than five-star hotels and multinational tourist ventures. The future undoubtedly holds change, but we're all praying that Loreto can avoid the kind of unplanned, runaway growth that has turned Cabo San Lucas into a piece of Very Southern California.

Campers will find everything they need in Loreto, from ice and ice cream to gasoline, restaurants, supermarkets, and excellent sunsets.

Free Camping: Access to the beaches north and south of Loreto is limited, as usual, by local road conditions and property owners. Because both can change without warning, your best bet is to explore and quiz other campers in the area. Some side roads get off to a good start but then peter out in narrow arroyos or tricky sand traps. Other roads may be freshly graded or cleverly repaired by industrious campers.

Baja's weather is very hard on dirt roads. Although sandy arroyo bottoms are traditionally used in this area to reach the beach, one good cloudburst in the Sierra de la Giganta can turn an improvised road into a temporary river. South of Puerto Escondido, for example, several seasonal dirt tracks wander from the highway to the beach near Km 88, and farther south, at Ligui. In good, dry years, these are passablo in vane and caro; at othor timoe thoy doad-ond in washouts and sand traps. Again, the answer is to explore and ask other travelers for suggestions.

Ejido Loreto RV and Trailer Park ($$): This is an excellent beachfront location on the southern edge of the town of Loreto. The well-managed campground is clearly the best of the ex-government RV parks. Happily, tent camping is allowed. Steve says, "This campground is great! You can get a shower for one dollar, even if you aren't a guest. Better yet, there's no extra charge for more than two people in a vehicle. I really appreciate this. There's nothing more irritating than having to pay extra to camp with a small child."

Fishermen and kayakers take note: small boats can be launched over the beach and clam digging is worth the effort. The park also offers storage for vehicles and boats.

If you visit Ejido Loreto, look up Hope Bartmass, the campground's unofficial greeter and resident artist. Following in the footsteps of many great Baja characters before her, Hope gave up her job as a country club hostess and left California with her belongings stuffed into a pickup camper. Now comfortably ensconced in Loreto, Hope's "work" in the trailer park provides rich material for her art and writing. She says, "I finally found a job where I don't have to wear panty hose." If you're looking for an unusual souvenir, Hope does a very attractive poster-style map of southern Baja.

Facilities and Rates: There are 72 full hookup sites and discounts without hookups, drive-through sites, and good access for big rigs. Facilities include nice bathrooms and hot showers and a washer and dryer. Loreto is within pleasant walking distance.

Puerto Escondido: Fifteen miles south of Loreto, this small, almost perfectly protected bay is among Baja's most-favored yacht anchorages and "hurricane holes." Until recent years, Puerto Escondido's mud flats and mangrove thickets were one of the peninsula's most interesting and informal campgrounds. On a typical visit, we might squeeze ourselves between a clapped-out Ford Econoline van with a homemade canvas "pop top" and a fully decked out, top-of-the-line Airstream. Though the camp's hard core winter population was made up of vacationing fishermen and divers who dedicated their free time to the pursuit of fresh seafood, Puerto Escondido also harbored backpackers huddled under tarps, desert-rat pickup rigs, motor homes both large and small, home-built boats, gleaming yachts, and enough VW vans to evacuate half of Berkeley.

John Steinbeck visited Puerto Escondido in 1940 and described it as "a place of magic. If one wished to design a secret personal bay, one would probably build something very like this little harbor." I'm sorry to report that Puerto Escondido is now being fully redesigned by French developers, its magic transformed into high-rise hotels and a state-of-the-art tourist colony.

Tripui RV Resort ($$$): Take the turnoff to Puerto Escondido; the park is near the highway and hard to miss. To call this a camping ground would be an understatement, and nothing about the Tripui RV Resort is understated. From its lighted tennis courts and carefully manicured lawns to its well-attended happy hour and hefty fees, this park adds another dimension to camping. Some people sing its praises, but Steve privately mutters that Tripui is "the next best thing to camping in your local mall." His greatest complaint (other than price) was the park's uninspiring location: on a thorny slope overlooking the highway instead of the bay.

Facilities and Rates: There are 116 spaces with full hookups; no pull-throughs. Tent sites are available at $3.00 per person. Showers are $1.50. There are discounts for longer stays and RV clubs, except AAA. The resort offers a laundry, groceries, a swimming pool, drinking water, a restaurant, a curio shop, and a playground.

South of Puerto Escondido, the unyielding peaks and ridges of the Sierra de la Giganta force Mex 1 up and away from the coast, diverting it westward, onto a long semiarid plateau. Shortly before the highway leaves the Sea of Cortez, campers will find an appealing shoreline of rocky bluffs, small beaches, and protected coves. Two islands, Isla Carmen and Isla Danzante, lie temptingly close to the mainland. Both are very popular with fishermen and kayakers.

For the person who wants more than just a fine beach and a stirring view, this area offers an unusually wide variety of activities, from snorkeling, sailboarding, and shelling to exploring for ancient Indian rock paintings.

Puerto Escondido to Ciudad Constitución: After leaving the coast at Ligui, you'll have about 30 miles of moderate mountain driving before reaching level ground. Pay close attention, especially if it has been raining. Falling rock is always a problem in Baja's mountains. Road shoulders are so narrow that whatever comes down—stones, mud, or water— usually ends up on the highway.

I was reminded of this one rainy autumn when Lorena and I merrily rolled around a curve west of Ligui and collided head-on with a large granite boulder. Fortunately, we only lost our oil pan, our radiator, and most of our composure. Once my knees stopped shaking, I was able to flag down a very helpful bus driver, who took me directly to the nearest tow truck—about 60 miles away. Heeding Lorena's advice to "look on the bright side, even if it hurts your eyes," I soon gained valuable and highly detailed knowledge of Ciudad Constitución's towing companies, junkyards, auto parts stores, and mechanic shops. Our crippled van was repaired in record time for an astonishingly low price.

Ciudad Constitución supplies local farmers, ranchers, and travelers with basic, no-frills accommodations, food, goods, and services. Camping facilities are very limited.

Side Trips: A good highway (Mex 22) leads west from Ciudad Constitución to San Carlos (36 miles) and Magdalena Bay. This coast is rather stark but the clamming, fishing, and late winter whale watching can be exceptional. There is also free camping, birding, and beachcombing. The potential for kite flying is virtually untapped. Regular gas and supplies are available at San Carlos.

Campestre La Pila ($): One and a half miles south of Ciudad Constitución, turn west and follow a dirt road for one mile. Watch for a sign and turn left into the campground.

Campestre La Pila not only has a down-on-the-farm atmosphere but it's right in the middle of one—hay bales, dust, barnyard "bouquet" and all. The attraction isn't the campground—which is adequate for overnight—but the swimming pool. In fact, Campestre La Pila (literally "country trough") is a pleasant local swimming hole and picnic ground with an RV park added as an afterthought. Although the landscaping doesn't extend to the campground, you can park your rig with the chickens, then relax around the pool or eat dinner, picnic-style, on the shaded lawn.

Ciudad Constitución has few competing attractions and La Pila's picnic area and pool are very popular on weekends. If you're interested in speaking Spanish and meeting friendly *Baja Californianos,* this is a perfect opportunity.

Ciudad Constitución to La Paz: This is a straightforward 135-mile drive through level to mildly rolling desert. The Sierra de la Giganta (Mountains of the Giantess) forms a virtually impassable barrier to the east. There are no reasonable side roads to the Sea of Cortez and only limited access to the Pacific coast. Unless you're well prepared, stick to the most heavily traveled roads. This region is quite arid; if you camp in the desert, nighttime skywatching is terrific.

RV Campgrounds: The only RV park on this stretch is Los Aripos, more than 9 miles before La Paz. See below.

La Paz: Other than Ensenada and Tijuana, La Paz is the only real city you'll find in Baja. It is also a pleasant surprise to most travelers. The city is not only attractive but its prices have yet to suffer resort-style inflation. Campers and boaters love La Paz for its well-stocked supermarkets, plentiful hardware stores, and auto parts shops—and curse it for frantic traffic and difficult parking.

La Paz is also a duty-free port and a very popular vacation and shopping destination for mainland Mexican tourists. With its pleasant, bayside *malecon* (quay), small plaza, busy shops, and traditional afternoon siesta, the city satisfies most visitors as authentically Mexican. After years of playing second fiddle to Cabo San Lucas and Loreto, La Paz is finally attracting attention from outdoor-oriented tourists. The city offers Mexico's first charter sailboat fleet as well as excellent guided diving, fishing, and nature trips. Lorena and I have used La Paz several times as a base camp for long kayaking expeditions in the Sea of Cortez.

There is daily car and passenger ferry service from La Paz to Mazatlán and twice weekly service to Topolobampo.

The tourist office on the waterfront malecon, at Paseo Obregon and 16 de Septiembre, has good city maps and information in English.

Compass directions are confusing in La Paz. Although Mex 1 runs roughly north to south, the highway curves from west to east around La Paz Bay. This causes many travelers—myself included—to confuse the west side of town (where Mex 1 comes in from Ciudad Constitución) with the north (Pichilingue and the ferry terminal).

Camping: The RV parks are all west of La Paz, with the exception of one in the southern suburbs. There is plenty of free camping within a one-hour radius as well. The closest free camping is beyond the ferry dock, in the area known as Pichilingue. This broad, hilly peninsula has a number of startlingly beautiful bays, lagoons, and white sand beaches. A few miles to the north, across the San Lorenzo Channel, the island of Espiritu Santo is a major attraction for divers, kayakers, and fishermen.

The La Paz peninsula's brushy flats are crisscrossed with

narrow dirt roads, many of which lead to wonderful camping and picnic sites. Be warned, however, that Pichilingue harbors some very aggressive *jejenes* (no-see-ums), a tiny stinging gnat that can drive even the most determined campers to the nearest bug-proofed hotel. Unless your RV or tent has fine-mesh screening specifically designed to stop these merciless insects, pick your campsite with extra care. Look for high, dry, wind-swept ground rather than protected hollows. Avoid mangroves, brush, lagoons, mud puddles, and damp sand. If the jejenes attack, your only protection is to huddle over a smoky fire or bury yourself deep within a sleeping bag. At their worst, no-see-ums are virtually impervious to insect repellent, including pure "jungle juice." (Lorena advises, "Mix 10 to 20 drops of pennyroyal oil to your repellent to increase its effectiveness against no-see-ums.") The more exposed eastern side of the peninsula has far fewer bugs than its western beaches.

In spite of what you may have heard about Baja's low rainfall, it does get wet on occasion. In fact, I've rarely camped in southern Baja during late winter and early spring without enjoying at least a few showers. Should it rain while you're camped at Pichilingue, low spots will quickly become ponds and the roads will be instantly coated with a very slick mud. We were in a group of campers who spent an extra two days at Tecolote Beach, stranded by a February drizzle that transformed the desert into a huge mud slick. Fortunately, a combination of ceaseless wind and cold, blowing rain kept the bugs at bay.

Why camp at Pichilingue at all? Because when the conditions are good—which is most of the time—they're *very good*. Catch a moonrise over the mountains, or a sierra mackerel off the beach and, believe me, you'll be hooked.

Free beach camping can also be reached at the end of several confusing dirt roads that lead from La Paz's eastern suburbs, past the municipal dump, to El Coyote. Follow the most heavily used roads, and when in doubt, bear east. Unless you have current local information on road conditions, however, larger RVs should avoid this area.

Better roads and excellent free camping are found at Los Planes, Bahia de Los Muertos, and Punta de la Ventana, about an hour southeast of La Paz. Todos Santos, on the Pacific Ocean an hour southwest of the city, also has great free camping.

Los Aripes RV Park ($$$): This park is at the village of El Centenario, 9.3 miles west of La Paz on Mex 1. (Because the highway curves around La Paz Bay, west actually feels like north.) If you're driving south from Ciudad Constitución, this is the first RV park you'll come to.

Los Aripes is sandwiched between the highway and a broad, shallow bay, but traffic is rarely heavy enough to be a nuisance, especially at night. Although boats can be launched at high tide, the bay is very shallow here. Kids love the wading, but swimming is another story, especially when the tide goes out and exposes a vast mudflat. Still, this is a pleasant park, and one we've camped at often in past years.

Lorena and I used Los Aripes as a base camp while preparing for (and recovering from) extended kayaking voyages. I enjoyed being well out of range of La Paz's traffic and turmoil, yet still within easy commuting distance of services and shopping. In fact, small stores in the campground's immediate neighborhood provide plenty of basic supplies.

Facilities and Services: There are 29 sites with full hookups, accessible to big rigs but no pull-throughs. There are no tent sites. Facilities include a restaurant and bar with satellite television, a laundromat, showers, and hot water. A new swimming pool may be completed by now.

El Cardon Trailer Park ($$): On Mex 1, at Km 4 (mile 2.5) on the west side of La Paz, El Cardon is an old standby—a very reliable, well-managed campground with a comfortable, lived-in atmosphere. The grounds are attractively land-

scaped, but Steve is positively enchanted by El Cardon's do-
it-yourself vehicle grease pit, a feature he believes is uni-
queto this trailer park.

El Cardon isn't fancy, but Norbert Hahnel, the owner,
provides each space with such thoughtful features as a
palapa with a built-in table and electric light. Another big
plus is long-distance international telephone and mail service, free maps, and car insurance.

Facilities and Services: There are 85 spaces with full
hookups, and access for rigs up to 40 feet, with 40 pull-
throughs. El Cardon offers a swimming pool, drinking water,
a curio shop, ice, sodas, weekly discounts, 17 tiled showers,
and 19 flush toilets.

La Paz Trailer Park ($$$): Between the waterfront and
Abasolo Street, just south of the VW agency, on the western
edge of La Paz, this new, modern park is very clean and well
kept but often quite crowded.

Facilities and Services: There are 96 full hookup sites
and a discount without hookups. The park has good access
for big rigs, with 9 pull-throughs. There are 10 tent sites, a
laundry, showers, a swimming pool, a jacuzzi, a tennis court,
a satellite television room, and a restaurant, bar, and curio
shop.

Gran Hotel Baja (Ramada Inn) Trailer Park ($): Just west
of the La Paz Trailer Park (see above) and behind the Ford
Agency, look for the Gran Baja hotel; you can't miss it. This
is a "good news/bad news" campground. The bad news is
traffic noise and a hot water heater that will be repaired next
week. The good news is that tents are allowed and RV sites,
including hookups, are quite cheap.

Facilities and Services: There are 18 spaces and clean
bathrooms but no laundry. This park is managed by the hotel
next door; campers have use of the hotel swimming pool,
restaurants, and bars.

Aquamarina RV Park ($$$): Near the Gran Baja Hotel,

on the west shore of La Paz at #10 Nayarit, just off Abasolo Street, the park was still under construction. According to Steve, ''It looks good, although the price for waterfront sites is too rich for my blood.'' Aquamarina is not only on the beach but it is also attached to a marina owned by the La Paz Diving Service. ''If you have a boat or are interested in diving,'' Steve says, ''check this park out.''

El Carrizal RV Park ($$): On the southern outskirts of La Paz, take Mex 13 to the southeast from Mex 1. The park is half a mile from the junction. This is a large, attractive, and easily overlooked park that suffers from its uninteresting location. The swimming pool is big, but for some reason it isn't filled until December.

Facilities and Services: There are 160 spaces with full hookups, bathrooms, showers, and a laundry.

La Paz to Land's End: Although it covers a relatively small area, the southernmost portion of the Baja peninsula includes some of its best camping, fishing, and outdoor recreation. It also includes Cabo San Lucas and San Jose del Cabo. A whirlwind of development, land speculation, and sudden wealth has transformed these once laid-back fishing villages into the gold dust twins of Baja tourism. Dubbed ''Los Cabos'' by promoters, these up-and-coming resorts bear almost no relation to the ''real'' Baja. Peeking between the T-shirt shops, $300-a-night hotel rooms, and glitzy tourist temples, however, Los Cabos' natural charms still exert a considerable attraction for campers.

Two paved highways connect La Paz to Land's End at Cabo San Lucas. Mex 19 crosses the peninsula to the southwest, meeting the Pacific Ocean near the charming village of Todos Santos. This is the fast track to Cabo San Lucas; buses cover the distance from La Paz in less than three hours. Saner drivers will enjoy good beachcombing, camping, wonderful views, and unusually lush and interesting desert vegetation along this route. Warning: with only a few exceptions, heavy Pacific surf makes this coast much too dangerous for swimmers.

Your second choice from La Paz is to stay on Mex 1. The "old road" to Cabo San Lucas is a much slower and longer route that is nonetheless quite interesting. Mex 1 also touches occasionally on the Sea of Cortez, and side roads branch out to wonderful beaches and camping.

When in doubt, my advice is to flip a coin. Or better yet, drive both highways as a loop trip. In fact, if you're biking or camping from a rental car, this loop can easily keep you occupied and happy for several days or weeks.

Free Camping: A little over a mile south of La Paz, turn east off Mex 1 onto a good gravel road (BC 13) to Los Planes and Bahia de Los Muertos (40 miles). At mile 24, a road goes north to the small fishing villages of El Sargento and La Ventana. Supplies are available in Los Planes, a fairly substantial farming community.

Camping is very good in this area, especially if the wind isn't howling. When the wind does blow, watch out. My brother and I endured a series of hair-raising adventures while kayaking along this coast during an especially blustery spring. After being sunburned, sandblasted, and swamped (twice), we finally limped into a protected cove on Bahia de los Muertos.

"Bay of the Dead?" Rob groaned, crawling into his sodden sleeping bag. "Couldn't you have spared me the translation?"

Fishing here can be excellent to exceptional. I'll repeat, howovor, that boaters should use great caution and carry survival gear.

Los Barriles: At Km 111 (actually about 65 miles) south of La Paz on Mex 1, turn east onto a dirt road toward Los Barriles. This road soon branches left to Punta Pescadero, a rough trip along an especially beautiful coast. Take your time and explore for campsites. (The side road to Punta Pescadero is passable, but it's rough as a cob and can be very hard on RVs and low-clearance cars.)

Martin Verdugo's RV Park ($): This park is at Los Barriles, half a mile east of Mex 1. Watch for signs on the highway. The park is something of an institution. Because it is well known, it is usually quite crowded. As Steve says, "Martin's is cheap and it's fine, but it's just not as fine as Playa de Oro."

Playa de Oro RV Park ($$): This park is at Los Barriles, just beyond Martin Verdugo's. Watch for signs on Mex 1. Steve's partner, Tina, thinks this park is a knockout. "This is a new, very well done campground with lots of plants. When the coconut palms grow a bit, it will be even nicer. The beach is great for swimming, wind surfing, and small boats. They even have potted plants in the bathrooms!"

Steve's attention was drawn to the park's well-used barbecue pit and communal potluck dinners on Saturday night. "We had the good fortune to be here on Thanksgiving. The entire camp turned out for a tremendous potluck." The manager earned Steve's undying affection by sharing a turkey and an entire roast pig. By the time Steve discovered the camp's book exchange and abundant supply of hot shower water, he was ready to set up permanent housekeeping.

"Believe it or not," Steve adds, "they even give Spanish lessons. The hell with objectivity; this place is great!"

Facilities and Services: There are 54 full hookup spaces. There is a higher rate for beachfront sites. Tents are allowed. Facilities are a laundry, ice, and sport fishing trips.

Free Camping: Seventy-eight miles south of La Paz, a dirt road goes east from Mex 1 to La Ribera, Cabo Pulmo, Los Frailes, and (possibly) San Jose del Cabo (82 miles). This road covers a lot of camping ground, not to mention excellent spots for fishing, kayaking, exploring, and diving. Baja's largest coral reef is at Cabo Pulmo, a tiny village that developers are already drooling over.

A few supplies and regular gasoline are available in La Ribera. Other than that, you're on your own. Drinking water can be begged and bartered in Cabo Pulmo and at occasional ranchos.

The road to Cabo Pulmo varies from fairly good to rather awful, depending on maintenance and the weather. Under normal conditions, adventurous RVs and passenger cars regularly reach Cabo Pulmo. The worst section is usually beyond Cabo Pulmo, between Los Frailes and San Jose del Cabo. I've done it in a gutless van without problems, but frequent slides, washouts,and other acts of nature make conditions unpredictable. For accurate road reports, ask a northbound driver—preferably someone driving a vehicle similar to yours.

Los Barriles to San Jose del Cabo: Mex 1 cuts inland here, skirting the eastern foothills of the Sierra de La Laguna. If you are interested in local wildlife, there is a small zoo in Santiago, about 83 miles south of La Paz. Follow a good side road west through the village. The zoo is on the outskirts of town.

If you're an experienced desert hiker, Santiago is a jump-off point into the Sierra La Trinidad and from there to the Sierra de La Laguna. I was told by locals, however, that the approach to the mountains is long (about two days) and dry, and the trail is easy to lose. A more direct approach to the Sierra de La Laguna can be made from the Pacific side, near Todos Santos.

San Jose del Cabo: This is the ''other Cabo,'' a relatively sedate town that seems almost stodgy in comparison to high-strung Cabo San Lucas. Although San Jose's golf course, condo developments, and beachfront hotels hint at dramatic change, there is a sense of history and community here that is almost entirely lacking at Land's End. San Jose even has a marketplace, albeit a very small one, and a town plaza where Spanish is still spoken. Bird-watchers and photographers will want to visit the lagoon, bordering the beach next to the Hotel Presidente. San Jose's beautiful beaches are unsafe for swimming because of heavy surf and strong undertows.

Free Camping: Although the beaches and hilltops are studded with surveyor's stakes, some of Baja's finest beach camping can still be found north of San Jose del Cabo. Look for a dirt road leading toward the beach about one-fourth mile from town, on the boulevard to the Hotel Presidente. Go two miles east to La Playita, a fishing village and former pirate stronghold. (La Playita's seafood restaurants are worth a visit.)

Continue through the village until you find a dirt road winding north along the coast. This eventually leads to Los Frailes and Cabo Pulmo (see Los Barriles). Expect washboard, crumbling shoulders, and traffic. Surfers love this area, and they tend to drive with their eyes on the waves, not the road.

You'll have to explore for campsites, especially in the bottoms of the larger arroyos. If you find yourself in loose sand, deflate your tires to 10 or 15 pounds pressure, drive softly, and carry a big shovel. We've camped out here for years; sooner or later, I always get stuck. Your best precaution is to park on the side of the road and scout ahead on foot.

Brisa del Mar Motel and RV Park ($$$): On the beach, three miles south of San Jose del Cabo, this large, attractive park has a devoted following, including a suntanned cadre of semiresident colorful characters. There's everything you need here, including a swimming pool, laundry, pool table, restaurant, motel, and very lively bar.

Ellie, the park's owner, says, "The service in our restaurant is slow, but I have the best burgers in Baja.'' Affectionately known as ''Mom'' by her guests, Ellie also has a reputation as a friendly but firm hostess who doesn't tolerate nonsense. This campground attracts every kind of camper, from lavish RV Land Yachts to surfers, backpackers, dune buggy jockeys, and Ma and Pa Kettle look-alikes. It's an interesting, never-a-dull-moment mixture. In fact, there was more happening in the trailer park than anywhere else in San Jose, including the discos. Although a local police car made regular circuits of the campground, the only disturbance I noticed was caused by a shapely European camper wearing a dazzling eye-patch bikini.

Facilities and Services: There are a variety of site options with a sliding price scale for beachfront spaces, tents, and campers who don't require hookups. The park is very full from December through February, but few campers are turned away. Facilities include a book exchange, gift shops, some RV and surfing supplies, and maps. There are some palapas and pleasant motel rooms and kitchenettes.

San Jose del Cabo to Cabo San Lucas: With 20 miles of curves, sandy coves, and speeding airport taxis, be careful. Traffic can be hot and heavy to Cabo San Lucas. This is the most dangerous road in southern Baja. Unfortunately, development has cut off virtually all access to free beach camping.

Shipwreck Beach ($): This site is about 14 miles south of San Jose del Cabo, at Km 10 (6 miles north of Cabo San Lucas). There is no sign, so watch closely for a narrow dirt road leading to the camping area from Mex 1.

Many people consider Shipwreck Beach to be one of Mexico's finest rustic campgrounds. Though camping was once free, the property owners (Cabo del Sol Hotel) now charge for the use of a well with ''good'' drinking water and a basic shower. The unmarked sites are first-come, first-serve.

This beautiful camp is very popular and tends to fill up during the winter. Long-term campers dig their own sewage holes. Garbage is picked up on Wednesday and Sunday at the side of the road.

In addition to the wreck of a Japanese fishing vessel, there is an excellent swimming beach, snorkeling, and good boat launching. Fishing is sometimes fantastic for dorado, bonita, wahoo, sailfish, and marlin.

A friend well into his seventies was trolling from a small home-built kayak near here when he hooked a giant marlin. In a courageous battle right out of *The Old Man and the Sea*, he was eventually towed far out to sea, beyond sight of land. By the time rescuers spotted the kayak many hours later, the fisherman was exhausted but unbowed and almost had to be physically restrained from continuing to fight the fish.

Shipwreck Beach is one of those rare and special places for which southern Baja is so famous. Rumors abound, however, that this beach will soon be developed as a golf course or major hotel.

Cabo San Lucas: This town's abrupt transformation from isolated fishing camp to high-rolling tourist resort has left it rather ragged around the edges. Cabo can either be fun or frustrating, depending on your needs. If you're looking for world-class marlin fishing, scuba diving, cheap T-shirts, tequila sunrises, a tan, or just plain "fun in the sun," this is the place. Cabo has supermarkets, laundromats, car parts, and other services, but if you're pinching pesos look elsewhere.

Free Camping: With waterfront lots selling for hundreds of thousands of dollars, not much real estate has been overlooked in Cabo. Van and small RV campers can sometimes find free camping, however, near the beach at the Hacienda Hotel, on the east side of the bay. You might also find campsites on dirt roads that weave east toward San Jose del Cabo along the low ridge overlooking the beach. Shortcuts from Mex 1 into this area can be found near the cemetery, two and one-half miles east of Cabo San Lucas.

If you're self-contained and hard up, Cabo tends to be sympathetic to discreet, overnight side street camping. There are several RV campgrounds in and around Cabo San Lucas. Most are on the east side of town, on the highway to San Jose del Cabo.

Cabo San Lucas suffers from a perennial shortage of fresh water, which must be piped in from San Jose del Cabo. Campers who insist on washing their vehicles, clothing, boats, and dogs run the risk of being ''86'ed'' by irate campground managers. A dust-caked RV is the sign of a savvy, desert-wise traveler.

El Arco ($$): Three miles east of Cabo San Lucas, on the east side of Mex 1, this is Cabo's best camping value. Though it isn't on the beach, the park has a good view of the sea. Shade is sparse, but the park is new and the manager assures us that the plants are growing just as fast as they can. A swimming pool is also in the works. In the meantime, there's a large restaurant and a bar with satellite television.

Facilities and Services: There are 60 overnight spaces with full hookups (discount without) and 60 residential spaces, storage for boats and vehicles, clean bathrooms, and showers.

Cabo Cielo RV Park ($$): Two and one-half miles east of Cabo San Lucas on Mex 1, next to the cemetery, this park is small, crowded, and rather stark.

Facilities and Services: There are 22 full hookup sites, no pull-throughs. There is room for caravans without hookups. Tents pay full price. The bathrooms are reasonably clean and have hot showers. Washing and drying clothes is not permitted. Pets must be leashed.

San Vicente RV Park: About two miles east of Cabo on Mex 1, this site is filled by long-term resident campers. Overnighters are only accepted in summertime, as vacancies permit.

Vagabundos del Mar ($$$): Two miles east of Cabo on Mex 1, this park is owned by the travel club of the same name. Although "Sea Gypsies" offers a wide range of services, the campground itself is stark and unappealing. As Steve says, "This is basically a full-service RV parking lot." Vagabundos take their security seriously: there is a no-nonsense fence, a watchman, and a 10:00 p.m. closing. Proving that it takes all kinds, Steve complains, "All this security makes me paranoid. Besides, the campground is expensive." Can he add anything of a positive nature? "Yeah," Steve laughs, "the manager is very nice, and there's an ice machine in the lobby."

Facilities and Services: There are 90 spaces, with 30-amp power and patios. A coin laundry, a pool, drinkable tap water, clean bathrooms, and hot showers are provided. Cable TV connections are coming soon.

El Faro Viejo: On Calle Matamoros, on a low hill just north of downtown Cabo San Lucas, the park sits in a maze of unmarked streets that is impossible to describe. In fact, El Faro Viejo is so hard to find that many people, including return visitors, swear that "The Old Lighthouse" actually exists only a few months out of the year. If this sounds too much like camping in the Twilight Zone, you can steady your nerves in the park's excellent restaurant. El Faro Viejo is known for its tender, aged beefsteaks and delicious seafood grills. Rumor has it that tables are often filled with campers, vacationing Hollywood celebrities, professional ballplayers, and other beautiful, hungry people.

Cabo San Lucas to Todos Santos: Completion of Mex 19 closed the final link in the southern Baja loop. At a sane speed, driving time from Cabo San Lucas to Todos Santos (about 51 miles) is one hour. Considering its proximity to Los

Cabos, the Pacific coastline is still surprisingly empty. One factor is the surf: big and definitely mean, with few beaches protected enough for more than shallow, cautious wading. Surf fishermen and beachcombers should be very careful of waves that can snatch them off steep, soft beaches. (Be watchful of your children!)

After leaving Cabo San Lucas, Mex 19 turns inland for about 15 miles before meeting the Pacific coast. There are excellent opportunities for beach and desert camping, though you'll have to watch carefully for side roads. Keep an eye peeled for newly bulldozed roads, ranch roads, and well-traveled arroyo bottoms. Watch the highway at the same time; traffic tends to be light but fast.

Almost as soon as you turn the corner at Land's End and head north along the Pacific, you'll notice a distinct cooling and an increase in moisture. As deserts go, this one is definitely lush, with dense forests of tall cardon cactus and grotesque elephant trees. It's one of our favorite areas of Baja for early morning and late evening desert walks.

Don't overlook camping in the desert itself. Although roads branching eastward can get very rough by the time they reach the foothills, some are well traveled and passable for several miles or more in standard cars. As these roads climb gently toward the mountains, they offer wonderful views of the Pacific Ocean, as well as good desert camping. As a general rule, the closer you get to the sierra, the tougher the roads become.

Playa Los Cerritos: About 44 miles north of Cabo San Lucas, follow a good dirt road west from Mex 19 to a former government campground on the beach. This park was abandoned, though I've heard rumors that it may be reopened soon. Until then, it makes a fine free campsite. In fact, when I last visited Los Cerritos, there were just two RVs there, parked in solitary splendor.

El Pescadero, about 48 miles north of Cabo, is a small farming town and seasonal surfer's mecca. Narrow dirt lanes lead from the highway to the beach, where you'll find good camping and interesting company. Several side roads go toward the beach between Pescadero and Todos Santos. A new RV park was scheduled to be opened in this area in late 1988; watch for signs or ask for directions in Todos Santos. As you enter Todos Santos from the south, the highway makes a sharp turn to the right. Just south and west of this turn, you'll see a small RV park on a dirt street. It was closed during our last visit, and no information was available.

Todos Santos: This is a small, very attractive farming town blessed with an abundant supply of pure spring water and a Mediterranean climate. You'll find regular gas, two modest supermarkets, and a few other supplies. Todos Santos is a great place to stretch your legs. Admire the town's colonial-style buildings, then take a relaxing walk toward the beach, through cool palm groves, cornfields, and luxuriant mango orchards.

Beach camping is available north of Todos Santos (follow dirt roads through the village and across the fertile valley), but due to extensive farming, ranching, and fencing, access is limited.

Sierra de La Laguna: Todos Santos lies between the Pacific Ocean and the 6,000-foot peaks of the Sierra de La Laguna. This small range of mountains is accessible only by foot or muleback. Trails lead into the sierra but they aren't easy to locate. The best trail begins at Rancho La Burrera, about 18 miles southeast of town. The final few miles of the dirt road into the ranch can be very tricky. Be careful.

The hike up to La Laguna isn't easy, but once you reach the top, you'll find ancient pine and oak forests, grassy meadows, springs, and abundant firewood. Inquire locally in Todos Santos for guides and directions. For an excellent description of these mountains, read *A Desert Country by the Sea* (see Recommended Reading) and *Parks of Northwest Mexico*.

Todos Santos to La Paz: This is a straightforward, one-hour drive; no campgrounds.

Baja Car Ferries

The Mexican government operates large oceangoing vehicle and passenger ferries between ports on the Pacific mainland and the eastern shore of the Baja peninsula. These fast, modern ferries are built in Europe and have an excellent safety record. Subsidies keep the cost of crossing the Sea of Cortez (Gulf of California) very low, even for large RVs. (The charge for a van on the Cabo San Lucas to Puerto Vallarta route was about $30 in late 1988.) Because Baja is such an attractive area for camping, many West Coast travelers enter Mexico via the Transpeninsular Highway, then cross to the mainland by ferry. A quick look at a map shows that this route is a considerable short-cut. That is the good news.

The bad news about the ferry system is that it is now too popular, especially during the busy winter camping season. Delays of a few days are common. One winter, while the ferry was plugged with RV caravans, Lorena and I twiddled our thumbs (on Shipwreck Beach) for almost two weeks before we got aboard at Cabo San Lucas.

Late update: *Mexico West Newsletter* (see Recommended Reading) reports that the Cabo San Lucas to Puerto Vallarta ferry is out of service, perhaps permanently.

Unfortunately, it varies from difficult to impossible to make advance ferry reservations. To complicate matters, the system also suffers from the ''trickle down'' effects of Mexico's faltering economy. Maintenance and cleaning have become lax and major breakdowns—and interruptions in service—plague the fleet. As Steve laments, ''The only thing consistent about the Mexican ferry system is that it isn't consistent.''

Reservations

Theoretically, advance reservations can be made by simply calling ferry offices in Mexico. In reality, it can take days of dialing to make the connection, or just minutes; it's all up to chance. Once the call is completed, the person at the other end of the line may or may not speak English and may or may not accept reservations. In our experience, however, once the reservation is successfully made, it will be honored.

Most people wait until they reach a ferry office in Mexico to make a reservation. You can only make a reservation or buy a ticket on a ferry that leaves from that ferry office's port. In Cabo San Lucas, for example, reservations can be made for the Cabo to Puerto Vallarta crossing, but not for the La Paz to Mazatlán run. If you have a vehicle, it is necessary to make separate reservations for it and for cabin space (see below).

Once a reservation has been made, you may be told to confirm it again in a few days. Though inconvenient, I'd do this even if it isn't mentioned. Standby lists may be available for specific dates and sailings. If you add your name to a standby list, check it regularly.

Accommodations

Ferries have uncomfortable bus-style reclining seats for ''salon'' class passengers as well as cabins on most runs. Cabins come in three types. *Especial* cabins have beds, bath, and sitting room. There are only a few of these and in spite of my best efforts, I've never been able to book a ''Special'' cabin.

A *cabina* has two comfortable bunks, a mini-bathroom

with a mini-shower, and a porthole. Lorena and I have used cabinas on several crossings. We found them cramped but quite adequate.

Turista cabins have no bath, a small sink, and a porthole if you're lucky. Claustrophobes take note: these smaller, below-decks compartments can be hot and stuffy.

Salon class is really steerage with a view. But for sobbing babies, serenading drunks, and an occasional overflowing toilet, it isn't too bad.

It is strictly prohibited to remain in your vehicle during the crossing. In fact, you won't be allowed onto the car deck at all until you've docked on the other side.

Food, Entertainment, and Pets

There are a restaurant and cafeteria on board, but we prefer to take a large picnic box. The food in the ship's restaurant is adequate, but cafeteria fare can be grimly institutional, with runny refried beans and greasy chicken.

Pets must be kept inside your vehicle, on the closed (and locked) car deck. It gets very hot, so a generous, spill-proof supply of drinking water is an absolute necessity. The crossing can be a hardship for pets.

Red Tape

Pay close attention; this is the part that confuses and frustrates many people.

1. Have a validated tourist card for yourself and each of your companions (see chap. 2, Red Tape).

2. With a validated tourist card in hand, get a vehicle importation permit, more commonly called "car papers." Car papers are available at the border, but the officials in Tijuana tend to be cranky and will tell you to get your papers in La Paz. That's fine, because the officials in La Paz are among the most helpful and courteous in all of Mexico. They smile, and they do not ask for bribes.

Unlike their colleagues in La Paz, the officials who issue car papers in Cabo San Lucas never smile and frequently extort bribes. I've complained about this situation for years, but it was still going on at last report. If you must deal with the Cabo San Lucas officials, be sure that all of your documents are in perfect legal order or you could be hassled for a bribe. When in doubt, go to La Paz, which has fewer bureaucratic obstacles and more sailings than all the other ports combined. The La Paz ferry office is in a large government building at the corner of Calle Ejido and Ramirez, on the northeast edge of the city.

3. Go to the ferry office early in the morning and make your reservation. Be prepared to stand in line for hours. Smile often and if you gripe, do it quietly. Ferry workers are undertrained, underpaid, and virtually immune to complaints. If you have a problem, state your case calmly or save it for the local turismo office.

4. Having made and reconfirmed your reservation, return to the ticket office early on the morning your ferry departs to actually purchase the tickets. Separate tickets are sold for vehicles and passengers. Rates are based on the length of a vehicle (in meters). Measure your vehicle bumper to bumper (including racks), and divide the length in feet by 3.24 to get the length in meters. Make a note of this figure. Don't fudge. Be prepared, in fact, to submit your vehicle to an immediate remeasuring at the ticket office.

5. Get in line at the ferry terminal several hours before departure. "Wait and bake" is the routine, so bring lunch and a fresh book. Sometime before boarding, customs officials will give tourist vehicles a cursory inspection. Because Baja has free-trade status, Mexican visitors are checked closely for contraband VCRs and other dutiable goodies they may be taking back to the mainland.

6. Drive aboard the ferry. Passengers: walk aboard, tickets in hand, carrying any luggage you might need. Drivers: expect tight, shoehorn-style parking. Set the hand

brake, apologize to the dog, and lock up. To reach the passenger deck, you'll probably have to exit the ferry against traffic and reboard via the passenger gangplank, with your ticket. If you have a cabin, stewards will show you the way. Everyone else races for a seat in the main salon.

7. Smile; you actually did it!

CHAPTER 9

Pacific Coast

For many people, the "Mexican Riviera" embodies everything that makes camping in Mexico so great, from palm-lined beaches, tropical sunsets, and offbeat fishing villages to cheap prices, easy access, and near-perfect weather. For years, the Pacific coast has attracted winter campers from all over the United States and Canada. It is no wonder that this area offers the best selection of RV parks and campgrounds in the country.

Whenever I'm dismayed by the "progress" of the past 20 years, I just remind myself that cities such as Guayma, Mazatlán, Ixtapa, and Acapulco are just minor intrusions on this 2,000-mile coastline.

Much of the region remains off the beaten track. Travelers who are willing to explore side roads and lesser known beaches will find countless opportunities to experience Mexico's timeless backcountry. Now that the final portion of Mex 15 has been completed along western Michoacán, almost all of Mexico's west coast is accessible to RV and vehicle campers. From Puerto Penasco south to Puerto Angel, this coast shelters innumerable winter colonies of RVers, fishermen, divers, and miscellaneous beach lizards.

The narrow Pacific lowlands are closely bounded to the east by a barrier of steep, deeply furrowed mountains. Once you reach Highway 15, though, the coastal route is surprisingly free of mountains and curves. Other than a few minor mountains and moderate switchbacks, by Mexican standards, this highway is relatively tame.

Note: Though your map may not show it, the highway has been paved along the Oaxaca coast from Pochutla to Salina Cruz. This is a good road, with only a couple of hours of curves south of Puerto Angel.

One of the Pacific coast's main attractions is the relative stability of its weather. I divide the region into three climate zones. (1) North of Mazatlán you're actually on the Sea of Cortez, not the Pacific Ocean. As in Baja, the climate is extremely dry. Temperatures can be cool in winter and blazing hot in summer. The heat tends to moderate in late October. This area attracts a large number of snowbird campers from the American Southwest. (2) Mazatlán to Manzanillo: In my opinion, the coastal ''midriff'' has Mexico's best winter weather—in the high 70s and 80s during the day, cooling to the high 50s and 60s at night. Though occasional storms may pass through during January and February, this deliciously temperate weather pattern dominates from November through May. (3) Ixtapa-Zihuatenejo to Tapachula: Warmer and more humid than the midriff. Winter camping is ideal, especially if you peel down to a bathing suit or shorts. By May, however, the heat packs a wallop.

The Pacific coast attracts more campers than any other region of Mexico. Although traffic near the border can be heavy, occasional sections of four-lane road between Nogales and Culiacán make this drive easier every year. Bypasses have also been built around virtually every major city.

Travelers coming from California or the American Southwest can cross into Mexico at several points between Tijuana and Nogales. Unless you'd like to visit Tijuana or drop down to San Felipe at the head of the Sea of Cortez, you

can save time by driving east on US 8 from San Diego, then turning south toward the border at Gila Bend or Tucson.

From the border crossing at Nogales, it is a relatively short drive to Hermosillo (172 miles), Guaymas (256 miles), and Mazatlán (743 miles). Another popular option is to cross from Baja to the mainland by car ferry (see chap. 8).

Although the main coastal highways, Mex 15 and Mex 200, are relatively straight and level, the mountains bordering the Pacific coast create a formidable barrier to east-west travel. There are only a few highways through the Sierra Madre. The most notorious, Mex 40 from Durango to Mazatlán, is an intimidating, brake-scorching series of hairpin curves, switchbacks, and steep grades that most drivers prefer to avoid. I've done this route in vans, but only very confident drivers with excellent brakes should attempt Mex 40 in large rigs. Get an early start, and plan on spending most of the day behind the wheel.

Our favorite route between central Mexico and the coast is via Mex 110, on the slower but quite scenic route from Guadalajara southwest to Jiquilpan and then west to Colim. This highway has been greatly improved in recent years and offers quick, convenient access to the beautiful highlands of Jalisco and Michoacán. It also can be used as a scenic route to Mexico City.

In this section of the directory, we'll explore the Pacific beaches from Mazatlán to Salina Cruz, Oaxaca. This route parallels two other major regions. From north to south, these are the central highlands and Oaxaca and Chiapas.

Mazatlán, Sinaloa: For many American and Canadian RVers, Mexico is synonymous with Mazatlán and beaches. In fact, Mazatlán's RV parks are often dominated by resident campers and repeat visitors. There are several reasons for this: Mazatlán is the northernmost of the "Mexican Riviera" beach resorts, with generally excellent winter and spring-time weather. Highway connections and driving conditions from the U.S. border are improving every year. Mazatlán's ferry connections to La Paz also make it a gateway to the Baja peninsula, a popular route for campers traveling to and from the west coast of the United States.

Although Mazatlán is a tourist-oriented city, most visitors find it satisfyingly Mexican in flavor, atmosphere, and customs. Add good fishing, sunbathing, and reasonable prices, and it's no wonder that Mazatlán attracts so much attention.

Free Camping: Unfortunately, we don't know of any good free camping areas close to Mazatlán. Former camping beaches north of town are now the *Zona Dorada* (Golden Zone) of hotels, restaurants, and condos. As with camping in any urban area, it pays to mind your "p's and q's." Cruisers and predatory cops can take the fun out of free camping near resort towns. For peace of mind, your best bet is to snuggle up with other campers or find a regular campground.

RV Parks: With over a dozen campgrounds to choose from, Steve dubbed Mazatlán ''Trailer Park City.'' Because of the town's popularity, most of these parks are crowded in winter. Many are booked in advance by caravans and regular customers. One, Las Canoas, is a private, members-only park.

All of the campgrounds are located to the north, along a broad boulevard that skirts Mazatlán's best beaches and sun-worshiping Golden Zone. We'll begin at Camaron Circle, a *glorieta* (traffic circle) about 2.5 miles north of downtown. Be aware that this boulevard changes names several times. Just north of the glorieta it is called Sabalo.

La Posta Trailer Park ($$$): This park is at Avenida Buelina #7, near the Pemex station about one block east (inland) of Camaron Circle. A pleasant, older park, it suffers from being located in a noisy, congested area. If you'd like to be close to Mazatlán's ''action,'' however, or are just passing through, La Posta is worth a look. The park is attractively landscaped and convenient to the huge Comercial Mexicana shopping center.

Facilities and Services: There are 165 spaces with hookups but no tent sites. There is access for big rigs. Facilities include bathrooms, showers, and a swimming pool. Insurance is available.

Mar Rosa Trailer Park ($$$): One and a half miles north of Camaron Circle on Sabalo (Tarpon) Boulevard. The palm-shaded Mar Rosa has a fine, beachfront location and adequate services. Its main disadvantage is crowding. The park has a large population of resident campers, especially during the high season. The overnight sites lack elbow room and are too close together for comfort or privacy.

Facilities and Services: There are 68 spaces, most with full hookups. Access is provided for rigs up to 35 feet. There are some tent sites and long-distance international telephone service.

Playa Escondida (Holiday) Trailer Park ($$): Four miles north of Camaron Circle on Sabalo Boulevard, this park is our long-time favorite in Mazatlán. Everything about it is authentically Mexican, including the confusing name. Though "officially" known as Holiday Trailer Park, a Mexican tourist guide lists it as "Holly Day," and signs say "Playa Escondida Bungalows and Trailer Park."

Hammock swingers take note: by whatever name, this is the place to kick off your shoes and relax on the sand beneath a coconut palm. Unlike some parking lot-style campgrounds, Playa Escondida's spacious grounds feel like a genuine "park": casual, comfortable, and "homey." Though the campground isn't right on the water, the beach is within easy walking distance. There is also a large, refreshing pool and plenty of shade.

A helpful Canadian who winters at Playa Escondida every year in his pickup camper considers Playa Escondido's location a benefit. He points out that being back from the beach protects the camp from stiff, salty sea breezes, which, in turn, significantly reduces corrosion on his rig. Without so much wind "it's a heck of a lot easier to rig my sun awning," he adds.

Facilities and Rates: There are 200 sites, and a discount is offered if you do not need hookups and for tent camping. Though the showers are slightly brackish and not very hot, they're clean and plentiful. Laundromat and do-it-yourself wash stands with lines for drying are available. There is a volleyball court, some groceries, insurance, and bungalow rentals. Note: early gate closing time, 8:00 p.m.

Mazatlán to San Blas (182 miles): Highway 15 skirts the eastern edge of a vast system of mangrove swamps, savannahs, saltwater lagoons, coconut plantations, and seemingly endless miles of broad, ocean beaches. Campers will find several reasonably good access roads from Mex 15 to the Pacific coast. This area is heaven for bird-watchers, fishermen, beachcombers and bug-slappers. The mosquitoes and no-see-ums aren't always bad here—but when they are, be prepared. The local people are quite friendly, prices are cheap, and tourists are few and far between.

We once camped for several days in a coco plantation at Playa El Novillero. Our most frequent visitors were semiwild burros foraging for handouts. Local kids helped us capture a few of these rambunctious beasts for an impromptu "burro busting" rodeo that left me hobbling for days.

The traffic in heavy trucks and stinking buses can be very heavy on Mex 15, so take your time. The slowest stretch is south of San Blas, where the road climbs into the mountains to Tepic. Unless you're pressed for time or driving a large rig, I'd take the longer, slower, more scenic coastal route via San Blas and Santa Cruz.

Just north of Acaponeta, you'll cross from Sinaloa into the state of Nayarit. Nayarit is lusher than states to the north and south, and though clear-cutting has reduced its forests, you can still find some very impressive jungle in this area.

San Blas, Nayarit: This small, attractive beach town has a long-time reputation for excellent surfing and bird-watching and absolutely awful no-see-ums. Steve points out, "We can probably thank the bugs for the fact that San Blas hasn't changed that much since we first visited it in the 60s. I'm learning to enjoy scratching."

Next to surfing, San Blas is best known for its fascinating boat trips into the bayous and jungles. Fishing is excellent.

Trailer Park Los Cocos ($): Turn left on the west side of the plaza in San Blas. Follow Batallón de San Blas Street south (toward the beach) for several blocks to the campground. This friendly, well-managed park has roomy, palm-shaded lawns and a good view of the beach, just a few minutes walk. The water is rather shallow for surf casting, but offshore fishing is good. Surfers assure me that the waves here are often "bitchin!" (I retired from the sport after my first attempt on a homemade board launched me into the midst of an extended Mexican family taking a Sunday swim. My runaway board nearly decapitated the elderly grandmother.)

Los Cocos probably owes its unusually low rates to local vampires. As mentioned earlier, San Blas' bloodthirsty jejenes and mosquitoes are lurking behind every bush, waiting for the "evening bite." When the sun is low, wear plenty of clothing and douse yourself liberally with *Autan* repellent, a Mexican product that supposedly stops no-see-ums.

Facilities and Services: There are 100 spaces and tent sites, hookups, and access for big rigs and pull-throughs. Especially nice bathrooms with very hot showers, a restaurant, and a bar are available. There is a laundromat next door and beach restaurants a short walk away.

San Blas to Santa Cruz: The road follows the ocean, giving views of beaches and coconut plantations. There are opportunities to camp, as well as a new trailer park at the village of Playa Los Cocos. A friend says the park is "cheap, with a very nice location."

Shortly before reaching the village of Santa Cruz, the road turns inland and winds slowly to Tepic, about 30 miles away. The highway has many curves and tight switchbacks, so take your time.

Tepic, Nayarit (altitude 3,000 ft.): Steve advises, "Don't miss the state museum. It displays some of the finest pre-Columbian ceramics I've ever seen. The museum is downtown, on the main street leading to the plaza."

Motel and Trailer Park Los Pinos ($): This park is located in the suburbs, 1.5 miles south of downtown Tepic, on the west side of Mex 200 to Puerto Vallarta. Pine trees shade this comfortable and unusually quiet park. The manager is friendly and very proud of the campground's tasty drinking water. "It is so good," she says, "that people from Mexico City take it back with them in jugs." They could also use some of Tepic's clean mountain air.

Los Pinos is an exceptional value, both for camping and motel rooms. Bungalows large enough for four people, including stove and refrigerator, aren't much more than campsites. Steve isn't the first traveler to consider taking an extended rest here. Ironically, tourists bound from one beach to the next rarely give Tepic more than a cursory visit. If you're searching for an off-the-beaten track hideaway or a place to practice Spanish, Los Pinos is worth a close look.

Facilities and Services: There are 22 sites with hookups, clean bathrooms, and hot showers, and public bus service. Shopping and other services are available in nearby Tepic. The park takes caravans and offers vehicle storage.

Linda Vista: Next to Los Pinos, this is a small, pleasant park, but we prefer the former.

Kampamento Cora (Kora) ($$$): Cora is off Mex 15 in an industrial/warehouse area. Your best bet is to look for signs, ask locally for directions or thumb the *seccion amarilla* (Yellow Pages). The Cora (sometimes called a KOA) is notoriously difficult to locate. Steve reports, "It is so hard to find that once we found it we couldn't bear to leave, even though it cost too much."

Tepic to Puerto Vallarta (105 miles): Once Mex 200 rejoins the coast, you'll have several RV parks and free camping areas to choose from. Before you charge ahead, keep in mind that Puerto Vallarta's growth has limited camping there. Rather than hurry south, I'd review the listings that follow very carefully. Beaches between Tepic and Puerto Vallarta are much cleaner, prettier, and less trampled than Puerto Vallarta's.

La Penita RV Park ($$$): Fifty-four miles south of Tepic, at Km 90 on Mex 200, just north of the village of Jaltemba, "The Little Peak" campground is appropriately situated on a hilltop with a very good view of the Pacific Ocean. In addition to full services, there is access to the beach. Steve says it is "a pleasant enough place, but it seems overpriced for not being on the beach."

Rincón de Guayabitos: This is a small beach resort just a couple of hours north of Puerto Vallarta on Mex 200. In spite of its proximity to "Pee Vee," Rincón de Guayabitos is known to relatively few travelers. Most of its visitors are Mexicans or gringos looking for peace, quiet, and budget prices.

Rincón is actually two parts: the village of La Penita de Jaltemba, with its modest shops, fruit stands, seafood restaurants, ice plant, and gas station, and just a few miles south, Rincón de Guayabitos, a planned community-style resort of bungalows, villas, trailer parks, and small hotels.

There are several small attractive RV parks in Rincón de Guayabitos, but overnighters won't find an abundance of spaces during the winter high season. For better or worse, most parks here are occupied by clannish resident campers. Jealous snowbirds have been known to duel with barbecue forks for choice beachfront sites, and many are reserved years ahead.

Steve reports that *El Dorado RV Park* was crowded in January, and the *Tropico Cabana* was jammed with resident campers, as was the *Villanueva*. We've camped in Rincón several times, and though our fellow campers were friendly enough, we clearly didn't belong to the "club." (Maybe it was our rig—a severely dented Chevy van with a homemade roof rack.) More than anything, Lorena and I enjoy Rincón's beautiful beach, snorkeling, and opportunities to meet Mexicans.

Rather than choose a park in advance which may already be filled, my advice is to slowly cruise Rincón de Guayabitos' streets until you find a place that appeals to you.

Delia's Trailer Park ($): This park is at the southern end of Rincón de Guayabitos. (From Mex 200, turn west at Km 94 near the Pemex station, then turn south on Avenida Sol Nuevo. It is about 2 km.) Delia's is by no means the fanciest park around, but in some ways that is its advantage. The grounds are slightly run down and the shower isn't hot, but the campground is rarely crowded. Also, the beach is close, the manager is very friendly, and the overnight rate is the best you'll find in Rincón. In fact, Delia's monthly rates are so low that judging from the suntans and smiles on several resident campers' faces, this pleasantly funky campground is just what they were looking for.

Facilities and Services: There are 16 spaces with water and power; no sewer. Access for big rigs is tight but possible. There are no tent sites. Facilities are one fairly clean bathroom and shower. A small store is nearby.

Lo de Marcos: This village is 64½ miles south of Tepic, 7.5 miles south of Rincón de Guayabitos, and 37 miles north of Puerto Vallarta. Everything about this small fishing village is picturesque, from its name (That of Marcos) to its palm-fringed beaches and whitewashed walls. Lo de Marcos is about a mile west of Mex 200.

Bungalows y Trailer Park El Caracol ($$$): Turn west at the sign for Lo de Marcos (about Km 108). Continue just over a mile to the church, then turn south and go about half a mile. The park is on a beach at the edge of town.

Although this park is on the high end of Steve's budget, he thinks El Caracol is worth it. ''The beach location is a knockout!'' he says. ''This park is exceptionally well maintained and landscaped,'' Steve adds, ''and very clean, comfortable, and attractive. You can launch a boat from the beach, and the fishing is good. I can easily imagine spending three months here.'' Hinting that he may need a long rest after this book is completed, Steve points out that the rates drop substantially for 90-day visits. Bungalows are also available.

Facilities and Services: There are 22 spaces with full hookups. Access for big rigs is rather tight, and no pull-throughs are possible. Tent sites are available. The bathrooms and showers are very clean. Laundry washstand and lines, filtered drinking water, and a fish cleaning area are offered. The gate closes at 10:00 p.m.; blow your horn if you're late.

El Pequeño Paraiso RV Park: Also in Lo de Marcos. Not visited.

Sayulita: Seventy-four miles south of Tepic, this is yet another small, picturesque fishing village on a beautiful beach. This is what camping in Mexico is all about!

Trailer Park Sayulita ($$): Approximately 9 miles north of Bucerias, turn west off Mex 200 (watch for a small trailer park sign on the highway). Go almost two miles, then turn north (right) on Adriana Street. Follow it to the end. The park entrance is in a stone wall on your left.

This small, very well kept campground is another of Steve's favorite hideouts. The park is located on an excellent, safe swimming beach. Small boats can be launched and fishing is good. The village stores and restaurants are only a five-minute walk away.

Facilities and Services: Facilities include 24 spaces with full hookups and access for 34-foot rigs but no pull-throughs. There are tent sites with shade. Very clean bathrooms, hot showers, do-it-yourself laundry tubs and lines, and Ping-Pong are available. Of special note is the camp's filtered tap water.

The Sayulita, a numberless road, cuts southward across the hills to Punta Mita. This is a very scenic drive through dense, hilly jungle. Watch for parrots, snakes, and killer chuckholes. The road was once fully paved, but because of seasonal washouts and ragtag repairs, it can be very tough on large and low-clearance vehicles.

Punta Mita: A few miles north of Bucerias, a road goes west from Mex 200 to Punta Mita (12 miles). Beaches along this side road are a favorite for picnics, fishing, snorkeling, and surfing. Unless you're willing to take a few lumps, however, it's best to be cautious while playing in the waves. The surf isn't huge here, but its tricky ''break'' can cause painful wipeouts.

Punta Mita itself is a collection of laid-back seafood restaurants and beautiful beaches. This area gets a lot of visitors from Puerto Vallarta, especially on weekends, so keep a close eye on your gear. If you're planning to overnight, look for other campers. The Punta Mita area has an unfortunate reputation for thefts.

Las Marietas islets, just offshore, can be reached by hiring a local *panga*. They have no shade or water, but the camping, diving, and fishing on the islands can be very good.

Bucerias: Eighty-four and a half miles south of Tepic on Mex 200, this small but sprawling village on Banderas Bay is really a bedroom community of Puerto Vallarta. The beaches are better than PV's and so are the prices, especially for meals and lodging. Bucerias and other outlying villages along Banderas Bay are known for their excellent, economical seafood.

Bucerias RV Park ($$$): At the south end of Bucerias, turn west on unmarked streets toward the beach. Watch for trailer park signs or just explore; there isn't much here, so you shouldn't be lost for long.

Believe it or not, Elizabeth Taylor almost slept here. In fact, this lovely, palm-shaded property was once owned by Ms. Taylor herself. Fortunately for the rest of us, the actress's would-be retreat is now a pleasant campground.

This is a well-managed park with all services, including a restaurant and a very popular bar. The park is small and undoubtedly fills up during the high season. During my last visit, rooms were being added. Liz has good taste; compared to Puerto Vallarta's hustle and bustle, the Bucerias RV Park is downright peaceful.

Time Zone Change: As you drive south across the Rio Ameca toll bridge, you'll enter the state of Jalisco. The time zone changes here from Mountain to Central. Advance your watch one hour. (Mexico has no daylight savings time, only year-round standard time.)

Puerto Vallarta: "Pee Vee" is one of Mexico's fastest-growing resort cities, with a population of more than a quarter of a million. On an average winter day, something like 80,000 foreign tourists will crowd the town and nearby beaches, catching a few rays. You'll find discos, parasailing, boutiques, high-rise hotels, and enough margaritas to float a cruise ship—but only two RV parks.

Free camping in Puerto Vallarta has gone the way of bulldozers and development. South of town several miles, Mismaloya Beach was a favorite camping area. I visited Mismaloya recently and found a single diehard gringo pickup camper squeezed between the shell of a new hotel and a crew operating jackhammers.

Tacho's Trailer Park ($$): On the north end of Puerto Vallarta. The turnoff to the east (inland) from Mex 200 is across from the big ferry terminal and marina. Look for signs. Before PV was discovered, Tacho's Trailer Park was in a pleasant, rural setting. With the "Golden Zone" extending its embrace toward the airport, however, the campground now finds itself surrounded by progress. No matter, because once you enter this park you might well ask, "Tacho, is this really Mexico or are we suddenly back in Kansas?"

Though I personally prefer starry skies to satellite television and Mother Nature to microwave ovens, this park is very popular with RVers. In fact, some guests swear that Tacho's paved lanes, sidewalks, trimmed lawns, and street lights are the next-best thing to camping in suburbia.

Facilities and Services: There are 155 sites with everything, including a community sink. There is excellent access for big rigs. A store, laundry, pool, and games are available. There is bus service to town, a genuine blessing if you've ever locked bumpers in PV's narrow streets.

Puerto Vallarta Trailer Park ($$): At Calle Francia #143, Colonia Versailles, in northern Puerto Vallarta, the park is east of Mex 200 (known here as Avenida Mexico), between Tacho's and downtown. Turn east at the hotel Suites del Mar.

Thanks to a busy gardener, this park is a pleasant, shaded refuge in an otherwise undistinguished setting. This is "town camping," Puerto Vallarta style. Once you leave the park, you'll have lots of traffic, hotel construction, and miscellaneous Mexican sound effects to keep you on your toes. Still, the trailer park is only a five-minute walk from the beach, and there is ridiculously cheap and entertaining bus service into town. The park is also convenient to supermarkets, restaurants, and shopping malls. Considering the bargain price, Steve rates Puerto Vallarta Trailer Park as his first choice.

Facilities and Services: There are 70 sites with all hookups but no pull-throughs and limited maneuvering room. Reasonably clean bathrooms and hot showers, an automatic laundry, and telephone service are offered.

Puerto Vallarta Bypass: To put it bluntly, Puerto Vallarta's northern suburbs are a mess. Traffic is dense and confusing and the bypass is poorly marked. It you're going south on Mex 200, you'll pass the airport, the ferry terminal, and then several high-rise hotels. At a busy intersection *north* of the gas station, the road makes a "Y." The bypass is toward the east; straight ahead is downtown.

Regular leaded gas is available 59 miles south of Puerto Vallarta and also in Chamela.

Chamela, Jalisco: This small resort community is 85 miles south of Puerto Vallarta and Melaque, roughly midway between PV and Manzanillo, on Mex 200. Chamela is a friendly village with a sparsely developed coastline of beautiful beaches and rugged headlands. Other than a Club Med resort tucked secretively into a cove to the south, there isn't much to Chamela. After observing its ups and downs for years, we concluded (happily) that the area is too far from the "action" to attract many tourists. Rumors abound that Chamela will one day be discovered, yet in some respects, tourist services (such as its sadly stocked supermarket) have actually gone downhill. But Chamela remains an excellent area for relaxed camping, fishing, and exploring rural Mexico. There is a bank and long-distance phone service in the supermarket.

Free camping is difficult on Chamela Bay because of limited access. North of Chamela, at mile 83 from Puerto Vallarta, a turnoff leads west to Ejido La Fortuna, a small collection of modest restaurants in a protected corner of the bay. La Fortuna is a good spot to eat seafood, buy fresh fish, or launch a small boat. Chamela's beaches are open to the Pacific and can be very tricky for swimming and boating.

Villa Polinesia and Camping Club ($$): Turn west at Chamela's combination supermarket, bank, and long-distance telephone office. Follow a gravel road half a mile to the campground. Villa Polinesia has a fine beachfront location, but the surf is often intimidating. Though the sea is sometimes relatively calm, conditions change rapidly. A quick, powerful "shore break" can make swimming, boat launching, and body surfing difficult to dangerous. Fortunately, the campground is building a swimming pool. For the time being, guests have the use of a pool in an adjoining property. The manager, Señor Aguilar, is enthusiastic and quite attentive. He was quick to point out that Villa Polinesia is very family oriented. "We cannot tolerate drunks or other disturbances." There are plans for a playground. The campground itself is small and very clean. Campsites have thatched ramadas, and three-prong electrical outlets are being installed.

Unlike many RV parks, Villa Polinesia welcomes tent camping at a very low fee. For tentless campers, there are odd little tentlike cabanas. A large house next to the park can be rented for groups of up to 15 persons at a very economical rate.

It's a beautiful, two-mile beach hike from Villa Polinesia to La Fortuna, at the north end of the bay. I ate a wonderful lunch here, a red snapper taken fresh from the boat and grilled over sizzling hardwood coals.

Facilities and Services: There are 16 spaces with full hookups and 8 tent sites. The bathrooms and hot showers are very clean. Ping-Pong tables are available. A restaurant is in the works.

Chamela to Barra de Navidad: Mex 200 cuts through steep, hilly country covered by low, deciduous jungle. The shore is rugged, and there are few access roads to the beach. Most side roads lead to private property where camping is not allowed. Because of deep arroyos, mudholes, and uncertain conditions, larger vehicles should stick to the pavement and most-traveled dirt roads.

Free camping is hit-or-miss, but when you find a place that's good, it'll be worth the effort. Supplies are very scarce, so carry food, fuel, water, and bug protection. The mosquitoes can be fierce, even in the dry season. Still, this is one of Mexico's most beautiful seacoasts and well worth exploring.

Plaza Careyes and the Club Med turnoff are at mile 98 south of Puerto Vallarta.

El Tecuan ($$): South of Puerto Vallarta at mile 110, look for a lighthouse sign on the highway. Several miles of narrow, twisting paved road bring you into the hotel and campground.

El Tecuan is typical of beaches in the area: broad, steep, and exposed to the full force of Pacific waves. Take my word for it: this is no place for weak swimmers or novice body surfers. After a couple of near-fatal encounters with surf along this coast, I now confine my swimming to the most protected waters.

El Tecuan has a small beachfront campground with basic services but no RV hookups. Horses can be rented, and local fishermen are usually willing to strike a bargain on fishing, diving, and birding trips. My favorite spot is El Tecuan's lagoon, both for swimming, bird watching, fishing, and catching crabs. Steve and I were bathing here one day when he suddenly came out of the water like a Trident missile. Sure enough, a large crab had pinched an impressive hole in his big toe.

There is an airstrip and a hotel at El Tecuan.

Boca de Iguanas ($$): This campground is 120 miles south of Puerto Vallarta and 10 miles north of Melaque on Mex 200. There is a sign. Follow a rough but quite passable dirt road about one mile to the beach.

On a coastline renowned for its natural beauty, Bahia de Los Angeles stands out as one of Mexico's most eye-catching bays. Within the bay, the palm-lined beach at Boca de Iguanas fulfills most travelers' expectations of a tropical paradise. The smooth, sandy shore is not only clean and inviting but offers near-perfect conditions for swimming, sailboarding, boating, and fishing.

Although the manager admitted that this park enjoys a presunset "happy hour of mosquitoes and no-see-ums," insects are not a particular problem. The sunsets at Boca de Iguanas aren't bad either.

Facilities and Services: There are 45 spaces with hookups, some sewers, and dump station. There are no pullthroughs and access for big rigs is tight. Tent sites are available. There are clean bathrooms but no hot water. A hand laundry service and do-it-yourself sink, a small store with drinking water, and a restaurant are on site.

Melaque/San Patricio: About 34 miles south of Chamela, Mex 200 meets the Pacific Ocean at the sister villages of Melaque and San Patricio. Even long-time visitors can't tell the difference between these friendly, Siamese-twin beach towns. In fact, San Patricio refers to the commercial, "downtown" area, whereas Melaque is the northern, resort portion of the town. Whatever you call it, San Patricio/Melaque is a convenient place to shop for pineapples, fresh-baked bread, and other staples. The town also has well-stocked hardware stores, shade tree mechanics, a reliable post office, gasoline, a bank, phones, and other basic services. I usually reward myself for doing errands by enjoying a long seafood lunch in one of the town's thatched-roof restaurants.

Melaque is a favorite weekend and holiday retreat for Mexican families from Guadalajara. If you'd like to take a room rather than camping, there is a broad selection of budget accommodations.

Free Camping: At the north end of the beach in Melaque, you'll find an informal, amiable community of RV and van campers. There are restaurants on the beach, but otherwise you're on your own, with no services or hookups.

Trailer Park Playa ($): In San Patricio, right on the beach, at the end of the main street. I agree wholeheartedly with Steve's bemused comment that "this park is obviously popular because it's always crowded, but for the life of me I don't know why."

In fact, this stark, shadeless campground is often packed rig-to-rig with resident campers. Overnight spaces are also quite limited. The manager assured Steve, however, that he can usually find room for another vehicle. Sure enough, Steve found himself parked so close to the bathroom that other campers were asking him to pass the soap.

On the positive side, Trailer Park Playa is very cheap and convenient to shopping and restaurants. It also has good security. "The gates close at 7:30 p.m.," Steve says, "so it must not attract the swinging crowd."

Facilities and Services: There are 45 spaces with full hookups. Access is tight, but possible for big rigs. There are some tent sites. The reasonably clean bathrooms and showers have no hot water. At 25 cents per person for nonguests, the showers here attract a devoted following of out-of-town campers.

Barra de Navidad: About four miles south of Melaque, this beach town was once a major hangout for surfers, hippies, backpackers, van vagabonds, and other chronic, low-budget travelers. For better or worse, "Barra" is now being groomed for a more affluent crowd. Fortunately, the changes are coming slowly, and the town retains much of its original personality and quirky charm, which includes several excellent seafood restaurants, an interesting lagoon, good sportfishing, and lots of budget hotels. Barra is also known for its surfing, sunbathing and vigorous nightlife. Considering its size, the town has more than enough cantinas, bars, discos, mariachis, and beer agencies.

Free Camping: All the way through town, at the far end of the beach. Campers of all types have been using the south end of the barra (sand bar) for many years. You'll find an interesting winter colony here of surfers, RVers, van campers, and backpackers. Privacy is limited, but the sunsets, conversation, and people-watching are great.

Barra de Navidad to Manzanillo (40 miles): Traffic can be fast and heavy along this stretch, particularly on weekends. Few roads lead to the coast, but one of the best branches off to Playa del Oro. About 19 miles south of Melaque, follow a cobblestone road several miles to a long, open beach. There is free camping, but the surf is hazardous and so are the mosquitoes, especially at dawn and dusk.

Manzanillo: An important commercial port that is doing its best to polish its image as a tourist resort. In many respects, Manzanillo is a ''poor man's Acapulco,'' a busy seaport with a long maritime history. From a developer's standpoint, Manzanillo suffers from a lack of photogenic beaches close to town. Most of the tourist action is to the north, at Las Brisas, Las Hadas, Santiago, and other postcard-perfect beaches.

RV Parks: As of this writing, the RV park and camping situation in Manzanillo isn't just limited, it's downright tragic. *Don Felipe's Trailer Park* at La Audiencia beach, a perennial ''Gringo Trail'' favorite, has been gobbled up by creeping condos. *Sunset Gardens* trailer park is also being converted to condominiums. Steve made a final, sentimental visit and found the caretaker on the verge of tears at the thought of losing his job after 23 years in the park. Long-time resident campers weren't too happy, either. Wishful rumors that Sunset Gardens would move to another location couldn't be confirmed.

Miguelito's ($$$): Continue south toward Las Brisas at a major intersection about 5 miles north of Manzanillo. Go just over a mile to the end of the road in Las Brisas. According to Steve, Miguelito's is the only place even resembling a campground in Manzanilllo. This park is run-down and unfenced and sits across the street from a noisy, exhaust-choked city bus turnaround. "On top of that," Steve says, "Miguelito's is expensive. I'd rather camp on the street, which we did." Facilities and Services: There are 13 full hookup spaces, with good access for large rigs. The park has a pool and some shade and is close to the beach.

Manzanillo to Tecomán (35 miles): Mex 200 skirts the eastern shore of a vast, shallow lagoon. There is no camping along this road until you reach Cuyutlán, Boca de Pascuales, and other Pacific beaches. You now have the option of going inland to Colima and the Michoacán highlands or following Mex 200 south from Tecomán to Playa Azul.

Tecomán, Colima to Playa Azul, Michoacán (about 110 miles): This is the final link in Mexico's long-awaited, border-to-border Pacific coast highway. As yet, there is very little traffic and virtually no tourist facilities. Don't expect to find gas stations (top off your tank in Tecomán), supermarkets, RV parks, or towns of any size—just mountains, canyons, small ranches, and mile after mile of undiscovered beaches.

In addition to its spectacular views and roller coaster curves, the Sierra Madre of Michoacán has a reputation for marijuana and opium cultivation. At highway checkpoints, you can expect to meet soldiers and federales inspecting vehicles for drugs and firearms. In fact, antidrug patrols operate throughout the states of Michoacán, Guerrero, and Oaxaca, giving special attention to coastal highways.

You may also hear rumors that the Michoacán coast is "bandit country." Though we've camped in and around this area for years, we've yet to meet with bandits or serious trouble.

We have had several nervous encounters, however, with zealous military patrols and heavily armed federales. It is also true that campesinos in such remote country always carry machetes and knives and sometimes guns—usually small calibre pistols and .22 rifles. In our experience, the people of this coast are honest, friendly, and hospitable but often very shy of strangers. Their contact with the outside world is often limited to portable radios and a rare newspaper.

My advice, in a nutshell, is to avoid drunks, drinking scenes, and drugs, be civil to the soldiers, camp near others, and don't be slow to move along if things feel weird. One additional point: it is strictly prohibited to buy or possess genuine artifacts and archaeological pieces in Mexico. You may be offered such items along this coast. Refuse politely, explaining that it is *prohibido*. If the preceding makes you too nervous to camp in comfort, save the Michoacán coast for a later trip.

Maruata: The village, about 70.5 miles south of the Tecomán junction with Mex 200 and Mex 110, offers sheltered coves and good fishing and diving. Pass through the village of Maruata and cross over the river. At the southern end of the bridge, turn east (inland) and loop back under the bridge, where a rough dirt road leads to the beach, half a mile away. There is a sea turtle research station at Maruata Beach, a pair of thatched restaurants, and a few gringo campers.

You'll find several small beach villages and unmarked dirt roads between Maruata and Playa Azul. We once camped for a month in a coconut plantation north of Chuquiápan. Our visit was not only a major event for the village and local ranchers but on two occasions, the schoolteacher brought the entire student body to chat with us.

Playa Azul: This small, rather nondescript town sits on a large, rather nondescript beach. After exploring the Michoacán coast to the north or Guerrero to the south, however, even Playa Azul's limited shops and services can be quite welcome. (The neighboring steel town of Lazaro Cardenas, 10 miles south, is the area's most important city and commercial center. It has a large supermarket.)

Playa Azul offers the only "official" RV campground between Manzanillo and Zihuatanejo. As more people explore Mexico's scenic Pacific coast highway, facilities for camping should gradually improve. In the meantime, it's either free camping or the Hotel Playa Azul Trailer Park.

Hotel Playa Azul Trailer Park ($): This park is in the backyard of the hotel, in the center of town. The entrance is on Francisco Sarabia, a dirt street. Go into the hotel and ask them to open the gate. The park is fenced and always locked.

This small park shares the hotel's facilities as well as its name. Steve remarks that what this campground lacks in beauty is compensated for by its lovely low price. Though this plain-and-simple establishment might not inspire long-term visits, it is quite adequate for overnight and short layovers. After a hot day on the road, a long, cool dip in the hotel's swimming pool is particularly welcome. The restaurant is also good and inexpensive. Local activities include eating seafood, playing dominoes, and watching the surf pound against the sand.

Facilities and Services: There are 10 spaces (more or less), some with power and sewer. Access is tight, but big rigs can be shoehorned in. One clean bathroom and hot shower serves everyone. There is laundry service in the hotel, a barbecue area, and Ping-Pong.

Playa Azul to Ixtapa-Zihuatanejo (75 miles): You'll have to backtrack from Playa Azul to the highway junction at La Mina. Unfortunately, the highway meets the ocean just once on this drive, at the village of Petacalco, 21 miles south of La Mina. This is a popular surfing spot, which usually means bad news for divers and swimmers. You'll probably meet several military roadblocks in this area. Smile and be patient.

Ixtapa-Zihuatanejo: Ixtapa is a high-rise beach resort that caters almost exclusively to well-heeled American and Canadian tourists. The nearby town of Zihuatanejo is much less expensive and, in my opinion, much more attractive. Zihuatanejo has quite a selection of budget and moderately priced hotels. There are good restaurants, shopping, and nightlife. It is no wonder that many guests at Ixtapa's high-rise hotels spend much of their time exploring Zihuatanejo. "Zihua," or "Zee," also has the best swimming beaches in the area, and day trips can be arranged for snorkeling, scuba diving, and picnicking.

Unfortunately, camping facilities are very limited. Unless you'd like to free camp or attach yourself to a hotel, there's just one RV park we can recommend. It is so expensive, however, that we've made an exception to our usual pricing code.

Hotel Playa Linda RV Park ($$$$): The park is located on the beach north of Ixtapa, at the end of the road. It you're coming south on Mex 200, follow the trailer park signs west.

Playa Linda lives up to its name (Pretty Beach). In fact, there are almost five miles of "pretty beach" here plus a swimming pool, inviting lawns, and shade from coconut palms. For the energetic, there are two tennis courts and basketball. The park's tap water is safe to drink and there is hourly microbus service to Ixtapa. Security includes a chain link fence (on all sides except the beach) and a guard at the gate. Considering these features, the question arises, Where is everybody? Why is Playa Linda virtually empty?

Steve thinks it's the price. "I'd rather find a budget hotel in Zihuatanejo or just park behind a gas station. Playa Linda may be the most expensive RV park in Mexico. He wasn't pleased, either, with the park's camping area: 50 individual sites (with hookups) designated by brightly painted lines on a flat expanse of pavement. "It's just like camping behind Safeway," Steve gripes. "Tent campers actually have to keep off the grass and sleep on the asphalt!"

Is this what Playa Linda's brochure calls "a new concept of recreation and rest"?

Free Camping: Steve camped under the palms, next to a small restaurant, just a stone's throw north of Playa Linda. In exchange for chatting with the owner and buying a few sodas and a snack, his family had the use of a less-than-immaculate bathroom and a very beautiful beach. Fresh water was available at the "water works" near the entrance to the trailer park.

"We enjoyed ourselves," Steve says, "but there are two possible disadvantages to this place. Every morning and evening someone comes around and sprays the mosquitoes with some noxious smelling substance. We were also told not to leave anything out at night because of thieves. We were careful and didn't have any trouble."

His final assessment of camping in Ixtapa: "If money is no object, Playa Linda is probably your best bet."

Steve wasn't nearly as charitable, however, by the time he left *Playa Ropa Campground* on the south side of Zihuatanejo Bay. The park is on the beach, but it's easy to miss. As Steve reports, missing this campground is probably a wise move. "Playa Ropa Campground is crowded to the point that some people couldn't get in. We camped so close to two converted school buses that we couldn't fully open the doors of our van. Worse yet, the bathrooms are filthy. I hate to say it, but there's also a problem with thieves."

In other words, we can't recommend Playa Ropa Campground.

What's left? The choices come down to free camping, making a temporary arrangement to park on private property, taking a hotel room, or getting out of town entirely and continuing your journey south to Acapulco. Fortunately, there are several free camping beaches between Zihuatanejo and Acapulco. RV parks in Acapulco are also relatively plentiful and attractive.

Zihuatanejo to Acapulco, Guerrero (150 miles): This is an easy, relatively straight-and-level drive with occasional hills. Expect several army checkpoints.

Access to the beach is good along this highway, but much of the coastline is exposed to the full force of the Pacific. There are several lagoon and estuary systems, with excellent birding, boating, and fishing. You should have little trouble finding free camping.

Las Salinas, 31 miles south of Zihuatanejo, is a major salt works. You'll see local kids standing beside the highway selling sacks of sea salt.

Acapulco Bypass: To avoid Acapulco entirely, follow signs east from Mex 200 to Mexico City at an intersection a few miles north of Pie de la Cuesta. There is a second, local bypass around the city as well. Look for a large Pemex station at a major intersection on the northern edge of Acapulco. Turn east on Avenida Cortines and continue over a large hill. At the bottom of the hill, take your choice: east to Mexico City or south on Mex 200 to Pinotepa Nacional.

Acapulco: Though I'm not a great fan of crowded resorts, I'm often surprised to find myself enjoying Acapulco, especially the older parts of town, where inexpensive hotels, restaurants, the market, and small neighborhood shops contribute to a lively, ''real'' Mexican ambiente.

Older beach resorts can usually be depended on to offer good services for RV campers at fair prices. There are several campgrounds from which to choose in the Acapulco area, but Steve's hands-down favorite is Quinta Dora.

Quinta Dora Trailer Park ($): Quinta Dora is about 6 miles north of Acapulco on Highway 200. Turn west toward the beach in the village of Pie de la Cuesta. Dora's is just over a mile down the road, on your right. The name is splashed prominently along a surrounding wall.

Quinta Dora straddles a narrow, palm-shaded sand pit that acts as a natural barrier between the pounding Pacific surf and the Coyuca Lagoon. The park is small, sandy, and attractively planted with shrubs and flowers.

To many travelers, Dora's Trailer Park is both a campground and a home away from home. The welcome usually begins at the gatehouse, where Frances, the park's unofficial hostess, greets new arrivals. Frances has been camping at Dora's for two decades, enjoying the camp's easy living and sunsets as well as painting her canvases. Though she used to drive a van down from New Orleans every year, Frances finally tired of the long haul and decided to fly to Mexico instead. She arrived at the camp with suitcase, paints, and brushes in hand. Dora immediately helped Frances clean the cobwebs and old Fanta bottles out of the gatehouse and set up housekeeping. Now, when Frances isn't "working the gate," she can usually be found in her improvised studio, pondering a canvas.

Among the interesting characters who follow the camping circuit in Mexico, one man merits special recognition. Don is a Florida refugee and long-time Quinta Dora regular. Like Frances, the campground's artist/gatekeeper-in-residence, Don is an energetic fellow who enjoys keeping busy. He also likes to take an occasional cooling dip.

Because of the surf, however, swimming from Dora's ocean beach can be very treacherous. As Don saw it, the solution was obvious: forget the ocean and swim on the other side of the park, in the warm, protected waters of the Laguna Coyuca. Don soon made a painful and frustrating discovery: after years of neglect, the shallow lagoon bottom was a minefield of broken glass and discarded tin cans. Instead of giving up, he decided to do something about it. Recruiting other campers, Don devoted many of his winters to carefully raking and picking junk from the lagoon bottom, gradually creating a pleasant, safe swimming beach. If you visit Dora's, you'll probably hear Don's distinctive voice booming through the palm trees. Don't be surprised if you're asked to volunteer for his latest camp improvement project.

Facilities and Services: There are 23 spaces, with good access for big rigs at most sites. Facilities include reasonably clean bathrooms and unheated showers, a laundry washstand and lines, beach chairs, ramadas, and daily truck delivery of pure water. Small local stores have ice and food, good bus service to Acapulco as available. Dora and her family are very friendly and helpful.

No pets! A sign at the entrance to Dora's also warns local mutts: *Se prohibe la entrada de perros bravos* (Mean dogs not allowed).

Acapulco Trailer Park ($$): On Pie de la Cuesta beach, just before you get to Quinta Dora campground, you'll find Acapulco Trailer Park. Though Steve personally prefers Dora's beachcomber atmosphere and exceptionally low prices, the choice here is pleasantly tough: this Acapulco trailer park is larger than Dora's, well-managed and very clean, and offers good services at very fair prices. Guests at the Acapulco have the use of a swimming pool across the street, at a restaurant owned by the same family. There is also a boat launch and mooring in the lagoon and even a water ski service. The park is well shaded by coconut palms and there are beach ramadas. Security is excellent.

The Acapulco's friendly owner promises ''Tranquil tropical life at surfside.'' Steve says, ''These folks have it covered!''

Facilities and Services: There are 60 spaces, some on the beach, with full hookups and concrete patios. Tent sites as well as inexpensive rooms are available. Bathrooms are very clean, tiled, and furnished with warm showers. There is a store on the premises and a restaurant, bar, and pool across the street. Regular bus service into Acapulco is available. Warning: Swimming in the ocean at Pie de la Cuesta is definitely not recommended. More than a few people have drowned or been seriously injured by this beach's notoriously powerful waves. Even strong swimmers can be viciously battered by crashing surf. No matter how tempting the sea may look, especially after a couple of margaritas, don't take the plunge.

Acapulco to Puerto Escondido (250 miles): The Costa Chica highway (Mex 200) winds between tropical lagoons and soaring mountains, with rare glimpses of Pacific beaches. The temperature ranges from warm to hot, and it is usually quite humid. Like the coastline north of Acapulco, you'll find lush vegetation, extensive lagoons, small villages, unmarked side roads, occasional gas stations, and very few tourist services. Though free camping is available at several beaches along the "Little Coast," there are no RV parks.

For most travelers, this is a straightforward, all-day trip with the usual army checkpoints. Adventurous campers will enjoy endless possibilities for backcountry exploring, but again, this is the real, sometimes "nitty gritty" side of Mexico.

Don't expect to find unleaded gasoline south of Acapulco; only regular is available.

Puerto Escondido, Oaxaca: In the late 1960s and early 1970s, this small fishing village was a favorite hideout for wave-crazed surfers and low-budget, long-haired van campers. Considering the beauty of Oaxaca's beaches, it's not surprising that Puerto Escondido has now sprouted hotels, discos, T-shirt shops and even an international airport. In spite of its growing tourist trade, Puerto Escondido is still small enough to be considered "offbeat" by most travelers. Development of the huge, Cancún-like resort of Huatulco just two hours to the south will undoubtedly speed the "discovery" of Puerto Escondido.

I'm sorry to say that Puerto Escondido also has a persistent reputation for thievery, especially on its most popular public beaches. Campgrounds aren't immune to local *rateros* (thieves) either, so be advised to keep your valuables and loose gear under lock and key or a watchful eye. Puerto Escondido's authorities are aware of the problem but seem unwilling to do much about it. Until they wake up to the fact that thievery hurts the community as much as the visitor, please don't judge the rest of Mexico by this town's standards.

Because of thievery, I cannot recommend free camping in the vicinity of Puerto Escondido. "Downtown" Puerto Escondido has three trailer parks. All tend to be crowded and noisy, especially when the local discos go to full, teeth-rattling power. Steve advises, "If you camp in town, bring earplugs." The security in these campgrounds won't win any public service awards, either. When we're in Puerto Escondido, we head directly to Puerto Escondido Trailer Park.

Puerto Escondido Trailer Park ($$): This park is just north of town, on Carrizalillo Bay. Turn west off Mex 200 at Km 139.5 and take a dirt road half a mile to the park. This spacious campground occupies a high bluff overlooking the Pacific Ocean. Steve has seen most, if not all, of Mexico's west coast and declares the view of sea and shoreline from this park "incredible!"

A path descends from the clifftop to a secluded beach with excellent swimming and snorkeling. If you don't have the energy to tackle the trail, the campground has a very inviting swimming pool. There is also a thatched, palapa-bar with cold drinks. If you need any final inducements, the management is very friendly and offers a 20 percent discount by the month if you pay in advance. Not too surprisingly, Steve intends to take advantage of the offer as soon as possible.

Facilities and Services: There are 149 spaces; 44 with full hookups, 65 with water and power, and 40 others. There are also some tent sites and very clean bathrooms with hot showers. Public bus service to Puerto Escondido can be found at the highway.

Considering Puerto Escondido's lamentable police protection, this park has one final and important attraction: good security, including a fence, a gate, and a toothy guard dog.

Beyond Puerto Escondido: You have two choices. Continue south on Mex 200 to Puerto Angel (mile 50), Huatulco (mile 75), Salina Cruz (mile 110) and eventually to Chiapas, or turn east at Pochutla (near Puerto Angel) and take Mex 175 to the highlands and city of Oaxaca (147 miles).

Mex 175 from Pochutla to Oaxaca is one of Mexico's slowest and most scenic highways. Other than a few seasonal washouts, the road is paved the entire way. It is also quite narrow. The mountainous portion—about 75 miles—has so many tight curves, steep grades, and switchbacks that I allow a full day to reach Oaxaca. Pull-outs are quite rare, but traffic is light.

This route ascends from humid, tropical *tierra caliente* (hot country), through banana and coffee plantations, past tree ferns, waterfalls, and near-vertical cornfields, to moss-draped forests of pine and oak at about 10,000 feet. The highlands are also the home of several interesting but reclusive Indian groups. After making an unforgettable two-week trek through these mountains, we now call them "Poor Man's Nepal."

You can expect occasional fog, rain, and very cool temperatures at higher elevations along this highway in summer and fall. There is often an army checkpoint near the summit at the village of San Jose del Pacifico.

Although a road also crosses the sierra from Puerto Escondido to Oaxaca, it is only partially paved. We once drove this so-called highway in a VW van, but it took two full and very tiring days. Don't attempt this road unless you're looking for an adventure.

RV Parks: Sorry, there aren't any. From Puerto Escondido south to Tuxtla Gutiérrez, Chiapas, and east to Oaxaca, you'll have to rely on motels, hotels, and free camping. Even these can be scarce, so if you see a place that looks inviting, don't pass it up.

Puerto Angel: This is a small fishing village that attracts budget tourists, backpackers, and end-of-the-road campers. Puerto Angel doesn't offer much more than the basics: food, gas, water, sunshine, clean sand, and interesting company. For great free camping, look north of the village.

Huatulco: Oaxaca's Cancún clone is being bulldozed out of a magnificent wilderness coast at this very moment. We've heard rumors that an RV park may be open by now. Future plans call for dozens of hotels, shopping centers, residential areas, and a new trans-sierra highway to the city of Oaxaca. Tourism officials expect two million tourists a year to visit Huatulco by the year 2010. For the moment, Huatulco is an awkward combination of frontier construction camp and fledgling resort. Only one thing is certain: while they last, the beaches are well worth visiting.

Puerto Angel to Tuxtla Gutiérrez, Chiapas (300 miles): This is a long haul through country that is best known for its hot winds.

Salina Cruz, Oaxaca: This small seaport dispenses petroleum to oceangoing tankers. For a Mexican town, it is remarkably unappealing.

Free camping is possible on the ocean beaches west of town. This region suffers, however, from sizzling temperatures, skimpy shade, and too much wind.

If you'll be continuing southward, turn to the Oaxaca and Chiapas section of this directory.

CHAPTER 10

Central (Colonial) Highlands

This is classic Mexico: cacti, burros, red tile roofs, cobblestone streets, and drowsy afternoon siestas. Central Mexico encompasses the country's greatest cities and colonial monuments as well as most of its population. In addition to its cathedrals, Aztec ruins, museums, markets, and crumbling haciendas, this region includes hundreds of hot springs, major peaks and national parks, rivers, volcanoes, caves, and other natural wonders. It would take years to explore Mexico's colonial heartland, and most of it is seldom visited by tourists.

Since all roads lead to Mexico City or Guadalajara, traffic tends to be heavy in this region. Smog, overpopulation, pollution, and urban crime are some of the pains this fast-growing area is experiencing.

Because the majority of its inhabitants are concentrated in large cities, most of the central region has a rustic, rural character. Campers will also find that RV parks in the central highlands are scarcer than they might wish. Fortunately, distances and driving times between campgrounds are not great. In addition, the highlands are dotted with public and private parks, spas, picnic grounds, and other informal campgrounds. Accommodations are a bargain and rates for small town hotels

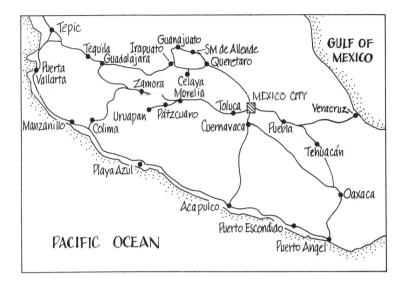

and motels are often competitive with RV parks. Your best strategy will be to find a comfortable place and to use it as a base camp for side trips and sightseeing. Rather than driving everywhere, try local buses and trains. Public transportation is one of Mexico's most inexpensive adventures.

Most of the central region is above 5,000 feet, with peaks soaring to more than 18,000 feet. Between the rain shadows of the heavily forested eastern and western sierras, the central plateaus are dry to arid. There are exceptions, of course, to this pattern of low rainfall: Guadalajara, Uruapán, and Cuernavaca enjoy a moist, semitropical climate that produces abundant and remarkably beautiful vegetation.

Compared to other parts of Mexico, the weather in the central region is relatively stable. Though winter temperatures can be frigid at higher elevations, most of the region is quite moderate year-round. In fact, this is my favorite area of Mexico for summer, rainy-season camping. During the winter months, cool nights and clear, warm days are strongly reminiscent of northern California or the American Southwest.

Driving

There are so many highways in central Mexico that single-sheet road maps can't possibly show every town or secondary road. If you're interested in exploring side roads and taking shortcuts, a Mexican *atlas de carreteras* (road atlas) will be very helpful. My favorite is published by Pemex, the Mexican federal oil company. Gasoline is easily available in the central highlands, but unleaded is found only in large cities and along major highways.

Because the central highlands cover a broad area, our campground descriptions do not follow a neat, north-to-south route. This section can be used as an itinerary or as an overview of the entire region.

If you're driving to central Mexico from El Paso, the fastest routes to Mexico City, Guadalajara, or the state of Michoacán are:

El Paso to Mexico City: Take Mex 45 to Jimenez, then Mex 49 to Torreón and Fresnillo. At Fresnillo, Mex 49 becomes Mex 45 again—take it to Zacatecas, where it changes back to Mex 49. Follow Mex 49 to San Luis Potosí, then take Mex 57 all the way to Mexico City.

El Paso to Guadalajara: Follow the directions above to Zacatecas, then take Mex 54 right to Guadalajara.

El Paso to Morelia, Michoacán: From Zacatecas, take Mex 49 toward San Luis Potosí. About 21 miles east of Zacatecas, turn south on Mex 45 to Aguascalientes, Lagos de Moreno, and Salamanca. At Salamanca, take Mex 43 to Morelia via Yuriria, Morolen, and Cuitzeo.

Eastern Texas to Mexico City: Take Mex 57 via Monterrey. The quickest route to Guadalajara is via Saltillo and Zacatecas on Mex 54. This same route gives quick access to the Pacific coast or the state of Michoacán.

If you're approaching central Mexico from the Pacific coast, you have a choice of several routes to Guadalajara. From north to south, these are:

Mex 15 via Tepic: This is a "grin and bear it" highway, with lots of traffic and one particularly slow canyon crossing. Still, it is a direct route with plenty of gas stations. Give yourself a generous margin of daylight; I would never tackle this congested highway at night.

San Patricio/Melaque to Guadalajara: Mex 80 is the most popular route between Guadalajara and the Pacific coast. The road is quite curvy and traffic tends to be thick and fast, especially on weekends. In fact, I avoid weekend travel on this route whenever possible. Allow five to six hours.

There are two relatively unknown "back door" routes to central Mexico from the Pacific coast: via Colima on Mex 110 or via Playa Azul on Mex 37. Both of these highways are scenic, yet not too challenging for large RVs. Traffic is light and regular gasoline is available. If you're not pressed for time, I'd take one of these highways.

Mex 95 from Acapulco gives access to a network of secondary highways that can be used to bypass Mexico City to the west. (See Avoiding Mexico City, after Michoacán, below.) This is slower and more mountainous than the highways already described, but the route is also quite scenic.

Guadalajara, Jalisco (5,140 ft.): With five million *habitantes,* Guadalajara invites comparison with mega-crowded Mexico City. Fortunately, the country's second-largest city is considerably less polluted, hectic, and intimidating than the capital. Driving in Guadalajara is easier, and its police force isn't as predatory as the capital's.

Of special interest to RV travelers and campers are the town's services and supplies, including several huge, modern shopping centers, and sporting goods stores. Guadalajara and its environs are home to a large number of foreign retirees and winter residents, including the largest group of Americans living outside the United States. This is a good place to recharge your gringo batteries, especially if you're homesick.

The Guadalajara area has a number of RV parks as well

as campgrounds associated with balnearios and hot springs. One of Steve's all-time favorites is conveniently located west of Guadalajara, within easy commuting distance of the city.

Chimulco Campground ($): The campground is just south of Mex 80 in the town of Villa Corona (at Km 15, about 30 miles west of Guadalajara). Watch for "Balneario" signs. If your map doesn't show Villa Corona, it is about 9 miles west of Acatlán (itself at the western junction of Mex 80 and the Mex 15 freeway into Guadalajara).

Chimulco is a large balneario and picnic ground on the north side of Lake Atotonilco. Tell the gatekeeper that you want to pay for the *campamento*, then follow signs to the trailer park. If the gatekeeper is missing, proceed to the campground and someone will eventually be by to collect.

Chimulco's gardens, lawns, trees, and flowering shrubs are a fine example of what can be done with a nearly perfect, semitropical climate and an abundant supply of fresh water. In addition to the lake, swimming pools, playgrounds, water-slides, and clubhouse, the campground is just minutes away from a four-lane freeway into Guadalajara. It's no wonder that Steve found several campers contentedly passing the winter here.

"A very friendly group," he commented. "As soon as I parked the van we were invited to watch a movie on a VCR in the clubhouse. It was an early John Wayne and I kept falling asleep."

Facilities and Services: There are 49 spaces with full hookups and bathrooms with showers and hot water.

Centro Vacacional Agua Caliente: At Km 16 in Villa Corona (see above), within sight of Mex 80. This large RV park has full services and a swimming pool. Note: Watch for a sign on the west side of Villa Corona that says "Las Delicias." This wonderful hot springs has roofless "bungalows" with huge, spring-fed hot tubs inside. The tubs will hold a crowd, and hourly rates are very cheap.

Also in Villa Corona, you can't help but notice the mouth-watering aroma of chicken barbecue drifting across the highway from a roadside stand. "This is Mexican carryout food at its best," Steve says, "with big, smoky grills, covered with hardwood roasted chicken. Get a whole bird with all the trimmings—tortillas, salt, and fresh salsa. I ate one all by myself."

Hacienda Trailer Park ($$): You will find this park on the west side of Guadalajara, in the Ciudad Granja suburb. One mile southeast of the intersection of Vallarta Street (Highway 15 to Tepic and Nogales) and the Perifrico, turn right at the Datsun agency and follow signs to the park. This park is very well managed and deservedly popular. The grounds are large, shady, and attractively landscaped. There is a wonderful swimming pool, a clubhouse with a fireplace for cool nights, Ping-Pong, shuffleboard, ice, and soft drinks.

Steve spent Christmas at the Hacienda and, though the park was nearly full, the owner says overnighters can always find a space. "The park's owners, Tony and Yvonne Lozano, are quite helpful and speak excellent English. This park has a good-humored, friendly feeling."

Facilities and Services: There are 98 spaces with full hookups. Access is tight but possible for big rigs, but there are no pull-throughs. Tent sites are available at full price. Good bathrooms with hot water, laundry service, and mail and telephone service are available. There is city bus service to downtown Guadalajara.

Pyramid Trailer Park ($): This park is at Km 15 on Perifrico Sur, the "south loop" around Guadalajara, next to El Ixtepete archaeological zone. The park looks ragged around the edges, but the price is right and there are usually plenty of vacancies. There is a full range of services, including pleasant shade beneath the eucalyptus trees.

PAL RV Park ($$): PAL is on the southwest side of Guadalajara, across from the huge Plaza del Sol shopping center. The park, on Mariano Otero Avenue next to the Allen E. Lloyd building, can be reached from the Periférico via Mariano Otero or Lopez Mateos Avenue.

PAL is an acronym for Parque Allen Lloyd, the adjacent investment firm. "Allen Lloyd's former parking lot might be more accurate," Steve jokes, rating this park "high on concrete, power, and water pressure, but low on atmosphere and aesthetics." Judging from the scant number of vacant sites, however, the PAL concept is well received by RVers. (A second, somewhat cozier PAL outside of town at Lake Chapala is described below.)

Facilities and Services: There are 56 concrete spaces with cement terrace and full hookups and rigs to 40 feet can be accommodated. No tents are allowed. Pure tap water, 30-amp power, good showers and bathrooms, a recreation room, bar, barbecue area, tables, and tight security are offered. There is also mail, telephone, and city bus service. There is a major shopping mall across the street.

Plaza del Sol Shopping Center: Between Lopez Mateos and Mariano Otero avenues, on the southwest side of Guadalajara, this shopping center provides a strong dose of gringolandia. The sprawling mall has 251 shops, including Deportes Marti and Black Bass, sporting goods stores with miscellaneous camping, fishing, and diving gear. If you're looking for whole bean coffee, try the Café Moca.

Lake Chapala: Mexico's largest lake is now one of the country's most polluted bodies of water. Thanks to a Garden-of-Eden climate, and in spite of the lake's deteriorating health, two small beach towns—Chapala and Ajijic—continue to attract crowds of tourists and foreign retirees. I'm sorry to say that camping is very limited. With the sad demise of Los Manglarcito Trailer Park, there's just one campground at Lake Chapala.

PAL Lake Chapala ($$): On the Chapala-Jocotepec road (Mex 44). Take Highway 23 from Guadalajara, then turn west on the Libramiento (bypass) around the town of Chapala. When you reach the lake, turn left (east, toward Chapala) on Mex 44. The park is one-fourth mile from the turn, next to the Chula Vista Country Club. Like its namesake in Guadalajara, this is definitely an American-style RV park. The Chapala PAL is much larger, however, with lawns and a heated swimming pool.
Facilities and Services: There are 110 spaces with terraces and hookups, including satellite TV. Facilities and services include a recreation room, bar, barbecue, laundromat, telephone, 30-amp power, street lights, guard, clean bathrooms, and dressing rooms.

Guadalajara to ?: I'd devote at least one afternoon and evening in Guadalajara to a review of guidebooks on Mexico. Your choice of itineraries through central Mexico is limited only by your time and curiosity. Though the region is shy on RV facilities, by occasionally using motels and hotels, you'll be able to explore in any direction.
The route we'll follow takes advantage of the region's RV parks and our favorite campgrounds. It follows a somewhat erratic path from north to south, beginning in Guadalajara and ending in the state of Puebla. If you're using the directory for sightseeing and relaxed camping, allow at least a couple of weeks to cover this part of Mexico.
Note: If you're pressed for time or would like to avoid traffic, I'd skip Guanajuato and San Miguel de Allende and go directly to Michoacán. Guadalajara is just 230 miles from Morelia. Take Mex 15 via Zamora.

Guadalajara to Guanajuato (185 miles): There are several options, but I recommend Mex 80 to Lagos de Moreno, then Mex 45 to Silao. This route is slightly longer but avoids some of the heavy truck and bus traffic between Guadalajara and

Mexico City. The most direct route is on Mex 90 via La Pieda and Irapuato.

Guanajuato, Guanajuato (6,725 ft.): An old and very beautiful mining town, Guanajuato is literally a maze of narrow colonial streets, unexpected tunnels, and disorienting intersections. Your best bet is to avoid the center of town until you can approach it on foot or in a cab.

Morril Trailer Park ($): This park is high on the north side of Guanajuato, overlooking the city. Take the Carretera Panoramica and look for small trailer park signs as you begin to climb above Guanajuato. The entrance to this park is quite steep. If you're driving a heavy rig or a gutless van, check it out on foot. Steve says, ''You wouldn't know this was a trailer park unless we told you.'' It is rather bare, with some hookups, bathrooms, and a good view.

San Miguel de Allende, Guanajuato (6,130 ft.): This small town is known for its well-preserved colonial buildings, colorful fiestas, and international community of artists, writers, and retirees. The surrounding countryside is semiarid, mountainous, and sparsely inhabited. Day hiking can be very good, especially in the deep, tree-shaded canyons south of town.

Lago Dorado KDA ($): This site is near the lake, southwest of San Miguel de Allende. Take Mex 51 toward Celaya; about a mile south of town, you'll see signs for the Hotel Mision and Lago Dorado KDA campground on top of a hill. Turn west toward the lake and follow a bumpy, twisting cobblestone lane one and a half miles. Signs are plentiful. There is a steep, rough railroad crossing just before the park entrance which could be tricky for large rigs.

Lago Dorado is an unusually pleasant and well-planned campground that manages to provide a wide range of services without sacrificing its relaxed, country atmosphere. Unlike so many ''American-style'' campgrounds that mistake sterility for neatness, Lago Dorado's grounds are not only immaculately kept but also quite comfortable and attractive. There is ample space within the camp, tables, shade, and a large swimming pool. The park's secluded setting near the reservoir provides good bird watching, excellent walks, and blessedly quiet nights. Considering Lago Dorado's setting, services, and bargain price, this campground rates among Mexico's best.

Facilities and Services: There are 60 roomy spaces with hookups and tent sites. Amenities include immaculate bathrooms and hot showers, a laundry, games, a recreation room, books. The park's cordial owner is Dutch and speaks excellent English.

Motel La Siesta ($): On the south side of town, very near the intersection with Mex 51 to Celaya and the bypass from Queretaro, there is a large sign for the campground, which is behind the motel. This very popular park is an easy 20-minute walk from San Miguel's central plaza. Though the campground is rather bare and sunburned, campers have the use of the motel's small swimming pool.

San Miguel de Allende has always attracted a stimulating cross-section of international travelers, and La Siesta's clientele is no exception. A typical grab bag of campers includes everyone from diehard hippies to spit-and-polish RV retirees, with a generous sprinkling of amiable characters, borderline eccentrics, and just plain folks thrown in for good measure. The conversation in this park is interesting, wide-ranging, and sometimes never-ending.

Facilities and Services: There are 90 spaces with full hookups. The driveway is a tight fit, but big rigs will find plenty of room inside the park. The bathrooms are reasonably clean and have hot showers. City bus service and inexpensive taxis are available.

Rancho San Ramon ($): Northwest of San Miguel de Allende at Km 5 on Mex 51 to Dolores Hidalgo, this is a small, bare campground attached to a motel and balneario. In fact, a room for two people doesn't cost much more than the campground. There isn't much in the way of services, but you'll have naturally warmed swimming and wading pools to relax in, lawns, a picnic area, and an excellent view of the surrounding countryside. Expect lots of company on weekends.

Facilities and Services: There are 5 spaces with all hookups as well as rooms.

Queretaro, Queretaro (6,075 ft.):

Hotel Azteca RV Park: Nine miles north of Queretaro on Mex 57 to San Luis Potosí, the park is on a hillside, next to a restaurant and huge Pemex station on the east side of the highway. The Azteca is a very large, efficient park that caters to caravans and overnighters. Considering that it sits beside one of Mexico's busiest highways, this campground manages to be as pleasant as possible. The Azteca is convenient, especially for travelers bound to and from Mexico City, about three hours away. It has all services, hookups, and rooms.

Queretaro to Michoacán (120 miles): There are several highways to the state of Michoacán across a broad, intensely cultivated plateau known as the Bajio (Lowlands). Traffic is moderate to heavy, with lots of slow trucks, buses, and farm workers on bicycles.

The most direct routes from the Queretaro area to Morelia are Mex 43 from Salamanca and Mex 51 from Celaya. If you're not in a hurry, consider Mex 120 from Tequisquiapán, via Acambaro. Whichever highway you choose, take your time and enjoy the scenery. Be sure to buy fresh strawberries along the way. My favorite roadside snack is lightly cooked young garbanzo (chick peas) doused with lime juice and mild red pepper.

MICHOACÁN

The highlands of Michoacán include some of Mexico's most interesting towns and villages as well as great expanses of pine and oak forest. Although the region is quite mountainous, there is an extensive system of paved two-lane highways and graded secondary roads. If you're interested in cooler weather, Tarascan Indian markets, hiking, or back road exploring, this is the place.

Pátzcuaro, Michoacán (7,130 ft.): Set near the shore of a beautiful lake, this highland Tarascan community is one of Mexico's most interesting small towns. Pátzcuaro is not only picturesque and inexpensive, but it makes an ideal base for side trips throughout Michoacán. Pátzcuaro's invigorating, high sierra climate can be surprisingly chilly on winter nights. Though it will be dependably sunny and warm during the day, the grass is often frosty at dawn in January and February.

El Pozo Trailer Park ($$): This park is on the eastern shore of Lake Pátzcuaro, one and a half miles east of the Pátzcuaro city limits, at Km 20 (Mex 120) toward Morelia. There is a sign on the highway for the park, near the Chalamu Motel. Turn toward the lake and cross the railroad tracks.

El Pozo rates very high on Steve's list of family favorites. The campground has a genuine parklike setting, with trees, picnic tables, expansive lawns, and a wonderful view of the lake. Bird-watching is good; Steve says he can count on seeing a pair of vermilion flycatchers in the camp. You can also depend on a few mosquitoes, so be prepared.

El Pozo is managed by a retired couple from Mexico City, Alberto and Pilar Olvera. The Olveras are very cordial and helpful. Alberto speaks good English. Steve often leaves his van in their care while making side trips by bus and train.

Facilities and Services: There are 20 large spaces with hookups and plenty of room for big rigs. The park has clean bathrooms and hot showers, tables, playground, grills, a laundry sink, pure tap water, and phone service, as well as good security. There is easy bus service to Pátzcuaro and other towns just outside the gate.

Motel Pátzcuaro and *Posada Don Vasco* are on the northeast side of town, along Mex 120 to Morelia. This road is variously known as Avenida de las Americas, Francisco Madero, or Lázaro Cardenas—take your pick. Both establishments have some facilities for RVs, though the Don Vasco caters primarily to caravans.

Motel Chupicuaro (6,560 ft.): On the north end of Lake Pátzcuaro, between Quiroga and Zacapu, three and one-half miles west of Quiroga, at Km 41 on Highway 15, this is a very small but attractive park with a view of the lake. There is electricity and water.

Lago Camecuaro Park ($): Just east of Zamora on Mex 15 to Tangancicuáro and Morelia. At Km 131 on the west side of Tangancicuáro, look for a picture sign for Lago Camecuaro. Turn south and go half a mile to the park.

This is a local *ojo de agua* (eye of water) swimming and picnic place, not an official campground. The gates are open from 9:00 a.m. to 8:00 p.m., and there is a small admission charge. On weekends, this lakeside park is filled with picnicking and partying families, wandering mariachi bands, busy food and soft drink stands, cuddling lovers, excited children, and all the other hubbub of a typical Mexican *dia campestre* (country day).

At dusk and during the week, however, the crowds disappear. Steve says, "If you stay on, the caretaker or guards will drop by. Politely ask, ¿Se puede pasar la noche? (May one spend the night?) They've never turned us down, though on a couple of occasions the caretaker asked for a small *propina* (tip)."

Lake Camecuaro is small, crystal clear, and unusually beautiful. Several tiny islands in the lake are covered with ancient, twisted cypress trees. Early in the morning, thick, swirling mists create an eerie, otherworldly scene. Other than rickety picnic tables, the only facilities are rickety outhouses that are locked during closing hours.

Paracho, Michoacán (5,140 ft.): On Mex 37 to Uruapán, Paracho is a small Tarascan town widely known for its fine handmade guitars and inexpensive musical instruments. The village lies within a mountainous region of volcanoes and forests.

Parque Comunal Patabasco (free): Just off Mex 37 to Uruapán, about a mile south of Paracho, look for the entrance at Km 42—on the left side of the highway, if you're coming from Paracho.

This secluded park is set in a pine forest. Though the park is fenced, there is no gate. At Steve's last visit, the caretaker was also missing. In fact, the park is virtually abandoned, except for occasional weekend picnickers. It is a great place to enjoy the peace and quiet and to walk in the forest.

Facilities: There are rustic outhouses and sagging barbecue grills.

Los Azufres, Michoacán (9,000 ft.) ($): Take Mex 15 east from Morelia toward Zitacuaro. Los Azufres is about 11 miles northwest of Ciudad Hidalgo. Look for signs. The road is good but quite steep.

''The Sulphurs'' is perhaps the best known of this state's many thermal springs. The setting, several small lakes in the forested crater of a dormant volcano, is strongly reminiscent of Colorado or the mountains of northern California. It can get quite cold here at night—into the teens and 20s during winter. This is great country for day hikes and genuine, get-away-from-them-all retreats. Firewood is abundant, but services and supplies are very limited. Some accommodations are available. As with most Mexican spas and parks, Los

Azufres will be almost empty except on weekends and holidays. Although we found the hot springs disappointingly shallow and less than scalding hot, they were quite welcome at the end of a day's hike.

Morelia to Mexico City Shortcut (about 170 miles): Your map may not show it, but the *ruta corta* (shortcut) is considerably quicker and less mountainous than Mex 15. Like Mex 15, however, the shortcut is very scenic.

From Morelia, take Mex 126 to Maravatio and El Oro de Hidalgo. From El Oro, follow Mex 6 to Atlacomulco. It is a straight shot from Atlacomulco to Toluca on Mex 55. Take the freeway from Toluca to Mexico City or follow our Mexico City bypass directions to avoid the capital entirely.

Avoiding Mexico City

Although I consider Mexico City's museums, historical monuments, and restaurants to be worthy of every traveler's attention, traffic in the capital is just plain awful. Campers should seriously consider leaving their vehicles in an outlying city and traveling to the D.F. (Distrito Federal) by public transportation. There are no RV parks within Mexico City, but you'll find plenty of good hotels in a wide range of prices.

I'm also sorry to say that Mexico City's *transitos* (traffic cops) tend to prey on passing RVers, citing them for imaginary traffic offenses. Those with more imagination will insist on escorting you through the city—for a fee, of course. Considering that some frazzled tourists hire cabs to lead them from one side of Mexico City to the other, this is one offer I wouldn't refuse. Barter like hell, however, on the price. Anything over $10 verges on highway robbery.

Fortunately, alternate routes around Mexico City do exist, though you'll have to follow a map carefully to avoid getting lost. Though these bypass routes may take a little longer, they're scenic and much less stressful than taking the plunge across the city.

Note: Because of heavy commuter traffic, avoid driving in or near Mexico City during the morning and evening rush hours. Late morning and midafternoon are the best times to make your move.

Eastern Bypass: Driving from north to south on Mex 57, you can bypass Mexico City and reach Puebla or Oaxaca by turning east at Lecheria. Lecheria is not shown on every road map, but there are clear signs on Mex 57. The turnoff is on the northern outskirts of Mexico City, in an area of light industries. Take the Lecheria exit and continue several miles east to Ecatepec and Texcoco. From Texcoco, take Mex 136 to a junction near Apizaco. This road is steep and curvy, so take your time (about three hours). At the junction with Mex 117 turn southwest, toward Tlaxcala. Take the bypass around Tlaxcala, following Mex 119 to the outskirts of Puebla.

The fastest route to Oaxaca from Puebla is Mex 150 to Tehuacán, then Highway 135 to Oaxaca. (For campgrounds, see Puebla, below.)

Western Bypass: This route to Acapulco, Cuernavaca, or Oaxaca is quite scenic, but it can also be very confusing, especially when you reach the area around Tres Marias. Still, I'd rather be confused here than in downtown Mexico City. Again, take your time and watch closely for signs. This region is mountainous and the roads are narrow. Allow a full day to drive and sightsee from Queretaro to Cuernavaca.

From north to south on Mex 57, take the Toluca exit near San Juan del Rio. Follow Mex 55 south, bypassing Toluca. The bypass is poorly marked; if you miss it, just continue south through the city.

To Acapulco: From Toluca, continue on Mex 55 to Ixtapán de la Sal and Taxco. This region, by the way, is loaded with parks, hot springs, caves, and mountain curves.

To Cuernavaca and Oaxaca: Continue south from Toluca on Mex 55. Your goal is Tres Marias, north of Cuernavaca. To reach Tres Marias, however, you'll have to wind through the mountains. There are several ways to do this on secondary roads, so if you get lost, just keep plugging away. Try this combination from Mex 55: Santiago Tianguistengo to Lagunas de Zempoala to Tres Marias. When in doubt, ask directions to Lagunas de Zempoala, a lovely high sierra park with excellent hiking, small lakes, and limited camping facilities.

From Tres Marias, take Mex 95 south to Cuernavaca. If you're headed for Oaxaca, take the 95D tollway toward Cuernavaca, then exit on 115D to Tepotzlan, Oaxtepec, and Cuautla. From Cuautla, follow Mex 190 to Oaxaca. This slow, scenic route offers very limited services. Though we've camped off the road several times, there are persistent rumors of ripoffs in this area. RVers usually make a dawn start from the Cuernavaca-Cuautla area and drive straight through to Oaxaca.

Cuernavaca, Morelos (5,060 ft.): This is a warm, lush, semitropical city long favored by affluent Mexican and foreign visitors. It offers something for everyone, including some unusual camping facilities.

Monasterio Benedictino Trailer Park ($): This is easier than it sounds: on the north side of Cuernavaca, take the turnoff to Tepotzlan via Ocotepec from toll highway 95D. (Don't take toll highway 115D.) Drive about a mile, through Ocotepec and into the adjacent village of Ahuatepec. These towns aren't clearly defined, so keep your eye peeled for signs to the monastery, which is on your left (roughly north). Follow the signs into the grounds of the monastery.

A trailer park in a monastery? Yes, and a cowled monk will actually take your money. "He was very friendly and spoke good English," Steve reports, "and he gladly told us about life in the monastery."

Other than chats with Brother Manager, you won't actually see the monastery and its monks unless you make a special visit. The park itself is a grassy pasture surrounded by quiet wooded hills. The monastery is a simple and very pleasant campground, one that is seldom, if ever, crowded. In other words, travelers will find it a welcome refuge from a sometimes too wacky world.

Facilities and Services: There are 34 spaces with water and electricity. As you might expect, the bathrooms are exceptionally clean. The monastery store sells fruit preserves and honey.

Cuernavaca Trailer Park: This park is at Calle Mesalina No. 3, Colonia Delicias, west of Mex 95D from Mexico City and just north of the exit to Cuautla. Watch for signs. This is a large, full-service RV park with all the modern conveniences.

During Steve's last visit, the *Trailer Park San Pablo* in Cuernavaca was missing and rumored to have been replaced by a factory.

Las Estacas, Morelos (4,550 ft.) ($): From Cuernavaca, take Mex 138 east toward Yautepec. Just before Yautepec, there is a sign for Las Estacas at an intersection. In fact, signs are abundant—follow them to the park.

From Mex 95D (the Mexico City-Acapulco toll road), take the Oacalco toll booth exit and follow the billboards for Las Estacas (toward Yautepec).

Las Estacas is a somewhat mind-boggling combination of trailer park, spa, picnic ground, nature park, sports arena, and convention center. The centerpiece of this sprawling vacation retreat is a huge natural spring, an upwelling of crystal clear warm water that pours from the earth at over 2,000 gallons per second, forming a half-mile-long river through the park.

Steve took a typical hard, objective look at Las Estacas and made this report: ''Las Estacas is absolutely wonderful, one of our favorite campgrounds in all of Mexico! You have to see this place to really appreciate it. Be sure to walk up the trail to the headwaters of the river to get the full impact of the spring.'' When he'd finished exclaiming, Steve spent most of his time lolling in the river and doing laps in one of the park's many swimming pools.

Thanks to a warm, lush climate, Las Estacas is crowded with semitropical plants and shaded by sleek royal palms. The campground itself is something of a jungle arboretum, with giant trees and overhanging branches wide enough to walk on.

Facilities and Services: There are lots of unmarked spaces without hookups, clean bathrooms with unheated showers, good security, a bar, restaurant, store, and medical services and just about anything else you can think of. Bungalows with electricity and hot water (but no kitchens) are available on the grounds. This is really a miniature resort city in a parklike setting.

Fees: You will be charged an entrance fee, per person, as well as a daily camping fee. The total cost is low, but the arithmetic can be confusing. To minimize confusion and to avoid overpaying, save your receipts.

PUEBLA
The mountainous state of Puebla, east of Mexico City, is rarely visited by campers. A government publication lists only three RV parks and campgrounds in the entire state. Of these, the Spa Agua Azul in the city of Puebla is now defunct, and a second in Izucar de Matamoros is marginal at best (see below). Steve was unable to confirm a rumor that a new RV park has opened near the city of Puebla. In the meantime, your best bet is clearly Las Americas.

Las Americas Trailer Park ($): Las Americas is just outside Cholula on the south side of Mex 190 to Puebla. This is the old highway to Mexico City, not the four-lane toll road (Mex 190D). There is a sign for the park and a long gravel driveway.

An older, well-kept campground, Las Americas has a large area for caravans. At 7,000 feet, the park's swimming pool tends to be quite bracing. You can expect frosty mornings here during the winter months. Water comes from a private well that is said to be safe for drinking.

Renate Reliford and her archaeologist husband live in a large fifth-wheel trailer near the back of the campground. When she wasn't out exploring the backcountry, Steve found Renate quite willing to share her encyclopedic knowledge of central Mexico. "She also collects folk art," Steve says, "and gave us some very helpful tips on our eternal quest for the unusual."

Facilities and Services: There are 32 spaces with hookups. There is an extra charge for very large rigs and a discount for tents. The bathrooms have lots of hot water. Amenities include a phone, watchman, and local bus service.

Izucar de Matamoros, Puebla (4,350 ft.): This town is on Mex 190, the old highway to Oaxaca. The newer, faster route from Mexico City to Oaxaca is via Puebla and Tehuacán.

Hotel Cristobal Colon ($): At Km 66.5 on the Mex 190 bypass around Izucar de Matamoros, on the north side of town. Steve minces no words: "This is for overnight only. The RV park is basically a hotel parking lot with a lot of traffic noise. When the mechanic next door finally finished testing a truck horn, the dogs started howling. It was a long night."

Campers have to go through the lobby and restaurant to use the hotel's pool and outside rest rooms. "The best thing about this place," Steve advises, "is the price and the sign at the entrance, Hotel Cristobal Colon—Island of Love."

Facilities and Services: There are 6 spaces with shared power and one water tap, clean bathrooms and showers, and a restaurant, bar, and pool. The property is fenced.

Oasis Xochiltepec (free): This park is located on Lago Epatlan, about nine miles east of Izucar de Matamoros. On the southern side of Izucar de Matamoros, take a narrow paved road east to Epatlan and Huehuetlan. You'll have to drive through Izucar de Matamoros, so don't take the bypass. When in doubt, ask for Epatlan. Go through Epatlan and follow the rough but passable gravel road for just under two miles to the lake. (Not recommended for big rigs.)

As you may have guessed, you are definitely off the tourist circuit. This is a local weekend picnic park, but the caretaker allows camping in a pleasant grassy area near the lake. The countryside here is dry and hilly, and the only shade is provided by a thatched palapa. A small restaurant run by the caretaker serves very inexpensive fish dinners and delicious homemade cake. (If you don't eat or buy drinks, it would be polite to offer payment for camping.) There is excellent birding in the reeds around the shore. Be prepared for mosquitoes.

Facilities and Services: There are two more or less adequate toilets. The gates are closed and locked at night. Other than the usual yapping mutts, the park is blessedly quiet.

CHAPTER 11

Oaxaca and Chiapas

In general, the farther south one travels in Mexico, the more traditionally Mexican the country and people become. Just a few hundred miles south of Mexico City, the country narrows and is dominated by the pine-forested Sierra Madre del Sur. This region includes Oaxaca and Chiapas and encompasses a vast territory of rugged mountain ranges, tropical rain forests, and perennially warm beaches. This, too, is "Old Mexico," an exotic land of centuries-old traditions and colonial architecture, of narrow cobbled streets and shy, colorfully costumed Indians. Though travel through these highlands isn't always easy, it takes in some of the country's most spectacular scenery. Drivers will find this mountainous region challenging—and passengers will gape at the views. We also call this region the "Indian highlands," for its large number of traditional Indian groups.

For centuries, southern Mexico's rugged geography has limited its development and contacts with the rest of the country. There are few cities of any size and most of the region seems immune to progress. Travelers who complain that Mexico has become too modern for their taste will find that the clock still runs very slowly in most of southern Mex-

ico. Isolation has not only preserved traditional ways of life in the southern highlands, but also kept prices (and standards of living) quite low. With the exception of a few tourist resorts, costs for food, lodging, and basic services are among the lowest in the country.

The "downside" of low prices, however, can often be seen in the poverty of the local campesinos and Indians. Though picturesque, this region is not without its problems. Many of the Indians in southern Mexico, especially those in the true backcountry, can be wary and fearful of strangers. Ironically, gringos are usually much more welcome than Mexicans, who have a long reputation of exploitation and oppression.

Although this area includes some of Mexico's most

interesting and picturesque archaeological sites, cities, and natural wonders, RV parks and camping facilities are quite limited. The vast majority of American and Canadian campers tends to congregate in campgrounds and traditional free camping areas along the Pacific beaches at Puerto Escondido, Puerto Angel, and Huatulco. The more adventurous follow a good, two-lane highway into Chiapas, climbing into the cool forests surrounding San Cristobal de Las Casas. From San Cristobal the route descends eastward once again in a daylong traverse of the Chiapas Mountains to the lush, tropical lowlands at Palenque.

In fact, there is enough to explore and experience in this part of Mexico to keep you busy for years. The possibilities range from beach camping, diving, and fishing to highland trekking and jungle river rafting. In addition to 10,000-foot mountains, these states contain Mexico's most extensive (and critically endangered) rain forests and canopy jungles. Despite relentless clearcutting and expanding cattle ranches, the variety of bird, animal, and plant life is among the richest in North America.

Climate

I call the beaches of Oaxaca the ''Iguana Coast,'' both for their languorous lizards and dedicated two-legged sun worshipers. In fact, the Pacific beaches here offer the warmest wintertime swimming and sunbathing in all of Mexico. In summer—forget it; only surfers can tolerate the temperature. Although humidity is usually not a problem between November and April, the beaches and lowlands tend to be muggy. Take light clothing and a fan.

To cool off and dry out, simply climb the nearest sierra. At elevations of 5,000 feet and higher, Oaxaca and Chiapas boast of ''eternal spring.'' These claims are only slightly exaggerated. Oaxaca City's climate is near-perfect, but San

Cristobal de Las Casas' thin mountain air can be too cold for comfort in winter. Freezing, foggy mornings are common in January, though the days are often sunny and mild. When headed for the Indian highlands, Lorena never fails to pack her lightweight long underwear and down vest.

The eastern mountain slopes and lowlands of both Oaxaca and Chiapas are very lush and humid, with almost year-round rains. Tree ferns, rubber trees, "Tarzan" vines, and other jungle vegetation can turn roads into exciting green tunnels. Take rain gear; the dry season, roughly from January to March or April, is never entirely rain-free.

Driving

Driving conditions in this mountainous region of southern Mexico are scenic but *sinuosa* (winding). With few exceptions, highways are two-lane and in good to fair condition. Oaxaca and Chiapas are sparsely inhabited and traffic is relatively light. There are lots of slow trucks, tractors, third-class buses, and ox carts, however, so be especially alert. Watch for roaming livestock and heavily burdened pedestrians. It is not unusual to see campesinos pedaling bicycles laden with immense bundles of cornstalks or Indians with tumplines bent beneath sacks of grain or coffee beans on the side of the highway.

Mexico City to Oaxaca (305 miles): Bypasses to Oaxaca around Mexico City are described in the Central Highlands portion of this directory. If you're coming directly through the capital, you have several choices. The most popular route to Oaxaca, and the one offering the most accommodations and services, is Mexico City to Puebla on Mex 190D and from Puebla to Tehuacán on Mex 150. From Tehuacán, take Mex 135 to Oaxaca.

The "old" way from Mexico City to Oaxaca is via Izucar

de Matamoros and Mex 190. I enjoy this route, but it has few accommodations or services, and the highway is rough in places. RVers will feel more comfortable on the better-used route described above via Tehuacán.

If you're coming to Oaxaca from the Gulf Coast and would like to try a more challenging approach, take Mex 175 through the Sierra de Juarez. This narrow, twisting mountain highway takes several hours to negotiate. I recommend it only for vans and smaller motor homes. There are virtually no services along the way, so be prepared.

Oaxaca, Oaxaca (5,084 ft.): This beautiful colonial city of 500,000 inhabitants is set at the junction of three major valleys. Oaxaca is one of our favorite places in Mexico. In addition to the city's own attractions (which include museums, markets, sidewalk cafés, and excellent shopping), Oaxaca makes an ideal base for side trips to surrounding Zapotec archaeological sites and Indian villages. While you're in Oaxaca, be sure to visit the fine English language library and the downtown tourist offices. All are excellent sources of information on local sights and activities.

Oaxaca Trailer Park ($$): This park is on the northeast side of Oaxaca. Turn north at the intersection of Mex 190 (known as Calzada Chapultepec) and Mex 175 (known as Escuela Militar). There is a large Volkswagen agency at the intersection. Watch for trailer park signs. The campground is several blocks north of Mex 190, at 900 Violetas. It is very large and surrounded by a brick wall.

The Oaxaca Trailer Park is something of an institution to dedicated RV gypsies and vagabonding ''Mex-trippers.'' Sooner or later, everyone seems to end up here. Among the more memorable guests, Steve recently met a retired truck driver towing a fifth-wheel trailer behind a full-sized, diesel-powered semitractor. After disconnecting his trailer, this fellow casually drove his semi around Oaxaca as if it were a car. He said it was the only vehicle in which he really felt comfortable.

The Oaxaca Trailer Park is set in one of the city's quieter residential neighborhoods, within healthy walking distance of stores and downtown. Cabs and city buses are available at the gate. A large Blanco supermarket is located nearby. The campground itself is spacious, nicely planted with shrubs and flowers, and shaded by large trees.

Facilities and Services: There are 94 spaces with full hookups and some pull-throughs. The sliding rate scale has a substantial discount for tents. Facilities are reasonably clean bathrooms with hot showers, mail and phone service, and pure water (for sale).

Rosa Isabel Trailer Park ($): On Mex 190 from Mexico City, a few miles northwest of the city of Oaxaca. The park is on the west side of the highway, next to the railroad tracks. If you've been using this directory on a regular basis, you must be aware by now that Steve doesn't put much stock in overly groomed, parking lot-style campgrounds. Nor does he allow objectivity to harden an obvious soft spot for more laid-back RV parks and casual, old-fashioned trailer camps.

Steve begins his inspection of the Rosa Isabel with the usual overall assessment: ''The Rosa Isabel is rundown but homey.'' He follows this benign comment with a hard-eyed look at the park's location—sandwiched between the Pan American Highway and the railroad tracks.

''There really aren't many trains,'' Steve says reassuringly, ''and if you camp near the back of the park, the highway noise isn't all that bad.'' He admits that the park's fallen fence bothered him—but only until the Rosa Isabel's friendly managers (a young couple he first mistook for teenagers) assured him the fence would be rebuilt ''soon.''

Anything else? The park is very cheap. The bathrooms are quite clean, and the showers are definitely hot. ''Don't ask me why, but I really like the place.''

Facilities and Services: There are 48 spaces with full hookups. Although there are no pull-throughs, there is ample maneuvering room for big rigs. The park has trees and shade and is close to city buses and taxis.

Hotel Loma Bonita ($): This site is a stone's throw west of the Rosa Isabel Trailer Park on Mex 190. The entrance is a steep incline. Although this is nothing more than several parking spaces next to the hotel with water and electric hookups, Steve considers the Loma Bonita a great bargain.

"We rented a plain but comfortable room in the hotel and a camping place for less than we'd pay in a fancier RV park. We put our computer in the room and used it as an office while writing our shopping guide to Mexico." They also rented an unused bathroom to warehouse a shipment of *artesana* (arts and crafts). "The family that runs the Loma Bonita is large and quite friendly," Steve concludes. "We felt very comfortable here. The hotel also has a spectacular view of the Oaxaca valley."

Facilities and Services: There are several cement spaces with water and power, some covered spaces, and bathrooms. The area is completely fenced and locked at night.

Oaxaca to Tehuantepec (156 miles): The direct route south, on the Pan American Highway (Mex 190) is curvy and not especially interesting. It takes several hours at any easy pace, including stops. The long way to Tehuantepec—over the Sierra Madre to Pochutla on the Pacific coast, then south via Salina Cruz—takes about two days. This is a challenging and exciting drive. For more details, see the Pacific Coast section of this directory.

Tehuantepec, Oaxaca: The town has an interesting market and a couple of good, inexpensive restaurants. Try the seafood joint—on your right, just after you turn off the highway and cross the railroad tracks.

Camping is so limited in this area that I'll hedge our "no rumor" rule and mention the *Santa Teresa Trailer Park*, suggested to Steve by a camper from Manitoba. Turn inland (north) to Mextequilla from Highway 190. The turnoff is about 1.5 miles east of Tehuantepec on the highway to Juchitan, not far from the Hotel Calli. If you don't have a compass, east feels like south here, so be careful. Once you leave the main highway, the trailer park is at Km 6.5 (mile 4). "The park is fine but had no electricity," is about all we've got so far on this one.

Hotel Calli ($$$): On the eastern outskirts of Tehuantepec, beside Mex 190, the Hotel Calli has a few parking/camping spaces with no services other than the use of a bathroom in the hotel. It's better than nothing, at least for overnight.

Tehuantepec to Tapanatepec, Oaxaca (80 miles): This is not my favorite part of Mexico, mainly because the country is flat, hot, humid, and usually quite windy. Gasoline is plentiful, but good accommodations are not. Most travelers take one look at this region's steaming savannahs and hurry on. There are no campgrounds to speak of, but you'll find lots of empty beaches along the Pacific coast.

At Tapanatepec, Mex 200 continues along the coast to Tapachula and the Guatemalan border. Mex 190 cuts inland, through the foothills to Tuxtla de Gutiérrez, Chiapas.

Tuxtla Gutiérrez, Chiapas (1,750 ft.): Tuxtla is the capital of Chiapas and the commercial center for the southwestern corner of Mexico. This busy city of about 100,000 inhabitants is worth more than the cursory look most tourists allow it. Set in the tropical foothills of the Sierra Madre, Tuxtla has one of the best zoos in the country, a botanical garden, and a small archaeological museum. Even if you don't overnight here, be sure to take a boat ride into the awesome Sumidero Canyon, just south of town.

La Hacienda Hotel-Trailer Park ($): This park is on the western side of town (toward Tehuantepec), at the traffic circle intersection of Belisario Dominguez and the Periférico (bypass, also called Libramiento). The hotel is easy to find; if you're on the main highway you pass right by it.
This is a small and rather crowded park, but the location is excellent for overnighters. There are full hookups and a very welcome swimming pool. The Hacienda is also convenient to buses, cabs, and local services.

Tuxtla Gutiérrez to San Cristóbal de Las Casas (52 miles): This is a moderately steep and visually dramatic climb from tierra caliente (hot country) to the cool highlands. Traffic is light but quite slow. Take your time and enjoy the views.

San Cristóbal de Las Casas, Chiapas (6,890 ft.): This charming colonial town (about 40,000 inhabitants) is an important market center for tens of thousands of highland Tzotzil Indians. San Cristóbal itself is quite interesting and attractive. Prices are good and there is excellent shopping for food and handicrafts. Like Oaxaca, San Cristóbal makes a wonderful base for side trips into the surrounding mountains and Indian villages. San Cristóbal can be surprisingly cool, especially in late autumn and winter.

Rancho San Nicolas Camping-Trailer Park ($): From Tuxtla Gutiérrez, the Pan American Highway (Mex 190) approaches San Cristóbal from the west and skirts the southern side of town. To reach the campground from the Pan American Highway, turn north on Insurgentes toward the center of town. Go several blocks to the Pemex station, then turn right (east) on Francisco Leon Street. Leon Street eventually becomes a narrow country lane that crosses a bridge and climbs a hill to the park. If you get lost, hire a cab to lead you to the park. Big rigs should avoid wandering through San Cristóbal's narrow colonial streets.

San Nicolas is a down-home, country-style campground. Steve says that the pine trees, green grass, and wood
smoke make him homesick for Oregon. The campground's
tiny wooden cabins remind his daughter, Churpa, of a Hobbit
village. Carlos Melendez, founder of the Monarch Camping
Club, says San Nicolas has "all the environment of a logging
camp, very attractive."

Whatever your reaction to the camp's high mountain setting, its rustic facilities will not please everyone. San Nicolas'
cordial owner isn't shy about his preference for backpackers,
van campers, and relaxed RVers. He told us that travelers who
are addicted to hookups "always complain a lot" about his
scattered and slightly jury-rigged services.

But if you're looking for a quiet, friendly, and very inexpensive retreat, you'll find good company here. In addition
to the usual international crowd of Mexico explorers, San
Nicolas is a popular stopover for travelers bound to and from
Guatemala and Central America. Chiapas was once part of
Guatemala, and the campground and its surroundings look,
feel, and even smell like that country's highlands. Adding to
the local color, Tzotzil Indians in full *traje* (traditional cos-
tume) regularly pass by the camp on their way to San
Cristóbal's marketplace.

Facilities and Services: There are 12 marked spaces with
water and power "here and there" and no sewer hookups.
The park has lots of room for tents and no-hookup campers,
"funky but clean" bathrooms, and hot showers. One bun-
galow and seven very inexpensive clapboard cabins without
bedding are also available as is a do-it-yourself laundry sink.
When hiring the services of the Indian laundress, agree on
the price beforehand. The customer provides the soap.

Grutas de San Cristóbal ($): The San Cristóbal Caverns
are 7 miles east of San Cristóbal, on Mex 190 to Comitan an
Guatemala. A dirt road turns south off the highway and

winds through the forest for about a quarter of a mile to the park. There is a small sign. We've been camping in this spot since long before it was turned into a "tourist attraction." Fortunately, development has been minor. Other than a rarely occupied gatehouse, a little-used picnic area, and a high, cement slide, this municipal park remains a quiet, secluded forest. There is no water and the only "facility" is a rather grim toilet. The caretaker will be around sooner or later to collect a modest camping fee. Tell him, *"Quisieramos acampar, por favor"* (We would like to camp, please).

In addition to walks in the forest and polishing the seat of your pants on the slide, don't miss the main attraction: La Gruta de San Cristóbal, a deep, natural cavern. There is a small charge for admission.

San Cristóbal de Las Casas to Ocosingo, Chiapas (130 miles): The turnoff to Ocosingo from Mex 190 is about 7 miles east of San Cristóbal (just over a mile beyond the Gruta de San Cristóbal).

Most maps show Mex 199 to Ocosingo and Palenque as gravel, if they show it at all. However, after years of patchwork progress, this twisting, up-and-down highway is now paved for its entire length. Considering the mountainous terrain it crosses, the road is in remarkably good condition—for the condition it's in. Traffic is light, and with the exception of tight curves, occasional washouts and slides during the rainy season, shoulder slippages, and roller-coaster *assentamientos* (settlings), you should encounter no particular problems. In fact, the views and side attractions make this one of my favorite drives in Mexico.

Ocosingo, Chiapas (2,980 ft.): Regular gasoline, supplies, and modest accommodations are available in this small, semitropical town.

Agua Azul Campground and Waterfalls ($): About 30 miles north of Ocosingo, take a paved road west from the highway to Palenque. It is a steep, curving three-mile descent to the river and campground. (Note: The usually reliable AAA road map of Mexico shows Agua Azul confusingly close to Tumbala, on another road entirely.)

If you don't have a vehicle, you'll have to hike in on the road or hitch a ride. Cabs, buses, and tour vans sometimes pass by, but don't count on a ride. Once you're in Agua Azul, it is usually easier to beg a lift back up to the main highway or even to Palenque.

Agua Azul, or Blue Water, is one of Mexico's most dazzling natural wonders, a magical river of shimmering pools, cataracts, and waterfalls that meanders through an impossibly green, vine-draped jungle. As the sun moves across the sky, mineral deposits on the river's rocky bottom capture the light and diffuse it into shifting rainbows of emerald and turquoise.

Agua Azul covers several square miles of river and rain forest. There are literally hundreds of pools of all shapes, colors, and sizes, from tinkling, ankle-deep faerie baths to deep, thundering cascades. The water is not only clear and refreshing but swimmers can cavort from pool to pool on a do-it-yourself float and fantasy trip, ogling parrots, butterflies, giant bromeliads, and tree-clinging orchids. It is no wonder that Steve says, "Agua Azul is numero uno!"

Landlubbers can walk a well-trodden trail that follows the river upstream from the grassy parking area for about a mile. Though it is steep at first and sometimes quite slippery, anyone in reasonable condition will be able to make this magnificent jungle hike.

Agua Azul is owned and managed by a local agricultural ejido. You will be charged a small entrance and camping fee, per person and per vehicle, at the gatehouse. You'll also be pestered by local children asking for tips to guard your car (presumably from other children). Politely but firmly ignore them and they'll eventually look for easier pickings. Lock your vehicle carefully. If you are tenting, keep an eye on the kids.

Agua Azul is visited by tour buses from Palenque. Once the midday tourist crowds depart, the pace of life slows dramatically. Expect the usual weekend picnickers, however.

The campground is a vaguely defined area of parking lot, meadow, and trees. There is a toilet, but you'll pay a nominal charge to use it. Thatched, palapa-style restaurants dispense sodas, cigarettes, and basic meals. Hammock space can also be rented. There are no other facilities or services.

Keep in mind that Agua Azul is located in a rain forest. Be prepared for damp ground and rain, even in the so-called winter dry season. A warning about the river: for all its beauty, the current can be strong and hazardous, especially to small kids and weak swimmers. There are warning signs posted at the most treacherous spots—and wooden crosses to commemorate those who ignored them. Also, no matter how clean the water looks at Agua Azul, it is never safe to drink. Purify it carefully.

Misol Ha Waterfall ($): This site is just off the main highway, about 30 miles north of Agua Azul and 12.5 miles south of Palenque. Turn at the sign and drive a short distance to the refreshment stand and waterfall. The Misol Ha waterfall is both beautiful and impressive, but it is simply outdone by Agua Azul. Misol Ha does make a good overnight campsite. The parking lot is large, more or less level, and well drained. The fee for camping is small. You'll also find fewer kids than at Agua Azul.

Palenque, Chiapas (690 ft.): On a typical Saturday morning, Palenque's busy main street will be crowded with ranchers, farmers, tourists, loggers, school kids, local housewives, and Chontal Indians. In addition to its famous Mayan ruins, the town serves as a frontier shopping center for remote settlements in the southern rain forests. Though its atmosphere is commercial rather than colonial, Palenque is lively, interesting, and friendly.

Maya Bell Campground ($): On the road to the Palenque ruins, just under four miles from town and one and a half miles from the ruins, the Maya Bell is inside the boundaries of the Palenque National Park, a short distance beyond the gatehouse. Watch for a small sign and a driveway on your left; the jungle screens the campground from the road.

The Maya Bell is within pleasant walking distance of the Palenque ruins. Morning and evening bird-watching is very good, both in the camp and along the road and trails to the ruins. There is also regular, inexpensive *colectivo* (VW *combi* shuttles) service to and from the town and ruins.

The Maya Bell is a broad, grassy, tree-shaded clearing surrounded on three sides by deep jungle. The campground is on a hillside, with the upper slope favored by tent and hammock campers. There are several open-sided thatched ramadas scattered along the fringes of the jungle. These are often shared in a communal, low-budget style strongly reminiscent of the late 1960s. Van and RV campers tend to congregate in the lower camping area, near the hookups, bathrooms, and restaurant.

Facilities and Services: There are 40 spaces with all hookups, tents, huts, hammocks, bathrooms and showers, and a do-it-yourself laundry area. The restaurant has good, inexpensive food.

This wonderful campground is as close as most travelers will ever get to actually camping in the jungle. In fact, when the howler monkeys cut loose with their disturbingly jaguarlike roars, nervous visitors think the Maya Bell is a little too close to nature for comfort. Throw in a snake sighting, the odd insect or two, and a few unidentified nocturnal cries, and they'll beat a hasty retreat to the nearest hotel room.

The exotic action isn't confined to the jungle. The Maya Bell is so inexpensive and popular that it attracts young, active travelers, backpackers, and long-haired VW van types. Between the guitar music, partying, and mushroom munching, aging hippies can sometimes find it difficult to sleep. "I hate to admit it," Steve says, "but when I need a good night's rest, I join the motor home set at the Maria del Mar Trailer Park, just up the road."

Maria del Mar Trailer Park ($$): This park is on the road to Palenque National Park, less than two miles from the town of Palenque and a little over three miles from the ruins. This relatively new establishment is the only "real" RV park for many miles around. As with most newer campgrounds, however, the Maria del Mar is shy on plants and shade. Considering the Jack-in-the-Beanstalk growing conditions in this hot, humid country, it won't be a problem for long. Until the shade appears, you can cool off in the park's swimming pool.

Facilities and Services: There are 75 to 100 spaces with all hookups. The Maria del Mar has a sliding price scale that benefits tent campers. It has very clean bathrooms with generous hot water, a clubhouse and dance floor, a restaurant, a bar, and purified water. Local tours and horse rental are available, and there is frequent local *combi* van service to town and the ruins.

Hotel Nututum ($): On the highway to Ocosingo, about 1.5 miles from Palenque, the hotel and camping area share parklike grounds on the bank of the Rio Tulija. This is actually a balneario-style picnic place and swimming hole, with camping allowed as a very pleasant afterthought. Both the shady setting and the cool swimming are great.

Nututum has no hookups, but bathrooms and water are available. The fee is quite reasonable.

Steve once camped next to the river here after a long, hot drive from Villahermosa. Following a long, lazy swim, he was just stretching out in the shade for a nap when a neighboring motor home began spewing exhaust fumes from a noisy auxiliary generator. Steve claims he kept his peace for a full 30 minutes, but when he'd finally exceeded his daily limit of noise and carbon monoxide pollution, something snapped.

"I did not beat the guy's door down," Steve swears. "I just knocked loud enough to be clearly heard over the sound of his generator." In any case, when the door flew open, the startled motor home owner found himself facing a very large and very harried visitor. As politely as possible, Steve asked him to kill the generator or else.

"I'm just cooking dinner," the fellow stammered. "It'll only take a few more minutes. Otherwise I'd shut 'er down right away. You see, I need the power for my microwave."

Steve's constant curiosity about food immediately overcame his anger. "Microwave? What are you cooking?"

The motor homer looked him straight in the eye. "A frozen TV dinner," he answered. "Enchiladas and refried beans. Can I offer you one?"

On to the Yucatán: For driving and camping suggestions from Palenque to the states of Campeche, Yucatán, and Quintana Roo, see the Yucatán Peninsula section.

Palenque to Villahermosa and Tabasco: If you're going north from Palenque, you'll find very few campgrounds until you reach the state of Veracruz. Your best bet is to look for free camping along gulf beaches or attach yourself to a hotel or motel. Because traffic is generally heavy on Gulf Coast highways, I do not advise camping close to the road.

Villahermosa to Mexico City (530 miles): For the quickest, most direct route take Mex 180 to Acayucan, then jog south on Mex 185 to Sayula and pick up Mex 145 through Loma Bonita and Tierra Blanca. This is pineapple country, so be sure to stop for fresh squeezed juice. When Mex 145 meets Mex 150, turn west to Cordoba and follow 150D to Puebla. From Puebla you can bypass Mexico City if you wish (see the Central Highlands driving tips).

The slower, more scenic route from Villahermosa to Veracruz follows Mex 180 along the Gulf Coast. You'll find many more camping opportunities here, especially at Lake Catemaco and on the beaches south of Veracruz.

Tabasco:

Hermanos Graham Trailer Park ($): This park, on the north side of Mex 180, at Km 38, is approximately 79 miles west of Villahermosa and 25 miles east of Coatzacoalcos, near the La Venta archaeological site and the turnoff to Agua Dulce. There is an easy-to-miss sign. Stop at the house to pay for camping, then follow the road into the park.

This campground is also known as *Campo* or *Rancho Hermanos Graham.* The trailer park, a spacious, savannah-like field nicely shaded by tropical trees, is just a small portion of this extensive property.

The campground includes a lake, swimming and wading pools, and a playground. Bird-watching in the park is good, and there is a lookout tower. "This is an exceptional park," Steve says, "a beautiful oasis in the midst of an area known more for its oil rigs than natural beauty."

Facilities and Services: There are lots of full hookup sites, plus room for caravans and tents, clean bathrooms and hot water, games, horses, and sports activities. The management is very friendly.

CHAPTER 12

Yucatán Peninsula and Gulf Coast

In a country of startling diversity, the Yucatán still manages to come up with a surprise: this 55,000-square-mile peninsula is as flat as a pancake, with only a few minor dimples rising above a level limestone plateau. The most prominent topographical features, other than Mayan pyramids, are the gentle 350-foot "peaks" of the Puuc Hills.

Because of the great porosity of its limestone foundation, the Yucatán has virtually no lakes, rivers, or significant surface water. Just mile after mile of low thorn jungle, *milpas* (cornfields), savannahs, and mangrove swamps. Lest this sound boring, you'll also find stone-and-thatch Mayan villages, countless eye-popping archaeological sites, a wealth of birds and wildlife, and some of the world's finest beaches, coral reefs, and diving.

The peninsula's large Mayan population gives this region's culture, customs, and food a distinct identity that is quite different from the rest of Mexico. There is a sense of personal warmth and humor among the Yucatec Mayans which travelers find both attractive and reassuring. In all our travels, Lorena and I have never met a friendlier or more hospitable group of people than the Yucatecos. It is no wonder that many visitors, especially women, feel at ease among the Mayans. Literacy is also high in the Yucatán and crime is exceptionally low.

It is only in recent years that the Yucatán Peninsula (which includes the states of Campeche, Yucatán, and Quintana Roo) has been connected to the outside world with highways and international air flights. Consequently, facilities for campers are scarce. The peninsula's unique geography also complicates free camping and exploring. Because the jungle is so dense and the ground rough, broken, and incredibly rocky, casual hiking and camping are difficult. Side roads are extremely narrow and "wide spots" few and far between. Most campers take the path of least resistance and congregate along the beautiful Caribbean and gulf beaches.

Even the most jaded beachcomber can't overlook the area's wealth of archaeological sites, however. From tiny coastal "watchtower" altars to genuine Lost Cities complete with stone causeways, palaces, temples, marketplaces, and overgrown suburbs, evidence of a once-great Mayan civilization can be found at every turn and on virtually every trail. Many of these sites are located next to highways and villages; others are hidden by the jungle and known only to local farmers.

The Mayans are active hunters, gatherers, and traders. Narrow, rocky trails, some in constant use for centuries, radiate from every village and rancho. None of these trails is marked, and finding your way is complicated by the fact that backcountry Mayans often don't speak Spanish. In my opinion, that only adds to the challenge. (A guide can solve many problems. Even Mayans get lost in these confusing, lookalike forests.)

There's more: although the Yucatán's beaches enjoy cooling breezes, the jungle is another story. The combination of heat, humidity, rocky terrain, and tough, tripwire vines can add an interesting challenge to a typical hike. As in any good jungle, there must be a balance between the beautiful and the bizarre, the exotic and the unnerving. In addition to parrots, toucans, monkeys, and butterflies, the Yucatán also supports a healthy population of poisonous snakes and plants, stinging ants, mosquitoes, and scorpions. With due caution and common sense, none of these should be especially hazardous. Be careful, however, to mind the aluxes, invisible but potent dwarf-spirits who do their best to protect cornfields, forests, and wild creatures from unwelcome interlopers.

The Yucatán's topographic uniformity is a blessing for drivers. The highways are flat, straight, and in remarkably good repair, and traffic is light. With the exception of Cancún's kamikaze cabbies and margarita-muddled tourists, Yucatecan drivers tend to be remarkably safe and sane.

While RV and van travelers love the Yucatán's well-maintained, straightedge highways, they soon curse the *topes* (speed bumps) found in virtually every village. Good driving conditions, however, make it possible to cross the peninsula in virtually any direction, including diagonally, in one determined day of travel.

Relentless publicity about Cancún's "eternal spring" has created a very inaccurate picture of the Yucatán's climate. In fact, the Yucatán is categorized as tierra caliente (hot land), though in winter it can be surprisingly chilly. When a winter norte sweeps down from the frozen midwestern United States and crosses the Gulf of Mexico, Cancún will be cloudly, cool, and quite windy for days on end. These storms are most common from January through March and can last anywhere from two to ten days.

Hurricanes are also possible in summer and autumn, but the usual summer weather pattern is high heat and humidity with occasional downpours. We've camped in the Yucatán in summer and found it bearable only on the beach, with a minimum of clothing and activity. Unless you're accustomed to the heat, the best time of year to travel in this region is from mid- to late-October through March or April.

I call the Gulf of Mexico region the "Forgotten Coast." Only two cities on the entire Gulf—Veracruz and Campeche—qualify as "official" tourist destinations and even their following is quite limited. With the exception of bird watchers, treasure divers, and fishermen, the gulf's sweeping arc of beaches, jungles, and wetlands sees few visitors. Of these, the vast majority seldom stray far from Mex 180, the main route to the Yucatán from southern Texas.

Unfortunately, much of this coast has been scarred and polluted by Pemex, the Mexican government's oil monopoly. During the great petro-boom of the late 1970s and early 1980s, all environmental caution was thrown to the winds in the race to pump oil. At the same time, a tremendous influx of money and population buried many of the gulf's picturesque towns under an avalanche of concrete, glass, and steel. Clearcutting of tropical forests and slash-and-burn agriculture on the steep slopes of the eastern Sierra Madre combined with industrial pollution to wreak havoc on the region's wildlife, rivers, wetlands, and beaches.

In spite of these problems, the Gulf Coast remains a very exciting area for camping and exploration. Campgrounds are scarce, but there is no shortage of beaches, side roads, archaeological sites, and exciting adventures. As an aid to exploring this region, I highly recommend *Adventuring Along the Gulf of Mexico* by Donald Schueler (see Recommended Reading).

The gulf's climate is quite moist and humid, with high temperatures in spring and summer. The storm-prone Gulf of Mexico can be schizophrenic in winter, when periods of warm calm alternate with harsh winds, cool temperatures, and heavy rains. With the Sierra Madre Oriental trapping rain clouds close to shore, it is no wonder that much of this coast is wet and waterlogged. Vast swamps and intertwining rivers at the bottom of the gulf's "dipper" arc have earned the state of Tabasco the nickname "Mexico's Holland." Rain or shine, the fishing here is hard to beat.

Once you've reached the flatlands of Tabasco and Campeche, there is a tendency to rush headlong into the Yucatán Peninsula. In fact, with a heavy foot on the accelerator and a complete disregard for sightseeing, it is possible to drive from Villahermosa to Cancún in one marathon day. Avoid the temptation; there is much more to see in this region than meets the eye at 60 mph.

Villahermosa marks the junction of two major routes into the Yucatán Peninsula: Mex 180, the older, slower, and very interesting Gulf Coast highway, and Mex 186, the quicker, "back door" track to the Caribbean and Cancún. The choice is difficult. I love bird-watching, camping, and shelling along the Gulf Coast beaches, but the Mayan ruins along Mex 186 are well worth exploring. The best solution is a compromise: make a huge loop trip through the Yucatán that includes both highways.

Villahermosa, Tabasco to Mérida, Yucatán (400 miles): Mex 180 includes ferry crossings, so allow a full day or more to travel from Villahermosa to Campeche (280 miles). In addition to some of Mexico's finest fishing and birding, this coast is known for its seafood cocktails. While walking off a delicious concoction known as *vuelve a la vida* (return to life), Steve and I stumbled across a beach ankle deep in seashells. Unfortunately for RVers, there are no developed facilities. Free camping is abundant, but so are the mosquitoes.

The most heavily traveled highway between Villahermosa and Campeche is Mex 186, via Escarcega. This region is very swampy and drivers should be wary of roller coaster road surfaces caused by settling and slippage.

Escarcega, Campeche: This grimy little town is noteworthy only for its Pemex station. Long lines at the pumps are common. The attendants aren't the most honest I've met, so use your calculator and count your change carefully.

Camping and accommodations are very scarce in this

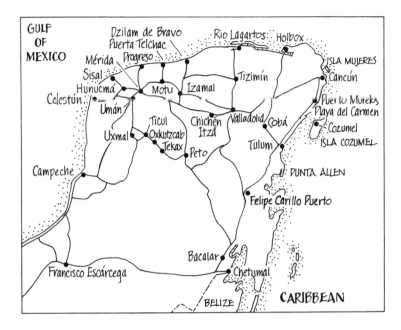

area, and you may have to overnight in Escarcega. Grin and bear it. You'll find a garishly painted hotel just east of the highway intersection, on the north side of the main street into town. The place is reasonably clean and cheap.

Escarcega to Chetumal, Quintana Roo (170 miles): Mex 186 cuts across low hills and broad expanses of uninhabited scrub jungle. Traffic is very light, and the early morning and late afternoon wildlife watching can be excellent. Allow at least a few hours to visit the Mayan ruins at Chicanna, Xpujil, Becan, and Kohunlich.

Escarcaega to Mérida: You have a choice of two routes from Escarcega to Mérida. The most direct is Mex 261 and Mex 180 to Campeche, then Mex 180 to Mérida. When I'm in the mood for ruins, however, I prefer the longer way round, via Uxmal. The Uxmal route includes several archaeological sites and caverns, as well as the usual trackless forests and seldom-visited Mayan villages.

Here again, you have two possible routes to Uxmal. North of Champoton, turn east to the ruins of Edzna. After touring Edzna, continue on Mex 261, a good but little-used secondary highway that will take you to Uxmal and several other noteworthy Mayan sites. From Uxmal it's an easy 90-minute drive to Mérida. Or, if you'd like to visit Campeche on your way to Uxmal, pick up Mex 261 east of Campeche and follow it to Uxmal.

Campeche, Campeche: This Gulf Coast city's history includes enough pirates, sieges, Indian revolts, and hurricanes to stock a dozen B-grade movies. In spite of its colonial architecture, outstanding seafood, and beautiful beaches, Campeche's tourism suffers from its out-of-the-way location.

Campeche Trailer Park ($): To find this park, don't take the Campeche bypass; stay on coastal Mex 180. About two miles south of town turn inland, following signs to the trailer park. Continue past the University of Campeche to colonial Samula and the campground.

This small, attractive park is set in a suburban citrus grove. Steve looks forward to giving his industrial-strength orange juice squeezer a good workout here. Though it isn't all that easy to locate, the park is a welcome overnight spot for Yucatán-bound travelers. Campeche is a fascinating city (and state) that most tourists overlook completely in their rush to the Caribbean. As a result, the Campeche Trailer Park is far enough from the beaten track to attract unusually interesting guests.

Facilities and Services: There are 22 spaces with hookups, clean bathrooms and showers and barbecue grills. The property is fenced.

Mérida, Yucatán: The largest city in the Yucatán Peninsula has only half a million inhabitants. In contrast to many mid-sized Mexican cities that have grown by leaps and bounds in recent years, Mérida is relatively unchanged. Food and accommodations are a bargain, especially when compared to inflated prices on the Caribbean. Also known as the ''White City,'' Mérida is exceptionally neat, clean, and conservative. Drivers will appreciate the city's logically numbered streets and surprisingly sane traffic.

Rainbow Trailer Park ($): This park is north of Mérida, at Km 8 on Mex 261 to Progreso. (In Mérida, this highway is called Paseo Montejo.) The park is just north of the huge Cordamex henequen processing factory, on the west side of the highway. The Rainbow's lawns are overgrown, the swimming pool is cracked and empty, and someone forgot to install the gate. In other words, this park has seen better days. Steve was not discouraged, however.

''The Rainbow is better than nothing. It's cheap, quiet, and has a rural setting. The grounds are rather bald, but there's some shade.'' The trailer park is also close to Mérida, with good bus service into the city.

Facilities and Services: The park has 70 spaces with all hookups, some pull-throughs, and good access for large rigs. There are clean rest rooms with hot showers and hand laundry service.

Mayan's Trailers Paradise ($): This park is on the southern outskirts of Mérida, on the west side of Mex 180 to Uxmal and Campeche, across from the Mérida International Airport. (When Mex 180 enters Mérida, it becomes Avenida de Los Itzaes.) There is a small sign for the park, but it is difficult to spot.

This park's location in Mérida's light industrial/airport district is both a curse and a blessing. As blessings go, this one isn't much: good access to downtown by bus or cab. The curse is noisy jetliners swooping so low that you can see the passenger's bemused expressions as they peer into the campground. Fortunately, night flights are rare.

Considering the scarcity of campgrounds in the Yucatán, I am reluctant to fault Mayan's Trailers Paradise for its
rather ragged appearance. Until more facilities open up,
campers need every park they can get. In its favor, the park
offers plenty of shade and a bargain basement price. "Paradise" is adequate for short visits.

Facilities and Services: The park has over 50 spaces
with full hookups, some with cement pads. There is good
access for large rigs. The bathrooms could use a scrubbing,
and there is no hot water. The park has a falling-down fence
and no gate.

Hacienda Yaxcopoil ($): On Highway 261 between
Uman and Muna, at Km 33. This is also the highway between
Uxmal and Mérida. If you're heading south toward Uxmal,
the highway doglegs to the left in front of the Hacienda's
weathered double arch. You can't miss the large billboard.

This former henequen and cattle estate is now a privately operated museum and gift shop. In addition to the
remarkably well-preserved residence, the grounds include
a large garden, corrals, gift shop, and a complete Industrial
Revolution-era henequen processing factory. The Hacienda's
friendly owner would also like to expand his tourist services
with a trailer park. Although there were no facilities at my
last visit, campers will be accommodated on a jury-rigged
basis. This is a fascinating place that makes an unusual overnight stop.

Rancho Uxmal Motel ($$): The Rancho Uxmal is about
three miles north of the Uxmal ruins on Highway 261. The
deep, grassy parking lot in front of the family owned and
operated Rancho Uxmal is the area's only campground.
Though this modest hotel's camping facilities are limited to
shade, two shared bathrooms, an outside faucet, and a few
electrical hookups, this is a pleasant and quite friendly base
from which to explore Ixmal and its environs. Lorena and I
tay here frequently, not only for the economy of the Rancho's

camping (and rooms) but also for its quiet location and excellent, home-cooked Mayan food.

Chichén Itzá, Yucatán

Piramide Inn Trailer Park ($$): On the north side of Mex 180 from Mérida, on the eastern edge of the village of Piste, less than a mile from Chichén Itzá. Look for the hotel of the same name. Chichén Itzá may well be the world's most visited archaeological site. This once-attractive campground has suffered as a result of the hotel's success. After a recent "remodeling," the trailer park has been squeezed up against the hotel. Once a grassy citrus grove, it has become a plain, graveled parking lot.

Facilities and Services: The park is small and crowded. It was under construction during our visit, but hookups should be in order by now. Campers have the use of the hotel swimming pool and restaurant/bar. There is good security. It is bearable for an overnight stop.

Hurricane Gilbert struck the coast of Quintana Roo and swept across northern Yucatán in 1988. There is little doubt that some of the campgrounds we've described have been damaged by Gilbert's 175 mph winds. I'd expect to find fewer coconut palms and thatched roofs but otherwise, repairs should be completed or well under way by the time you reach the Yucatán.

Puerto Juárez, Quintana Roo: Located on the northern fringe of Cancún's sprawling suburbs. Puerto Juárez is just a collection of seafood joints and a dock for the passenger ferry to Isla de Mujeres.

La Playa Trailer Park ($): This park is 2½ miles beyond Puerto Juárez on the road to Punta Sam. Punta Sam, the car ferry terminal to Isla Mujeres, is about 0.6 mile beyond the trailer park.

The "yellow plague" coconut virus has left this once palm-shaded coastline bald and sunburned. Fortunately, La Playa's beach is still beautiful and close at hand, with good swimming and boat launching in calm weather. Like many of the peninsula's campgrounds, however, La Playa is showing the effects of long-term neglect. The hot water heater rarely, if ever, works, and the caretaker, though amiable, is often absent. Still, the place is cheap, convenient, quiet, and seldom crowded. What more can you ask? (Answer: pray that the skyrocketing value of Caribbean real estate doesn't cause this trailer park to be sacrificed for more condos.)

Facilities and Services: There are 50 spaces with water and power, a dump station, and some beachfront spaces. Bathrooms are reasonably clean and have cold showers. A do-it-yourself laundry sink and clothesline are available.

Cancún, Quintana Roo: A city of over 250,000 people built on a sandbar between the Caribbean and a once pristine lagoon, Cancún is the incarnation of "fun in the sun" tourism, a resort that deliberately bears little resemblance to the "real" Mexico. I consider the city's main attraction to be its well-stocked supermarkets.

With the emphasis on high-rise hotels and discos, it's no wonder that camping is limited. Since Cancún's building boom has yet to peak, there is always hope (however vague) that someone will decide to provide comfortable and convenient facilities for visiting campers and RVs. For this reason, I suggest that you visit the tourist department and ask for their suggestions. If nothing else, they might direct you to secure parking areas. Otherwise, the pickings are extremely slim.

CREA Youth Hostel ($$): On the north side of busy Kukulkan Boulevard, east of downtown. The hostel is so large and fancy that many travelers mistake it for a tourist hotel. This is the "Hilton" of Mexico's government-sponsored youth hostels. With a swimming pool and nearby beach, lawns (for tenting), restaurant, and many other services, this hostel looks like a tremendous bargain, at least for tourists. Unfortunately, its rates reflect Cancún's gold rush economy and put the hostel beyond the budget of the very travelers it is supposed to help—Mexico's young people.

Depending on current policy, RV and van campers may be allowed to use the hostel's grounds and facilities. Check at the office.

Rainbow Trailer Park ($): A little over a mile south of the airport turnoff, on the west side of Mex 307 to Tulum. Look for a sign with a rainbow and the words "Trailer Park."

This is similar to Mérida's flight path Paradise Trailer Park except that Cancún's airport is busier and even noisier. Steve says, "Other than the fact that this campground is cheap, I can't imagine staying here on purpose." I agree; the Rainbow has all the appeal of an emergency runway.

Facilities and Services: There are 60 spaces with all hookups. The park is roomy and seems to cater to caravans. Tenting can be accommodated. There is no shade, and the facilities are generally unkempt and grimy.

Cancún to Tulum (80 miles): Mex 307 follows the Caribbean shore, but you'll have to take side roads in order to see the beach. Traffic is rarely heavy on this highway, but it's often dangerously fast. Tour buses, speeding tourists, and stalled vehicles are the main hazards. Because there are no shoulders, you can expect to find disabled buses, bicyclists, carts, and pedestrians in your lane.

Rising property values and increased development are beginning to limit the free camping possibilities along this coast, especially for RVers. Van and car campers will find a few narrow unused side roads, but in general, beach access is very limited.

Xcalacoco ($): The turnoff from Mex 307 to Punta Bete and Xcalacoco is roughly 63 miles south of Cancún and 5 miles north of Playa del Carmen at Km 297. There is a sign on the highway. Follow a rough, rocky road east one-plus miles to the campgrounds.

Until Hurricane Beulah laid waste to this coast in 1967, Xcalacoco was a thriving coconut plantation with a full mile of paradise-quality beach. Hard times, coconut blight, and family squabbles have reduced these holdings to a pair of small but still quite beautiful beachfront campgrounds, split down the middle by a barbed wire "spite fence." Approaching from the highway, I call them Xcalacoco Left and Xcalacoco Right. Though they evidently aren't on speaking terms, these family-owned camps share an exceptional beach, with excellent access to reefs, snorkeling, and good boating. Playa del Carmen can be reached by hiking the beach.

Xcalacoco Right has sandy parking spaces for up to thirty rigs. There is no electricity, but the bathrooms are clean and the showers hot. Water for both camps comes from nearby wells. Plain-and-simple bungalows can also be rented. There is a small restaurant.

Xcalacoco Left is even more down home, with small palapas for shade and shelter if you didn't bring your own. The old Mayan couple are exceptionally friendly. As part of Steve's selfless research into Mexico's best kitchens, he rates the señora's conch soup as "unreal." She will also cook your catch if you have luck while fishing.

Playa del Carmen: This is a small, lively town with an unusually nice beach. Ice, water, gas, and other supplies are available, but you'll save money by shopping in Cancún.

Las Ruinas ($): On the beach, one block north of the plaza. The Ruins is one of those quirky parks that you'll either love or hate; it all depends on your tastes and tolerances.

Las Ruinas is named for the small, chapel-sized Mayan temple that squats near the entrance. Park lore says that to preserve this ruin, the Mexican government will not allow Las Ruinas' owners to expand or significantly improve the park; hence its semiruinous condition. Like Yasser Arafat's perennial five-day beard, this campground's sagging, sand-floored cabanas, wood-and-cement tables, ramshackle barbecue, and communal bathrooms are carefully but scruffily maintained. With a motley crew of international backpackers, pickup and van campers, hippie hammock swingers, slumming southern Californians, and peso-pinching eccentrics, it's no wonder they call this town Playa del Karma.

Keep an eye on your gear. Most of the campers are quite honest, but with such interesting company, common sense says, "Be prudent."

Facilities and Services: There are several spaces for vans and pickups with electrical hookups only. There is no room for large rigs. The park has shaded, sandy tent sites right on the beach, reasonably clean bathrooms with cold showers, a laundry sink, and a clothesline.

Brisa del Mar Campground ($): Two blocks north of the plaza, close to the beach, this is a very small campground with space for just a few vehicles. Las Brisas is dirty, depressing, and definitely not recommended.

CREA Youth Hostel ($): Off a dirt road to the northwest of town. If you're on Mex 307, turn east (toward the sea) at the CFE electrical station about ¼ mile north of the intersection to Playa del Carmen. Go about two blocks on a dirt road. The driveway for the hostel will be on your left (north). If you continue on this road, it eventually leads to the beach, on the north side of town. When in doubt, ask directions to *el albergue*.

The youth hostel is a former boarding school that includes several low cement block buildings. There are segregated dormitories, a communal kitchen-dining hall (with refrigerators and stoves), and a thatched roof rec room. Several bare but clean private rooms with double beds and bath are also available for couples and families.

The albergue won't win any landscaping and design awards, but it offers clean, straightforward accommodations at a bargain price. The mood is friendly and very informal, but you don't have to be young to stay here. The management is helpful and will allow vehicle camping in the parking lot. The beach and town are within a ten-minute walk. We've enjoyed staying here and the hostel gets good marks from other guests I've talked to.

Facilities and Services: There are 200 beds, sheets, lockers, and locks, a kitchen, cold showers, and a basketball court. Five cabana rooms are also available. Be prepared for evening mosquitoes.

Public Parking Lot: Overnight parking is allowed on the beach side of Playa del Carmen's plaza, next to the small naval station. Though it's a very public place with no shade or services, I've seen RVs here on many occasions. With the marines close at hand, security should be good.

Paamul ($$$): At Km 85 between Playa del Carmen and Akumal, 53 miles south of Cancún. Turn east off Mex 307 and drive about a mile to the beach on a dirt road.

This small park is squeezed between beachfront bungalows and a low jungle. At the rate the palms are dying, it will also be without shade before long. Still, Paamul has the usual beautiful beach, with excellent snorkeling. It is one of the few Caribbean parks with full hookups, a feature that may account for its relatively stiff rates. Paamul is often full during the peak winter season.

Chemuyil ($): About 67 miles south of Cancún, between Akumal and Xel-Ha. A large sign at the highway brags that this is the world's most beautiful beach. They may be correct; follow a grandiose four-lane road about 100 yards to the campground and judge for yourself. Stop at the gatehouse and pay a small per-person admission for day use and camping. If no one is there, pick a spot and they'll catch you later. The staff, by the way, is very attentive and friendly.

As the sign so boldly states, Chemuyil is an exceptionally beautiful beach, shaded by a still-healthy grove of coconut palms and protected by a coral reef. With gentle waves lapping against white powdery sand and palm fronds rustling in the wind, this campground seems almost too good to be true.

Chemuyil is also incredibly cheap, with artificially low government subsidized prices for camping and picnicking. A hotellike building on the north side of the beach is used by vacationing bureaucrats, but the rest of this sprawling property is open to the public.

The south end of the beach, to your right as you pass through the gatehouse, is favored by tent campers. Take your pick of innumerable shaded, sandy view sites.

RV campers seem to prefer the camping area between the gatehouse and the beach. There is grass, shade, and good access to the rest rooms and restaurant. Screened palapas can also be rented for picnics or camping. RV caravans visit Chemuyil, but either through clever planning or simple oversight, hookups are not available and the campground is seldom full for long. Even during busy holidays, the southern parking lot and coconut grove are rarely too crowded for comfort. In spite of busy weekends, Chemuyil's staff keeps the campground and beach as neat as a pin.

To protect swimmers, private power boats are not allowed inside Chemuyil's protected cove. The dive shop does hire out a *panga*, however, for fishing and diving trips.

Facilities and Services: There are large, very clean community bathrooms with cold showers. Well water is available at the gatehouse. Drinking water is periodically sold from a delivery truck. No other supplies are available. There is a privately operated bar, a restaurant, and a dive shop. (The owner is friendly and full of good information about this area.)

Xcacel ($): Just over a mile south of Chemuyil (see above) on Mex 307. Look for a large sign. The same government agency that administers Chemuyil operates this lovely, inexpensive campground. Although Xcacel's beach is clean and beautiful, it is exposed to the wind and waves. In winter, when the nortes blow, swimming can be tricky here. As in Chemuyil, the campground occupies a large, sandy coconut grove. Xcacel's campground is set behind a low sand ridge that cuts off both the view and the wind. This is an advantage when nortes are in season, but it also shelters mosquitoes, especially on the jungle side of the camp.

There are no hookups; only a bathroom and shower, and a privately operated (expensive) restaurant/bar.

Tulum:

There are two Tulums: *Tulum pueblo,* the village, sits astride Mex 307. The *ruinas de Tulum,* the Mayan archaeological site, is a few miles to the northeast, on the beach. The village of Tulum is growing fast, but it's still just a modest collection of thatched houses and tiny stores. There is a gas station just north of the village, two backyard bakeries, and a couple of shade-tree mechanics.

If you're coming into Tulum on the bus, it's a long, hot mile from the highway to the campgrounds described below. Fortunately, cabs are plentiful.

El Mirador and Santa Fe Campgrounds ($): Just south of the ruins and within walking distance. Look for signs and narrow driveways toward the beach.

Backpackers and occasional van campers favor these low-budget campgrounds. I have a sentimental affection for these campgrounds based on memories from the early 1970s, before Tulum was a major tourist attraction. I'm sorry to say that fame has not meant good fortune for this particular spot. Coconut blight has ravaged a once hauntingly beautiful beach, and the campgrounds have become "scenes," surrounded by sad, unkempt stick-and-frond cabanas. Because their services and sanitary facilities leave a lot to be desired, most self-reliant campers tend to avoid these Caribbean-style crash pads.

Cabanas Chac Mool ($): On the beach road to Boca Paila and Punta Allen. The pavement ends a few miles south of the Tulum ruins. Chac Mool is another hundred yards to the south.

Chac Mool is a picture-perfect collection of thatch-and-stone cabanas set on a smooth white sand beach. By tourist hotel standards, the cabanas are decidedly rustic, but the Robinson Crusoe decor suits most beach lovers. There is a small restaurant with a limited but very tasty menu (closed Sunday).

Though Chac Mool does not advertise camping, there is space to park or tent camp beneath the dwindling palms on the south side of the property. Check at the restaurant before setting up camp. Other than communal bathrooms with occasional hot water, there are no services or electricity. Bring your own candles and drinking water.

Cabanas Arrecife and *Cabanas Tulum*: About half a mile south of the pavement, on the beach. Like Chac Mool, these cabanas charge hotel rates for pleasant but spartan accommodations. There isn't much room for RVs, but the managers are usually open to negotiations. Tent campers should find space beneath the palms.

South to Punta Allen: From the end of the pavement at Cabanas Chac Mool, it is about 30 miles to the village of Punta Allen. Punta Allen faces the Caribbean, near the tip of a sandy, palm-covered peninsula that juts southward into Bahia Ascención. After camping on the fringes of this huge wilderness of shallow lagoons and mangrove thickets, we nicknamed it the Mosquito Coast.

The road to Punta Allen is narrow, rutted, sandy, and sometimes very wet. Though it is interesting country, there are few good camping places along this road. The better spots are privately owned or inaccessible to vehicles. Our nickname isn't a joke—the mosquitoes and no-see-ums can be murderous, even at midday.

Other than barging through the underbrush, your best bets are a very rustic campground midway to Boca Paila or an exposed campsite near the Boca Paila bridge, at the mouth of the lagoon. About seven miles south of the bridge, Cabanas El Retiro is on an attractive but very shallow bay with lots of mosquitoes. From here to Punta Allen, the prospects aren't much better.

Punta Allen is a small Mayan lobster fishing village. Drinking water and limited supplies are available, but there are no campgrounds. If you'd like to stay overnight, ask for permission from local property owners to park on the waterfront. There is a small detachment of marines at the north end of the village, next to the road. These soldiers patrol the beaches for castaway smugglers and bales of "square grouper" marijuana. You may be given a quick once-over.

Cruzan Guest House: If you'd like to explore and camp the remote beaches of Ascención and Espiritu Santo bays, check at Sonya and Armando's guest house on the south end of Punta Allen. Sonya, a transplanted Californian, offers rustic, cabana-style accommodations and excellent homecooked meals. Her partner, Armando, is a diver, lobster fisherman, and guide. Together they operate the guest house and boat camping adventures, as well as local birding, diving, and fishing trips.

Coba: Just north of Tulum on Mex 307, a good paved road branches northwest to Coba (26 miles) and Nuevo Xcan (28 miles). The village of Nuevo Xcan is also on Mex 180, the Mérida-Cancún highway. The Coba highway can be used as a shortcut from Tulum to Chichén Itzá and Mérida, or to complete a loop trip originating in Cancún. (Some maps show a road between Chemax and Coba. Unless you're prepared for genuinely rough travel, don't try it.)

Coba is one of the Yucatán Peninsula's largest and least-explored archaeological sites. A once-great Mayan city, it includes major temples, palaces, and ceremonial buildings as well as five lakes, more than three dozen *sacbes* (raised stone highways), remnant stands of tall jungle, and the present-day village of Coba. Rather than cutting and grooming this site, the Mexican government has wisely designated Coba an "ecological-archaeological park." Excavations have been kept to a minimum, and trees continue to grow on major structures. To encourage the return of birds and other wildlife, hunting and logging have also been prohibited within the boundaries of the park.

Although there are no RV parks or designated campgrounds in Coba, this is an area that almost begs to be explored. Whenever someone asks me for a tip on getting close to nature in the Yucatán or on visiting a jungle without too much hassle, I recommend Coba. The site is easily accessible by private and public transportation, food and lodging costs are low, and the people are very friendly.

If you're intimidated by the peninsula's trackless jungles (and you probably should be), the central area of the archaeological site is crisscrossed by several good, clear trails. Lorena and I have spent weeks exploring and birding in the park, and yet we can always find something new. It is possible to get lost in Coba, but I don't consider it a major hazard, especially if you use common sense.

As for camping, the bed-and-cold-shower accommodations in Coba will satisfy most people's urge to rough it for a few days. Our favorite is El Bocadito, a small Mayan hotel and restaurant on the side of the highway, just as you enter the village.

Sian Ka'an: About ten miles south of Tulum, you'll find the Mayan ruins of Chunyaxche, a major site that has only recently been surveyed. This ruined city is part of Sian Ka'an (Enchantment from the Sky), Mexico's second largest Biosphere Reserve. Although the prohibition against camping within the main area of the archaeological site is enforced by the caretakers, vehicle campers can probably use the parking lot at the main entrance.

The 1,345,000-acre reserve was created by presidential decree on January 20, 1986. This vast area lies south of the Mayan ruins of Tulum and north of the Mexican port of Chetumal. Sian Ka'an is bordered on the west by Mex 307 and on the east by the Caribbean Sea. It includes 70 miles of coral reef and the largest lobster nursery grounds on the eastern coast of Mexico. In addition to tapir, manatee, jaguar, howler monkeys, snakes, and sea turtles, there are over 1,000 species of plants and 300 species of birds. Parrots, toucans, flamingos, wood storks, and LYBs (Little Yellow Birds) provide enough action to satisfy the most jaded bird watcher.

Because Sian Ka'an is a genuine reserve, access is very limited. Other than a small interpretive center beside Mex 307 at Chunyaxche and a few trails and rough roads through the jungle, the Biosphere is virtually inaccessible.

Felipe Carrillo Puerto: Gasoline, supplies, and modest accommodations. South of Carrillo Puerto, a road branches east to the Caribbean coast at Majahual. Though this region is similar to the Sian Ka'an Biosphere, it is being opened to homesteading. Free camping is plentiful but the bugs can be fierce. Supplies are not easily available so bring your own.

Lake Bacalar: An exceptionally beautiful lake bordered by mangroves and jungle, complete with a fortress to protect it from pirates.

Los Coquitos Park ($): On the *costera* (lakeshore) road, about half a mile south of the town of Bacalar. Don't take the bypass around Bacalar or you'll miss both the park and beautiful drive along the lake. Los Coquitos (The Little Palms) is a modest park with an exceptionally attractive location on the shore of Lake Bacalar. Steve remarks that this campground's safe, shallow swimming is wonderful for kids.

Los Coquitos is a local picnic and camping area; there are no hookups or services, unless you count a malodorous outhouse. The park's amiable codger-caretaker collects a modest fee for camping.

Cenote Azul Trailer Park ($): Less than a mile south of Los Coquitos Park (see above) at the junction of the costera highway and the Chetumal-Bacalar highway. The ''Blue Cenote'' is a stunningly beautiful turquoise pool surrounded by vibrantly green jungle. Across the highway, Cenote Azul Trailer Park is a balding field with too little shade. ''It's cheap,'' Steve says, ''but so is Los Coquitos, which I much prefer.''

Facilities and Services: There are 45 spaces with a few electrical hookups. The rates go up to the $$ range if you use electricity. Full hookups are planned, but until then there are a dump station, bathrooms, shower, and water faucet. There's also a palapa with hammocks for rent. The restaurant and swimming are across the street at the cenote.

Chetumal, Quintana Roo: An uninspiring port city that serves as a gateway to Belize and as a duty-free shopping center for Mexican tourists. Supplies and accommodations are available. There are customs inspections on the highway near Chetumal, so be sure to have your car papers in order.

Sunrise on the Caribbean Trailer Park: On the Caribbean coast, a few miles north of Chetumal, in the small town of Calderitas. We haven't visited this park, but it has a good word-of-mouth reputation as a comfortable, friendly place to stay.

Chetumal to Points Beyond? If you're feeling adventurous, consider crossing into Belize. This tiny, Central American country has fantastic diving and coral reefs, Mayan ruins, and especially fine jungles. Though it is possible to drive across Belize and on into Guatemala, road conditions in the Peten district of Guatemala are generally bad-to-awful. Unless you're traveling in a strong vehicle during the dry season, it's best not to attempt the long stretch between Flores and Puerto Barrios on Highway CA 13.

If you prefer to remain in Mexico, complete your Yucatán loop trip by traveling west on Mex 186 to Escarcega. Allow plenty of time to visit Mayan archaeological sites along the way.

Appendix

Recommended Reading

Books

With the exception of Baja, surprisingly little has been published about camping and exploring in Mexico. Because no single book can possibly cover such a broad topic, you'll have to rely on several sources.

Don't overlook the local library and used book stores. I often find books on Mexico by small presses as well as out-of-print publications that are fascinating. A classic, for example, is *The Enchanted Vagabonds* by Dana Lamb (see below). One of the finest books ever written on life and travel in Mexico's backcountry is *Unknown Mexico* by Carl Lumholtz. After more than 80 years, his insights and information are still quite useful.

Out-of-print guidebooks can still provide useful information. Look in used book stores and flea markets for Cliff Cross's camping "field guides," a series that was popular in the seventies. Cross's large format, soft cover books are rather dated by now, but I still enjoy his homespun style and excellent maps.

If you're serious about Mexico, request catalogs from

regional and university presses in the American Southwest and California (ask your librarian for addresses). Most publications on Mexico are considered regional or special interest and won't be distributed nationwide. For example, the fine book, *Backcountry Mexico* (University of Texas Press; see below) is rarely seen east of the Mississippi.

Books in Print is your best bet for locating new and little-known titles. You'll find this massive reference book at libraries and bookstores. Browse through it carefully; you never know what you'll find.

Index of Periodicals is another excellent source of information on camping in Mexico. This reference source lists virtually every magazine article written. The *Index* will lead you to articles in *Trailer Life* magazine about RV travel in Mexico, *Outside,* and *Backpacker* on hiking the Copper Canyon, and many others.

If you're looking for a specific book on Mexico or just want to browse, Mexico Book Service, 204 Worthington Drive, Exton, PA 19341, 215/524-0397, has everything: guidebooks, books on archaeology, cooking, and history, atlases, fiction, classics, Spanish-English bilingual editions, and more.

Tolliver's Books (1634 Stearns Dr., Los Angeles, CA 90035, 213/939-6054) has new, used, and out-of-print books on "Life and Earth Services," a broad term since they carry everything from guidebooks to scientific monographs. Tell them what you're interested in and they'll send you a specific catalog that will drive you wild with temptation. Book lovers beware: they've got something for everyone.

The Rio Grande Press, Inc. (Glorieta, NM 87535), has fine reprints of classic works on the Southwest and Mexico. These are the kinds of books you won't loan out casually.

Mexico Desconocido, Editorial Jilguero, Monte Pelvoux 110, Primer Piso, Lomas de Chapultepec, Mexico, D.F., Mexico CP 11000. Previously available only in Spanish, *Unknown Mexico* magazine now publishes an English translation of its articles as a centerfold. This excellent periodical covers everything from exploring Mexico's backcountry and beaches to treasure hunting, unusual fiestas, historical sites, arts and crafts, flora and fauna, etc., etc. Over the years, *Mexico Desconocido* has compiled a unique inventory of Mexico's fascinating natural and cultural treasures. (For subscription information, write them—in English, if you wish—or look for *Mexico Desconocido* at newsstands in Mexico.)

Sanborn's Mexico Travelog by Dan Sanborn, Sanborn's Mexico Insurance, P.O. Box 1210, McAllen, TX 78502, (512) 682-3401. Dan Sanborn sweetens his insurance policies for Mexico travelers by throwing in a free copy of his looseleaf Mexico Travelog. The travelog is designed to guide motorists along Mexico's major highways. The detail is awesome: ''VW agency at right and Coca-Cola bottling plant at left. Start working your way to right lane.'' His RV and campground information is useful but scanty. However, considering that the book is free and Sanborn's insurance is competitively priced, it's a deal worth considering.

AAA Travel Publications, from Automobile Club of Southern California, 2601 South Figueroa Street, Los Angeles, CA 90007. ''Triple A'' maps and publications on driving, campgrounds and accommodations in Mexico are available to members only. I like the AAA road map of Mexico, but the books are cold and impersonal. Unless you're already a member, spend your money on books listed below.

Mexico Camping Directory by Carlos Melendez A., Travelmex, Apdo 31-750, Guadalajara, Jalisco, Mexico CP 45050.

The *Mexico Camping Directory* is a compact, 85-page directory of campgrounds, trailer parks, and motels offering RV accommodations. Though updates are provided through *TravelMex* newsletter, we've found it difficult to combine the updates with the Camping Directory. Unless you're familiar with Mexico and have a detailed map at hand, the Directory's alphabetical listings can be very confusing.

TravelMex, P.O. Box 220407, El Paso, TX 79913, (915) 584-7817. Monthly. U.S. airmail subscriptions $15 per year.

TravelMex is the ''official newsletter'' of the Monarch Camping Club. In fact, most of this generally excellent newsletter is devoted to subjects other than camping: popular and lesser-known Mexican destinations, restaurant and book reviews, highway reports, retirement, and so on.

Issues also include a recent sample of Lloyd's Mexican Economic Report. *TravelMex* is published in Guadalajara but gives a nice balance of countrywide information. Good writing and research, and an obvious appreciation for all things Mexican, makes this my favorite newsletter on Mexico.

Mexico West Newsletter, P.O. Box 1646, Bonita, CA 92002, (619) 585-3033. Tom Miller, the author of several excellent books on Baja, offers a monthly newsletter through his Mexico West Travel Club. The club's focus, and that of the newsletter, is Baja and the northwest coast of Mexico. Typical issues have updates on driving and fishing conditions, Baja lore and history, restaurant reviews, campground updates, and club tours and activities. Letters from readers and reports from people just returned from Baja provide excellent up-to-the-moment information. If you're interested in Baja, this newsletter (and the club's other services) will be quite helpful.

The Baja Book III by Tom Miller. This very popular book is an easy-to-read collection of maps, road logs, and commentary on Baja's Transpeninsular Highway and important side roads.

A Desert Country Near the Sea by Ann Zwinger, Harper & Row. Prize-winning naturalist Ann Zwinger takes a close look at the flora, fauna, marine biology and geology of Baja's southern tip as well as detailed observations on the region's history and geography. This book is a wonderful combination of field guide, travelogue, and personal adventure.

Camping and Climbing in Baja by John W. Robinson, La Siesta Press, Box 406, Glendale, CA. Another oldie (mid-70s) but goodie; I keep running across copies in used book stores. Detailed information, including trail directions, maps, and nice photos.

National Parks of Northwest Mexico II by Richard D. Fisher, Sunracer Publications, P.O. Box 40092, Tucson, AZ 85717. Description, maps, charts, and color photographs of the Copper Canyon, Pinacate desert, Sea of Cortez islands, and Sierra de la Laguna Park in southern Baja. This book beautifully demonstrates the author's love for the people and wilderness parks of northwestern Mexico. A dedicated, do-it-yourself explorer, Fisher gives an excellent overview of the adventure possibilities in this vast region, with tips on specific hikes, maps, and accommodations. If you read this book, be prepared to trade that armchair for a pair of desert boots.

Backcountry Mexico: A Traveler's Guide and Phrase Book by Bob Burleson and David H. Riskind, 311 pages, 1986, University of Texas Press, Box 7819, Austin, TX 78713. More than half of this book is devoted to down-to-earth Spanish-English vocabularies and sample conversations, making it both a self-contained dictionary and language guide. It also includes valuable advice and information on how to conduct yourself in the backcountry, with a strong emphasis on northern Mexico. There are brief but useful discussions of driving, health, hiking, canoeing, and mule trekking. The book is well written and meticulously researched and demonstrates a real compassion for the Mexican people. Anyone interested in life and travel in Mexico's backcountry or colloquial, everyday Spanish should have this book.

Trails of the Sierra Madre by Eugene Boudreau, Capra Press and Pleasant Hill Press, 2600 Pleasant Hill Road, Sebastopol, CA 95472. Though slim in size, this book is full of information and fun to read. Eugene Boudreau's knowledge of northwestern Mexico is impressive. Specific suggestions for two walking or pack animal trips are given. The book is not new (1973), but like most well thought out books on Mexico's backcountry, the information is almost timeless. Boudreau's other books on the area are also good: *Ways of the Sierra Madre*, R. F. Grigsby's *Sierra Madre Journal: 1864*, and *Move Over Don Porfirio: Tales from the Sierra Madre*.

Mexican Wilderness and Wildlife by Ben Tinker, University of Texas Press, Austin, TX. Ben Tinker was appointed Game Guardian of Sonora by President Obregón in 1923. This book, beautifully illustrated by Doris Tischler, draws on many years of travel, by foot and horseback, in remote regions of northwestern Mexico. Mr. Tinker was a rancher and hunter; his love and knowledge of Mexican wildlife made him unusually well suited to act as its protector. I especially enjoy the short chapter entitled Desert Water. He includes brief tips on how and where to observe big game. A fine book.

Adventuring Along the Gulf of Mexico by Donald G. Schueler, Sierra Club Books. Though only a third of this book's 300 pages is devoted to Mexico's Gulf Coast (and Yucatán Peninsula), I consider it a "must read." Schueler's description of Gulf Coast wildlife, parks, beaches, accommodations, and tourist attractions is presented in a knowledgeable, highly readable narrative style. I only wish he'd keep going.

Backpacking in Mexico and Central America by Hilary and George Bradt. Brief (134 pages) but informative, though the Bradt Enterprises (409 Beacon Street, Boston, MA 02115) title is rather misleading; most of the book is about Central America, with the emphasis on hiking in parks. Nonetheless, the book should be valuable if you're heading south of Mexico.

Where There Is No Doctor by David Werner, The Hesperian Foundation, Box 1692, Palo Alto, CA 94302. A truly great book: readable, practical advice designed to keep you healthy with a minimum of treatment and expense. Used extensively in the Third World and originally written on the basis of the author's extensive experience in Mexico's backcountry. A nonprofit publication, also available in Spanish. Take at least one extra copy in Spanish to give away to someone who needs it.

Quest for the Lost City by Dana and Ginger Lamb, Santa Barbara Press, 1129 State Street, Santa Barbara, CA 93101. When I first began exploring Mexico, I was strongly influenced by the Lambs' gutsy yet humorous approach to adventure. Half a century after the Lambs plunged across the border with $10.16 in their jeans, this book still reads like the real Mexico.

Foraging Along the California Coast by Peter Howorth, Capra Press, 631 State Street, Santa Barbara, CA 93101. How to find and collect everything from clams to striped bass, with good, clear tips on equipment, cleaning, and preparation, and recipes. Nice illustrations by Jane Jolley Howorth. The book applies to much of Mexico as well as California; I recommend it highly.

A Field Guide to the Gems and Minerals of Mexico by Paul W. Johnson, Gembooks, Mentone, CA (1965). A detailed guide to mineral and gem collecting, one that we use not for "rock hounding" but to locate interesting hiking and camping areas. Mining is usually done in places that are rugged and scenic. This book, unfortunately, is hard to find; I got one copy at a jeweler's supply shop, another at a flea market.

How to Keep Your Volkswagen Alive by John Muir, $17.95, John Muir Publications, Box 613, Santa Fe, NM 87501. If you don't have this book in your VW, get one; you'll certainly need it, if only to check what that mechanic is doing. Now in Spanish ($10.00). A great gift for a Spanish-speaking friend or mecanico.

How to Keep Your VW Rabbit Alive by Richard Sealey, $17.95, John Muir Publications. Covers the Rabbit and Scirocco, including carburetors, diesel, and fuel injection. Spiral bound and profusely illustrated by Peter Aschwanden.

Maps

In the late 1950s, the Mexican Society of History and Geography estimated that 75 percent of Mexico was essentially unmapped and unknown, except in a general sense. In 1968, a program of detailed mapping was begun, relying heavily on aerial photography. This project is still incomplete, though a great deal of progress has been made. This means that detailed and accurate maps of Mexico are hard to come by and, for some areas, next to impossible. What's the solution, especially if you plan to travel into a remote area? Gather as many different maps as you can and compare them constantly. This leads to unexpected discoveries and revelations: if a river is shown on two out of three maps, there's a reasonable chance that it actually exists. Do your maps agree on the location of a huge canyon in a relatively rainy area but show no river at the bottom? Logic tells you, even if the maps don't, that there's water there and perhaps a lot of it, especially during the late summer rains.

Learning to read maps doesn't require special skills, just a good dose of imagination. Can you identify a maguey plant from a fuzzy photo in a field guide? I couldn't; it takes more than one view or angle and time to compare the suspected maguey with other similar plants. The same is true of maps; once you're familiar with each map's idiosyncrasies and shortcomings, your mind will combine these images to form a clearer, overall picture of the countryside.

In general, our experience has been that topo maps aren't nearly as accurate as those in the United States, especially if you need several to cover a proposed trip or an area of interest. Major foot trails may not be shown, rivers are missing, villages are misplaced, and so on. This doesn't make them useless; just keep on your toes and orient yourself with major ridges and mountains.

The following types and sources of maps are the best

and most obvious I could find. Keep an eye open, however, for unexpected sources of maps. *The Handbook of American Indians,* for example, publishes hundreds of very small and very detailed maps in its scholarly works. These maps are for the use of archaeologists and anthropologists, but by carefully comparing them to larger-scale maps, you can find details that are otherwise unavailable. Don't overlook old maps from outdated guidebooks, magazines, and scholarly works. Many are still accurate, especially for the backcountry, and may even have been used as the basis for a supposedly ''new'' map.

Road Maps

Don't expect to find road maps in Mexican gas stations—or even in Mexican bookstores. In fact, it's best to buy your maps before you leave home, unless you want map hunting to be your first errand in Mexico. I suggest you contact one of the map sources listed here, especially if you're looking for more than a basic single-sheet road map.

Road maps of Mexico are sometimes available in the United States at gas stations near the border, tourist agencies, large hotels, insurance offices, and Mexican Consulate and National Tourism offices. Get two maps; you'll lose or loan one almost immediately.

Inside Mexico, maps are available at INEGI offices (see below) and some bookstores. Don't expect to find maps of the entire country in local tourist offices or travel agencies. Larger bookstores and sidewalk news stands are your best bet for state and countrywide maps.

Road maps and travel logs for Mexico are available to members of AAA. Travel clubs and insurance companies also give out maps and road logs (see Books).

The best road atlas of Mexico is the Spanish-English *Atlas de Carreteras* by Pemex, the government oil monopoly.

This soft, folded atlas is often sold in Mexico by sidewalk vendors and newsstands. It's cheap and very good.

A complete geographic atlas published by Porrua (*Nuevo Atlas de la Republica Mexicana*) is sold in some Mexican bookstores. It is inexpensive and well worth having.

Carta Turistica: There are eight "Tourist" maps in this series, including seven regional maps and a single sheet map of the entire country. The single sheet map isn't as good as an AAA road map, but it's better than nothing. The regional maps, however, are outstanding. Though Carta Turistica maps aren't entirely accurate or up-to-date, this series is loaded with good information. They're also quite large, easy to read and have some topographic shading. (scale 1: 1,000,000)

Guia Roji maps and road atlases are produced in Mexico City. Guia Roji produces a wide variety of city, state, and road maps, but they all suffer from a common problem: the maps are simply too tightly drawn. Unless you have excellent vision, Guia Roji maps are difficult to read. Drawbacks aside, Roji maps are widely available in Mexico. By the way, most gringos mistakenly call these maps Guia Roja (Red Guide). Roji Guides are named for their founder, Señor Roji.

Serie Patria or *Serie Azul:* The "Blue Series" of state maps is now out of print, but you'll occasionally find sources (see San Diego Map Centre). Best used for general driving and city orientation, not hiking.

Guatemala: Road maps of Guatemala are hard to find, especially in Guatemalan gas stations. Topo maps are even worse; because of the military situation, most of Guatemala is "classified" and maps are not sold to the public. Ironically, you can buy Guatemalan topo maps in the United States from Guatemala. Write to Instituto Geographico Nacional, Avenida las Americas 5-76, Zona 13, Guatemala, C.A.

Map and Chart Sources

San Diego Map Centre, Inc., 2611 University Avenue, San Diego, CA 92104-2894. If you're confused and frustrated by now about Mexican maps, I don't blame you. Collecting good maps of Mexico takes time, patience, and a little money. Fortunately, the San Diego Map Centre can relieve a great deal of the burden. Their stock of maps, charts, cruising guides, and books on Mexico is outstanding. Service is quick and their imported map prices are very fair. Ask for a catalog. I recommend them highly.

Wide World of Books, 401 N.E. 45th Street, Seattle, WA 98105, (206) 634-3453. Perhaps as a result of once being hopelessly lost in downtown Coatzacoalcos, I now have an irresistible urge to collect maps of Mexico, sometimes by the sackful. Thanks to Joan Marsden at Wide World of Books, I can now share my hoard with other travelers. If you're interested in the *Carta Turistica*, Pemex Highway Atlas, or other Mexico maps and books, get in touch with Joan.

Tucson Blueprint, P.O. Box 27266, Tucson, AZ 85726. Topos and historical maps of Mexico.

Wide World of Maps, 2626 W. Indian School Road, Phoenix, AZ 85017, (602) 279-2323. Maps and charts; travel, camping, fishing, and natural history books; field guides.

Geocentro, San Francisco 1375, Esquina Tlacoquemecatl, Colonia del Valle, Mexico, D.F. This Mexico City map store has aerial photos, topos, road maps, atlases, and books.

Instituto Nacional de Estadistica Geografia E Informacion. Mexico's federal mapping agency, INEGI (National Institute of Statistics, Geography, and Information), is the best "in-country" source of topographic and relief maps, Carta Turistica road maps, and charts. Their prices are very low. The selection, especially of topos, is broad but unpredictable. If you need a specific topo badly, I'd query sources in the United States first.

My first stop when flying into Mexico is INEGI's excellent hole-in-the-wall shop (#65) in the airport's main concourse. I've visited many of INEGI's offices in Mexico and have been impressed with their enthusiasm and helpful service. (By a bureaucratic quirk, the agency's main office is not in Mexico City but Aguascalientes.)

INEGI INFORMATION AND SALES CENTERS IN MEXICO

Aguascalientes, Aguascalientes: Plaza de la Republica No. 111, Esquina Plaza Patria, Centro.

Mexico City (Distrito Federal): Aeropuerto de la Ciudad de Mexico "Benito Juarez," Local 65 and also at Insurgentes Sur No. 795, P.B., Colonia Napoles.

Riio Rhin No. 56, Colonia Cuahtemoc (no showroom).

Francisco Sosa No. 383, Esquina Salvador Novo, Colonia Coyoacan.

Hermosillo, Sonora: Carretera a Bahia Kino Km. 0.5 (Highway to Bahia Kino).

Monterrey, Nuevo Leon: Avenida Eugenio Garza Sada No. 1702 Sur, Colonia Nuevo Repueblo.

San Luis Potosí, S.L.P.: Independencia No. 1025, Centro.

Durango, Durango: Felipe Pescador No. 706 Oriente entre Laureano Roncal y Voladores.

Guadalajara, Jalisco: Avenida Alcade No. 788, Esquina Jesus Garcia, Sector Hidalgo.

Puebla, Puebla: 19 Sur No. 1102, Esquina 11 Poniente, Colonia San Matias.

Toluca, Estado de Mexico: Hidalgo Oriente No. 1227, Esquina Jaime Nuno.

Oaxaca, Oaxaca: Calzada Porfirio Dias, No. 317, Esquina Dr. Demetrio Mayoral Pardo, Colonia Reforma.

Mérida, Yucatán: Paseo Montejo, No. 442, Edificio Oasis.

Aeronautical Charts

Large-scale aeronautical charts are published by the U.S. Department of Commerce, National Oceanic and Atmospheric Administration, National Ocean Survey C-44, Riverdale, MD 20840. Four big charts cover all of Mexico, Guatemala, and Belize. These charts are cheap and surprisingly accurate. We prefer them, mainly because of cost, over topo maps and use them for boating as well as backpacking or back road exploring.

Camping and Travel Clubs

Monarch Camping Club, Apdo 31-750, Guadalajara, Jalisco, Mexico CP 45050. This is the only camping club that covers all of Mexico. Membership is $25 a year and benefits include discounts on RV campgrounds, rental cars, repair shops, and restaurants; maps, routing service, phrase book, and campground directory. The club's newsletter, *TravelMex,* is very good (see Recommended Reading).

Mexico West Travel Club, Inc., P.O. Box 1646, Bonita, CA 92002, (619) 585-3033. Founded by travel writer Tom Miller, Mexico West focuses on Baja and western Mexico. Membership is $35 a year. Benefits include: an excellent monthly newsletter (see Recommended Reading), updated telephone "hotline" reports on fishing, road conditions, and gas availability in Baja; discounts on books, hotels, campgrounds, tours, fishing trips, and all types of Mexican insurance. If you'll be spending more than a few days in Baja, the club's discounts can easily defray most, if not all, of the cost of membership.

Vagabundos Del Mar, Oxbow Marina, P.O. Box 824, Isleton, CA 95641, (707) 374-5511. The "Gypsies of the Sea" boat and travel club is a nonprofit organization of trailer-boaters and cruisers, fishermen,and RVers. The Vagabundos began in Baja but their membership and activities now extend to Canada and Alaska. Membership is $30 a year (plus $10 initiation fee). Benefits include discounts on insurance, RV parks, and services in Baja. The club sponsors fiestas and regattas in California and Baja. *Chubasco,* an informative bimonthly newsletter, relates club activities, members' experiences, advice, and sea stories.

RV Tour Operators

Point South R.V. Tours, Inc., 8463 Aura Avenue, Northridge, CA 91324, (800) 421-1394 or (CA) (800) 282-3673 or (818) 701-6944. If you don't have a motor home, Point South can provide one. This well-known company tours all of Mexico, including "piggyback" RV train trips through the Copper Canyon.

Tracks to Adventure, 2811 Jackson Avenue, El Paso, TX 79930, (915) 565-9627.

Amigo R.V. Tours, P.O. Box 43201, Las Vegas, NV 89116, (902) 452-8271.

Caravanas Voyagers, 1155 Larry Mahan Suite H, El Paso, TX 79925, (915) 592-2113.

RV Clubs

Good Sam, 29901 Agoura Road, Agoura, CA 91301, (818) 991-4980.

Winnebago, P.O. Box 268, Forest City, IA 50436.

Airstream, 419 West Pike Street, Jackson Center, OH 45334, (513) 596-6111.

Vocabulary

The Spanish used in the backcountry tends to be much simpler than you might expect. The term *feo*, for example, not only means "ugly" but also rough, harsh, unpleasant, uncomfortable (the weather is *feo*), uncooperative. Country people are close-mouthed; you'll soon learn how they manage to convey a great deal in a few words.

A special note: In Mexico, the words stupid (*estupido*), *idiota*, and *payaso* (clown) are very insulting in most circumstances and are not used casually to describe people or their actions. Insults of any kind are best kept out of your working vocabulary; their power is too often destructive.

In describing animals, such as a burro, do not say "*El burro de Juan*" to mean "John's burro." In Mexico, this is heard instead as John-the-burro. The correct form is "*El burro es de Juan*" (The burro is "of" John). It's one of those easily made mistakes that can be embarrassing to all concerned.

Camping Gear, Tools and Hardware, Odds and Ends

Acetylene torch   *soplete oxiacetilenico, autógeno*
allen wrench   *llave de alán*
aluminum   *aluminio*
ax   *hacha*
ayate   **carrying net**
backpack   *mochila*
bag   *bolsa, costal, morral*
barrel   *tambor, tambo, barril, tinaco*
basket   *canasta, cesto*
battery   *pila, batería*
bent   *doblado, chueco*
blade   *hoja*
blanket   *cobija, frazada, cubierta*
bolt   *tornillo*
bottle   *botella, pomo*
  5 gallon   *garrafón*
box   *caja, cartón*
box end wrench   *llave ástria*
blacksmith   *herrero*
broken   *roto, quebrado*
bucket   *cubeta, cubo, balde*
cable   *cable*
canteen   *cantimplora*
carbide   *carburo*
catalyst   *catalizador*
CB radio   *transceptor, CB*
chain   *cadena*
charcoal   *carbón*
charcoal stove   *avafre, brasero*
chingado   **all screwed up (impolite)**
chisel   *cincel*
clamp   *abrazadera*
compass   *brújula*

cord   cuerda
cot   catre
cotter pin   chaveta
crescent wrench   perico
crowbar   barra
dog cage, house   perreta
drill and bits   taladro y brocas
emery paper   lija de esmeril
enamelware   peltre
epoxy   epoxy
equipment   equipo, trastos
extension cord   cuerda, cable de extensión
fiberglass   fibra de vidrio
file   lima
film; 35mm   rollo; rollo para transparencias, diapositiva (slide)
filter   filtro
flare   bengala
flashlight   foco, luz
flit gun   rociador
foam rubber   espuma de ule
folding   plegable
fuel   combustible
funnel   embudo
gate   puerto, portal
gear, provisions   menesteres
glue   pegamiento, Resistol
gourd   jícara
grease   grasa
grill   parilla
hack saw   ceget
hammer   martillo
hammock   hamaca
hardware store   ferretería
hatchet   hacha, hachachica
helmet   casco

hose   *mangera, tubo*
huacal   **stick box**
ice chest   *hielera*
inflatable   *inflable. . . .de aire*
iron   *férreo*
jícara   **gourd**
key   *llave*
knife   *cuchillo, navaja*
knot   *nudo*
lamp chimney (glass)   *bombilla*
lantern   *linterna*
lariat   *riata*
light bulb   *foco*
lighter   *encendedor*
Liquid Wrench   *Alfloja Todo*
lock   *cerradura, retén*
luggage   *equipaje*
mantle (lantern)   *camisa, capuchón, mecha*
map   *mapa*
mat   *petate*
mattress   *colchón*
    air   *colchón de aire*
mosquito net   *pabellón, mosquitero*
nail   *clavo*
needle   *aguja*
needle-nose pliers   *alicates*
nut   *tuerca*
open end wrench   *llave española*
padlock   *candado*
patch   *parche*
phillips screwdriver   *desarmador decruz*
pin   *perno*
pipe   *pipa, tubo*
pipe wrench   *llave stillson*
plastic sheet   *plastíco, ule*

pliers   *pinzas*
plug   *tapón, tapadera*
pole   *palo*
portable   *portátil*
pump   *bomba*
ratchet   *matraca, llave de trinquete*
razor   *navaja*
refrigerator   *refrigerador*
rivet   *remache*
rope   *mecate, soga*
saddle   *silla de montar*
sandpaper   *papel de lija*
scissors   *tijeras*
screw   *tornillo*
screwdriver   *desarmador*
sharpening stone   *afiladera*
sheet metal   *lámina*
shovel   *pala*
siphon   *sifón*
sleeping bag   *bolsa de dormir*
socket   *soquet, dado*
socket extension   *extensión*
socket wrench   *llave de dado*
solder   *soldadura*
soldering iron   *soldador*
sponge   *esponja*
sprayer   *rociador*
spring   *resorte*
stake   *estaca*
stainless steel   *acero inoxidable*
stirrup   *estribo*
stove   *estufa*
strap, belt   *cincho*
string   *cuerda, hilillo*
stuck   *pegado*
swimming pool   *alberca, balneario, piscina*

tank   tanque, tinaja
tape   cinta
   electrical   cinta de Plástico
tarp   lona, carpa
tent   casita de campaña, tiendado campaña
thread   hilo
tin   lámina, hoja de lata
tin snips   tijeras para lámina
tools   herramientas, fierros
top, plug   tapón, tapadera
torch   antorcha, bengala, soplete (pressurized)
tow   remolque
tow truck   grúa, remolque
trailer   trayler, remolque, casa rodante (house)
transceiver   transceptor
trap   trampa
   rodent   ratonera
truck   camioneta, pickup troque, camión (big)
tub   tina, tinaco
twine   hilillo, hilo, cuerda
vado   **dip or ford**
van   combi, camioneta
vehicle   vehículo, mueble
vise   tornillo
vise grip pliers   pinzas depresión
washer   rondana
water pump pliers   pinzas de extensión
wick   mecha
winch   malacate, winch
wire   alambre
wrench   llave
zipper   cierre, zipper

Gas Stations, Repairs

Fill it up, please. — Lleno, por favor.
Check the oil and water, please. — Vea el aceite y agua, por favor.
I want an oil change and grease job. — Quiero un cambio de aceite y lubricación.
Check the oil in the transmission and differential. — Vea el aceite en la caja y diferencial.
Put in a liter of 30 weight oil, please. — Eche un litro de aceite   número treinta, por favor.
Where is the rest room? — Dónde está el baño?

accelerator   acelerador
adjust   adjustar
adjusting stars (brakes)   ajustadores de frenos
a-frame   horguilla
air filter   filtro de aire
air filter cartridge   cartucho del filtro de aire
alternator   alternador
armature   rotor
assemble   armar
auto electric shop   taller auto-eléctrico
auto parts   refacciones
auto parts store   refaccionería
axle   eje
brake shoe   zapata
ball bearings   baleros
ball joints   rótulas
batteria   acumulador, batería
battery cable   cable de acumulador
block   monoblock
body and paint shop   hojalatería y pintura
boot (tire)   huarache
brakes   frenos
brake drum   tambor

brake fluid	líquido de frenos
brake line	mangera de frenos
brake lining	balata
brake pedal	pedal de frenos
brake plate	plato de frenos
brushes	carbones
bumper	defensa
bus	autobús, camión
bushing	bushing, buje
cable	cable
camshaft	árbol de levas
camshaft bearings	metales de árbol de levas
car	coche, automóvil, carro
carburetor	carburador
carburetor float	flotador
carburetor jet	esprea
choke	ahogador
clutch	clutch
clutch disc	disco de clutch
clutch pedal	pedal de clutch
coil	bohina
coil springs	resortes
condenser	condensador
crankcase	monoblock
crankshaft	cigüeñal
cylinder	cilindro
cylinder sleeve	camisa
differential	diferencial
dismantle	desarmar
distributor	distribuidor
distributor cap	tapa de distribuidor
drive	manejar
drive shaft	flecha cardán
electrical system	sistema eléctrica
fan	ventilador
fan belt	banda de ventilador

fender   guardabarros
fields   campos
fly wheel   engrane volante
frame   bastidor
front wheel alignment   alineación
front wheel bearings   baleros de las ruidas adelantes
front wheel spindle   mango
fuel pump   bomba de gasolina
fuse   fusible
garage (repair)   taller mecánico, taller automotriz
gas cap   tapón de gasolina
gas line   tubo, mangera de gasolina
gas tank   tanque de gasolina
gasket   empaque, junta
gasket set   juego de empaques
gear   engrane
gear shift lever   palanca de cambios
generator   generador
ground   tierra
hand brake   freno de mano
head   cabeza
head gasket   empaque de cabeza
headlights   focos
horn   klaxón, bocina
hose   mangera
hose clamp   abrazadera
ignition switch   switch
jack   gato
kingpin   perno, pivote de dirección
kingpin carrier   portamango
leaf springs   muelles
lever   palanca
main bearings   metales de bancada
manifold   múltiple
   exhaust   múltiple de escape
   intake   múltiple de admisión

master cylinder   *cilindro maestro de frenos*
mechanic   *mecánico, maestro*
mechanic shop   *taller mecánico*
motor   *motor, maquina*
motor home   *casa rodante*
muffler   *mofle*
oil   *aceite*
oil filter   *filtro de aceite*
oil pump   *bomba de aceite*
panel truck   *camioneta, panel*
patch   *parche*
pickup truck   *camioneta*
piston   *pistón*
Pitman arm   *brazo Pitman*
points   *platinos*
pressure plate   *plato de presión*
pulley   *polea*
push rod   *levador, puntería*
radiator   *radiador*
radiator cap   *tapón de radiador*
radiator hose   *mangera de radiador*
recap (tire)   *recubierta*
relay   *relais*
rings   *anillos*
    compression ring   *anillo de compresión*
    oil ring   *anillo de aceite*
rocker arm   *balancín*
rod   *biela*
rod bearing (insert)   *metales de bielas*
rotor   *rotor*
RV   *vehiculo recreativo*

seal   *retén*
shaft   *flecha*
shock absorber   *amortiguador*
solenoid   *solenoide*

spark plug   *buja (candela in Guatemala)*
spark plug wire   *cable de jujía*
starter   *marcha*
starter ring gear   *cremallera*
station wagon   *guayin*
steering gear   *caja de dirección*
steering wheel   *volante*
stoplight   *luz de stop*
stud   *birlo, perno prisionero*
tail pipe   *tubo de escape*
thermostat   *toma de agua, termósi*
throw out bearing   *cojarín*
tie rod   *barrilla de dirección*
tie rod end   *terminal de barrilla de dirección*
tighten   *apretar*
timing gear   *engrange de árbol de levas*
tire   *llanta*
tire balancing   *balanceo*
tire gauge   *calibrador*
tire repair shop   *vulcanízadora*
tire tube   *cámara* **or** *tubo*
tire, tubeless   *llanta sin cámara*
tire valve   *válvula*
tow truck   *grúa*
torsion bar   *barra de torsión*
transmission   *transmisión, caja* **(box)**
truck, heavy   *camión*
tune   *afinar*
tune-up   *afinación*
turn signals   *direccionales*
turn signal flasher   *destallador*
universal joint   *cruceta y yugo, cardán*
upholstery shop (auto)   *cubreasientos*
vacuum advance   *avance*

valves   *válvulas*
   exhaust   *válvula de escape*
   intake   *válvula de admisión*
valve cover   *tapa de pulerias*
valve guide   *guía de válvula*
valve lifter   *buso, levanta-válvulas*
valve springs   *resorte de válvula*
valve spring keeper   *cazuela de válvula*
valve stem   *vastigo de válvula*
van   *camioneta*
voltage regulator   *regulador de voltage*
water pump   *bomba de agua*
weld   *soldar*
wheel   *rueda*
wheel cylinder   *cilindro de frenos*
windshield   *parabrisas*
windshield wiper   *limpia parabrisas* **or** *limpiadores*
windshield wiper blade   *pluma*
wire   *alambre*
wrist pin   *perno, pasador de émbolo*

It's bent. — *Está doblado.*
Adjust the clutch. — *Ajuste el clutch.*
Adjust the brakes. — *Ajuste los frenos.*
To bleed the brakes — *Purgar los frenos*
To rebuild the wheel cylinders — *Cambiar las gomas*
To turn the brake drums — *Rectificar los tambores*
Adjust the valves. — *Ajuste las válvulas.*
To grind the valves — *Asentar las válvulas*
Engine overhaul — *Ajuste general*
To turn the crankshaft — *Rectificar la cigüeñal*
To charge the battery — *Cargar la acumulador*
The engine is knocking. — *Suena la máquina.*
The engine is overheating. — *El motor se salienta.*
The engine is throwing oil. — *La máquina está tirando aceite.*

The engine is burning oil. — *La máquina está quemando aceite.*
The radiator is leaking. — *Está tirando la radiador.*
I want a major tune-up. — *Quiero una afinación mayor.*
Pack the front wheel bearings. — *Engrace los baleros de las ruedas adelantes.*
The tire is punctured. — *Está ponchada la llanta.*
The tire has a slow leak. — *La llanta está bajando poco a poco.*
Put a boot in the tire. — *Vucanice la llanta.*
Put 30 pounds of air in the tires. — *Ponga treinta libras de aire in las llantas.*

Red Tape

age   *edad*
baggage   *equipaje*
border   *frontera*
car permit   *permiso de automóvil*
customs   *aduana*
divorced   *divorciado (a)*
driver's license   *licencia de manejar*
immigration   *migración*
inspection   *revisión*
insurance   *seguros*
license plates   *placas*
marital status   *estado civil*
married   *casado (a)*
minor   *menor de edad*
passport   *pasaporte*
profession or occupation   *profesión or ocupación*
registration   *registración*
single   *soltero (a)*
suitcase   *maleta*
tourist card   *tarjeta de turista*
widowed   *viudo (a)*
vaccination certificate   *certificado de vacunación*

Index

Other Books from John Muir Publications

22 Days Series
These pocket-size itineraries are a refreshing departure from ordinary guidebooks. Each author has an in-depth knowledge of the region covered and offers 22 tested daily itineraries through their favorite destinations. Included are not only "must see" attractions but also little-known villages and hidden "jewels" as well as valuable general information.

22 Days Around the World by R. Rapoport and B. Willes (65-31-9)
22 Days in Alaska by Pamela Lanier (28-68-0)
22 Days in the American Southwest by R. Harris (28-88-5)
22 Days in Asia by R. Rapoport and B. Willes (65-17-3)
22 Days in Australia by John Gottberg (65-40-8)
22 Days in California by Roger Rapoport (28-93-1)
22 Days in China by Gaylon Duke and Zenia Victor (28-72-9)
22 Days in Dixie by Richard Polese (65-18-1)
22 Days in Europe by Rick Steves (65-05-X)
22 Days in Florida by Richard Harris (65-27-0)
22 Days in France by Rick Steves (65-07-6)
22 Days in Germany, Austria & Switzerland by R. Steves (65-39-4)
22 Days in Great Britain by Rick Steves (65-38-6)
22 Days in Hawaii by Arnold Schuchter (28-92-3)
22 Days in India by Anurag Mathur (28-87-7)
22 Days in Japan by David Old (28-73-7)
22 Days in Mexico by S. Rogers and T. Rosa (65-41-6)
22 Days in New England by Anne Wright (28-96-6)
22 Days in New Zealand by Arnold Schuchter (28-86-9)
22 Days in Norway, Denmark & Sweden by R. Steves (28-83-4)
22 Days in the Pacific Northwest by R. Harris (28-97-4)
22 Days in Spain & Portugal by Rick Steves (65-06-8)
22 Days in the West Indies by C. & S. Morreale (28-74-5)
All 22 Days titles are 128 to 152 pp. and $7.95 each, except 22 Days Around the World, which is 192 pp. and $9.95.

"Kidding Around" Travel Guides for Children
Written for kids eight years of age and older. Generously illustrated in two colors with imaginative characters and images. An adventure to read and a treasure to keep.
Kidding Around Atlanta, Anne Pedersen (65-35-1) 64 pp. $9.95
Kidding Around London, Sarah Lovett (65-24-6) 64 pp. $9.95
Kidding Around Los Angeles, Judy Cash (65-34-3) 64 pp. $9.95
Kidding Around New York City, Sarah Lovett (65-33-5) 64 pp. $9.95
Kidding Around San Francisco, Rosemary Zibart (65-23-8) 64 pp. $9.95
Kidding Around Washington, D.C., Anne Pedersen (65-25-4) 64 pp. $9.95

Asia Through the Back Door, Rick Steves and John Gottberg (28-76-1) 336 pp. $13.95

Buddhist America: Centers, Retreats, Practices, Don Morreale (28-94-X) 400 pp. $12.95

Bus Touring: Charter Vacations, U.S.A., Stuart Warren (28-95-8) 168 pp. $9.95

Catholic America: Self-Renewal Centers and Retreats, Patricia Christian-Meyer (65-20-3) 325 pp. $13.95

Choices & Changes: Preparing for Pregnancy and Parenthood, Brenda E. Aikey-Keller (65-44-0) 256 pp. $13.95

Complete Guide to Bed & Breakfasts, Inns & Guesthouses, 1989-90 Edition, Pamela Lanier (65-09-2) 520 pp. $14.95

Elderhostels: The Students' Choice, Mildred Hyman (65-28-9) 224 pp. $12.95

Europe 101: History & Art for the Traveler, Rick Steves and Gene Openshaw (28-78-8) 372 pp. $12.95

Europe Through the Back Door, Rick Steves (28-84-2) 404 pp. $12.95

Floating Vacations: River, Lake, and Ocean Adventures, Michael White (65-32-7) 256 pp. $17.95

Gypsying After 40: A Guide to Adventure and Self-Discovery, Bob Harris (28-71-0) 264 pp. $12.95

The Heart of Jerusalem, Arlynn Nellhaus (28-79-6) 312 pp. $12.95

Indian America: A Traveler's Companion, Eagle/Walking Turtle (65-29-7) 336 pp. $14.95

Mona Winks: Self-Guided Tours of Europe's Top Museums, Rick Steves (28-85-0) 450 pp. $14.95

The On and Off the Road Cookbook, Carl Franz (28-27-3) 272 pp. $8.50

The People's Guide to Mexico, Carl Franz (28-99-0) 608 pp. $15.95

The People's Guide to RV Camping in Mexico, Carl Franz with Steve Rogers (28-91-5) 256 pp. $13.95

Ranch Vacations: The Complete Guide to Guest, Fly-Fishing, and Cross-Country Skiing Ranches, Eugene Kilgore (65-30-0) 256 pp. $17.95

The Shopper's Guide to Mexico, Steve Rogers and Tina Rosa (28-90-7) 224 pp. $9.95

Ski Tech's Guide to Equipment, Skiwear, and Accessories, edited by Bill Tanler (65-45-9) 200 pp. $14.95

Ski Tech's Guide to Maintenance and Repair, edited by Bill Tanler (65-46-7) 200 pp. $14.95

Traveler's Guide to Asian Culture, Kevin Chambers (65-14-9) 356 pp. $13.95

Traveler's Guide to Healing Centers and Retreats in North America, Martine Rudee and Jonathan Blease (65-15-7) 240 pp. $11.95

Undiscovered Islands of the Caribbean, Burl Willes (28-80-X) 216 pp. $12.95

Automotive Repair Manuals

Each JMP automotive manual gives clear step-by-step instructions together with illustrations that show exactly how each system in the vehicle comes apart and goes back together. They tell everything a novice or experienced mechanic needs to know to perform periodic maintenance, tuneups, troubleshooting, and repair of the brake, fuel and emission control, electrical, cooling, clutch, transmission, driveline, steering, and suspension systems and even rebuild the engine.

How to Keep Your VW Alive (65-12-2) 424 pp. $17.95
How to Keep Your Golf/Jetta/Rabbit/Scirocco Alive (65-21-1) 420 pp. $17.95
How to Keep Your Honda Car Alive (28-55-9) 272 pp. $17.95
How to Keep Your Subaru Alive (65-11-4) 480 pp. $17.95
How to Keep Your Toyota Pickup Alive (28-81-3) 392 pp. $17.95
How to Keep Your Datsun/Nissan Alive (28-65-6) 544 pp. $17.95

Other Automotive Books

The Greaseless Guide to Car Care Confidence: Take the Terror Out of Talking to Your Mechanic, Mary Jackson (65-19-X) 224 pp. $14.95

Off-Road Emergency Repair & Survival, James Ristow (65-26-2) 160 pp. $9.95

Road & Track's Used Car Classics, edited by Peter Bohr (28-69-9) 272 pp. $12.95

Ordering Information

If you cannot find our books in your local bookstore, you can order directly from us. Your books will be sent to you via UPS (for U.S. destinations), and you will receive them approximately 10 days from the time that we receive your order. Include $2.75 for the first item ordered and $.50 for each additional item to cover shipping and handling costs. UPS shipments to post office boxes take longer to arrive; if possible, please give us a street address. For airmail within the U.S., enclose $4.00 per book for shipping and handling. All foreign orders will be shipped surface rate. Please enclose $3.00 for the first item and $1.00 for each additional item. Please inquire for airmail rates.

Method of Payment

Your order may be paid by check, money order, or credit card. We cannot be responsible for cash sent through the mail. All payments must be made in U.S. dollars drawn on a U.S. bank. Canadian postal money orders in U.S. dollars are also acceptable. For VISA, MasterCard, or American Express orders, include your card number, expiration date, and your signature, or call (505)982-4078. Books ordered on American Express cards can be shipped only to the billing address of the cardholder. Sorry, no C.O.D.'s. Residents of sunny New Mexico, add 5.625% tax to the total.

Address all orders and inquiries to:
John Muir Publications
P.O. Box 613
Santa Fe, NM 87504
(505)982-4078